# CONFESSIONS
## OF ST. AUGUSTINE

# THE
# CONFESSIONS
# OF ST. AUGUSTINE

*Translated by* F. J. SHEED

*New York*

SHEED & WARD

*First Printing, April, 1943*
*Ninth Printing, October, 1947*
*Tenth Printing, May, 1948*
*Eleventh Printing, August, 1948*
*Twelfth Printing, April, 1949*
*Thirteenth Printing, October, 1949*
*Fourteenth Printing, March, 1950*
*Fifteenth Printing, December, 1951*
*Sixteenth Printing, November, 1954*
*Seventeenth Printing, July, 1957*

MANUFACTURED IN THE UNITED STATES OF AMERICA

# CONFESSIONS
## OF ST. AUGUSTINE

# FOREWORD

It should be noted how astoundingly providential was St. Augustine's appearance at that particular moment of history. He was born in North Africa in 354. He was converted in September 386 and baptised at the age of 33 during the Easter of 387. He was made a priest in 391, the year before Theodosius became sole ruler of the whole Empire, and a bishop in 396, the year after Theodosius's death left the way wide open to the Barbarians. He wrote the *Confessions* in 399, having then been twelve years a Catholic and three years a bishop. He began his greatest work *The City of God* as a consequence of the Sack of Rome in 410, as a reply to the Pagans who attributed the catastrophe to the anger of the old gods against Christianity. He died in 430 (two years before St. Patrick came as apostle to Ireland) while the Vandals were actually besieging his episcopal city of Hippo. His immediate work against the Donatists, Manichees and Pelagians, great as it was, is as nothing compared to his function in the whole history of mankind. "He was, to a far greater degree than any emperor or barbarian war-lord, a maker of history and a builder of the bridge which was to lead from the old world to the new." *

The Barbarian invasion meant two great severances; in culture it threatened the thousand year old Classical tradition, with which the new rulers had no hereditary contact; in religion it cut off the Western Church from the Eastern—the hierarchical breach was not to come finally for centuries, but the old closeness was at an end: and this mattered immensely, for it was in the East that the great theological thinking had been done. Augustine prevented both severances—the severance of Western Europe from the Classical Tradition, the severance of the Western Church from its intellectual sources. In himself he summed up and by his prestige

* *St. Augustine and His Age,* Christopher Dawson.

gave to the new Europe all that was richest in the Classics: "The course of studies which St. Augustine had described in his treatise *On Christian Doctrine* became the programme of the monastic schools." * And in him the Western Church produced its first towering intellect—and indeed its last for another six hundred years. Just that one man, just when he was wanted. The great German non-Catholic scholar Harnack says: "It would seem that the miserable existence of the Roman Empire in the West was prolonged until then only to permit Augustine's influence to be exercised on universal history." *

What he was to mean for the future can only be indicated. All the men who had to bring Europe through the six or seven centuries that followed fed upon him. We see Pope Gregory the Great at the end of the sixth century reading and re-reading the *Confessions*. We see the Emperor Charlemagne at the end of the eighth century using the *City of God* as a kind of Bible. As Christopher Dawson has said: "To the materialist nothing could be more futile than the spectacle of Augustine busying himself with the reunion of the African church and the refutation of the Pelagians, while civilisation was falling about his ears. It would seem like the activity of an ant which works on while its nest is being destroyed. But St. Augustine saw things otherwise. To him the ruin of civilisation and the destruction of the Empire were not very important things. He looked beyond the aimless and bloody chaos of history to the world of eternal realities." *

If you wonder why that one man should have been able to send his message as far as we have seen that Augustine sent his, read the *Confessions* and find the sort of man he was.

* *Ibid.*

# A NOTE ON THE MANICHEES

The founder of Manichaeism, called Mani or (by the Greeks and Romans) Manes, was born in Babylonia about 215. At the age of 25 or 26 he first propounded his new religion in Persia; he was persecuted by the Zoroastrians, travelled widely, spreading his doctrines, and about the year 276 was crucified in Persia by Bahram I.

His religion, made up of borrowings from all the religions he met (including Christianity) with additional items and a general framework supplied by himself, is far too complicated to be set down shortly. There is much uncertainty as to almost every point of his teaching, and indeed it probably varied in different times and places. But these would seem to be its main points:

(1) In the beginning were two Principles, one Good, one Evil, God and Satan. Each of these has his kingdom, the Kingdom of Light and the Kingdom of Darkness. The two Kingdoms have one border in common, but in every other direction they are infinite.

(2) Each of these kingdoms is organised with incredible complexity. God, the Father of Light, has his kingdom proper with its Five Tabernacles (Intelligence, Reason, Thought, Reflection, Will) which are also called Aeons, and sometimes Angels. He also has his sub-kingdoms, Light-Air and Light-Earth, and each of these has five attributes. (The figure 5 is a key figure in Manes' doctrine because of some astrological significance he found in it.)

The Kingdom of Darkness has an organisation roughly parallel: the kingdom proper with its five Aeons (Wells of Poison, Columns of Smoke, Abysmal Depths, Fetid Marshes, Pillars of Fire) and sub-kingdoms each with five attributes.

(3) Satan invaded the Kingdom of Light. God himself did not fight Satan, but emanated Primal-Man (he is not to be confused with Adam) who in turn emanated Five Sons and these battled

against Satan and his Five Elements. Satan won and devoured Primal-Man and his Five Elements; which thus remained as scattered Elements of Light in the Kingdom of Darkness.

(4) A male and female devil in the Kingdom of Darkness bring forth Adam and Eve; in Adam's body are a vast number of these Seeds of Light, in Eve's a smaller number (this remains true of men and women generally). Cain and Abel are sons of Satan and Eve, Seth and the rest of the human race of Adam and Eve. Adam's fall consisted in yielding to the seductions of sex: the generation of Seth was his primary sin.

(5) The Spirits of Light took pity on men and sent Aeons to help them. One of the Aeons thus sent to deliver man is Jesus— not Jesus of Nazareth, who, according to Manes, was an imposter, a devil, who interfered in the work of the real Jesus. It is difficult to be quite clear about the Manichaean Jesus. He personifies the Light imprisoned in matter. As such all that happens in matter happens to him, so that he is always being born and suffering and dying. In particular he is eaten in all food. But some part of that imprisoned Light has already been released, and this is the same Jesus, but luminous. It is in this capacity that he works to deliver man; in the other he is in need of deliverance himself.

There is a continuing war for Men between Aeons of Light and Demons. The Aeons try to deliver men by teaching them the truth about nature and the powers of nature, and calling men from sensuality. The Aeons work through Prophets of whom Manes is the last and greatest, the "Paraclete."

(6) The whole of history is concerned with the effort to free the Light elements imprisoned in the Kingdom of Darkness and restore them to the Kingdom of Light. When all are thus restored, a conflagration will destroy the world, the Kingdom of Light and Darkness will be once more separated, and there will be no further invasion.

(7) Men could co-operate either with the Aeons of Light or the Demons. In general the use of matter was a co-operation with the Demons: and the act of generation was the extreme point of this co-operation. If at death a man was purified, his soul would

go to the Kingdom of Light; if not, there was a long process of purification. Some, of course, were beyond purification: they would be damned: among these is Eve who went to eternal damnation for seducing Adam. Here upon earth all believers were not in this purified state. There were the small number of Elect and the great body of Hearers. The Elect were bound to celibacy and were forbidden all flesh meat (for this is a special weapon of the powers of Darkness); they ate vegetables, and some vegetables were especially favored as containing a greater number of Light elements—of the cosmic Jesus in fact; and when the Elect ate them, these Light particles were set free. For the Hearers there were no such strict rules. They were urged to virtue, but if they fell into sin they had the consolation of knowing that these sins were something they were not responsible for but the acts of a foreign power working in them.

(8) Almost all rulers—Christian and pagan—persecuted Manichaeism as an enemy of morality. But it proved hard to destroy, and in the form of Albigensianism was an immense threat to mediaeval civilisation.

# CONTENTS

*Book Four*

# FROM EIGHTEEN TO TWENTY-SEVEN

### I–III  *Searching for Deliverance*

### IV–IX  *Loss of a Friend*

### X–XII  *The Transience of Created Things*

### XIII–XV  *He Writes a Book*

### XVI  *Reads Aristotle on the Categories*

*Book Five*

# AGED TWENTY-EIGHT

### I–II  *Prayer*

### XVIII–XXI   *The Need for Christ*

### *Book Eight*

## AGED THIRTY-ONE

### I–IV   *The Conversion of Victorinus*

### V–XII   *Augustine's Conversion*

### Book Nine

## AGED THIRTY-TWO

### I–VII   *Reception into the Church*

### VIII–XIII   *The Death of Monica*

### Book Ten

## CONCLUDES AUGUSTINE'S CONFESSION

### I–V   *Why He Makes This Confession*

## Book Eleven

# IN THE BEGINNING GOD CREATED . . .
## (Genesis I, 1)

## Book Twelve

# . . . HEAVEN AND EARTH
## (Genesis I, 1-2)

## *Book Thirteen*

## THE DAYS OF CREATION

### (Genesis I, 2-31)

## TRANSLATOR'S NOTE

The use of *Thou* or *You* in speaking to God presented a real problem. St. Augustine, of course, knew nothing of *Thou* as a term reserved for religious use. He, like any other writer of Latin, used *Tu* when he was talking to one (whether it were God or his mother or his mistress or an opponent in controversy), *Vos* when he was talking to more than one. It would seem therefore that our usage of *Thou*, with the special religious atmosphere that now goes with it, introduces a note into the translation that was not in the original.

On the other hand, Christians of the English tongue are so accustomed to using *Thou* in their prayers, that *You* would sound odd.

St. Augustine is addressing God all the time: he relates the story of his life to God, discusses philosophical problems with God, and from time to time breaks into what we should more naturally regard as prayer to God. If *Thou* is used throughout, the effect is quite intolerably archaic and untrue to the extreme modernness of St. Augustine's Latin. I have therefore made a compromise: in passages of straight prayer, I have used *Thou*; but when he addresses God in narrative or discussion, I have used *You*.

The border-line between prayer and discussion (or narrative) is not always quite clear. And, even apart from that, it has not been possible to apply the rule with entire consistency. Where St. Augustine uses Scripture passages in which our English version uses *Thou*, I have kept *Thou*; and in his own comments arising out of or linking such Scripture passages, it seemed best to keep to *Thou*.

Texts of Scripture, even where Augustine modifies them a little, are printed in italics; but not scattered phrases from Scripture.

I have occasionally inserted a phrase for greater clarity. Such phrases will be found in square brackets.

# CONFESSIONS
# OF ST. AUGUSTINE

# BOOK ONE

## THE FIRST FIFTEEN YEARS

GREAT *art Thou, O Lord, and greatly to be praised; great is Thy power, and of Thy wisdom there is no number.* And man desires to praise Thee. He is but a tiny part of all that Thou hast created. He bears about him his mortality, the evidence of his sinfulness, and the evidence that *Thou dost resist the proud:* yet this tiny part of all that Thou hast created desires to praise Thee.

Thou dost so excite him that to praise Thee is his joy. For Thou hast made us for Thyself and our hearts are restless till they rest in Thee. Grant me, O Lord, to know which is the soul's first movement toward Thee—to implore Thy aid or to utter its praise of Thee; and whether it must know Thee before it can implore. For it would seem clear that no one can call upon Thee without knowing Thee, for if he did he might invoke another than Thee, knowing Thee not. Yet may it be that a man must implore Thee before he can know Thee? But, *how shall they call on Him in Whom they have not believed? or how shall they believe without a preacher?* And, *they shall praise the Lord that seek Him;* for those that seek shall find; and finding Him they will praise Him. Let me seek Thee, Lord, by praying Thy aid, and let me utter my prayer believing in Thee: for Thou hast been preached to us. My faith, Lord, cries to Thee, the faith that Thou hast given me, that Thou hast inbreathed in me, through the humanity of Thy Son and by the ministry of Thy Preacher.

## II

But how can I call unto my God, my God and Lord? For in calling unto Him, I am calling Him to me: and what room is there in me for my God, the God who made heaven and earth? Is there anything in me, O God, that can contain You? All heaven and earth cannot contain You for You made them, and me in them. Yet, since nothing that is could exist without You, You must in some way be in all that is: [therefore also in me, since I am]. And if You are already in me, since otherwise I should not be, why do I cry to You to enter into me? Even if I were in Hell You would be there *for if I go down into hell, Thou art there also.* Thus, O God, I should be nothing, utterly nothing, unless You were in me—or rather unless I were in You, *of Whom and by Whom and in Whom are all things.* So it is, Lord; so it is. Where do I call You to come to, since I am in You? Or where else are You that You can come to me? Where shall I go, beyond the bounds of heaven and earth, that God may come to me, since He has said: *Heaven and earth do I fill.*

### III

But if You fill heaven and earth, do they contain You? Or do You fill them, and yet have much over since they cannot contain You? Is there some other place into which that overplus of You pours that heaven and earth cannot hold? Surely You have no need of any place to contain You since You contain all things, and fill them indeed precisely by containing them. The vessels thus filled with You do not render You any support: for though they perished utterly, You would not be spilt out. And in pouring Yourself out upon us, You do not come down to us but rather elevate us to You: You are not scattered over us, but we are gathered into one by You. You fill all things: but with Your whole being? It is true that all things cannot wholly contain You: but does this mean that they contain part of You? and do they all contain the same part at the same time? or do different parts of creation contain different parts of You—greater parts or smaller according to their own magnitude? But are there in You parts greater and smaller? Or are You not in every place at once in the totality of Your being, while yet nothing contains You wholly?

IV

What then is my God, what but the Lord God? *For Who is Lord but the Lord, or Who is God but our God?* O Thou, the greatest and the best, mightiest, almighty, most merciful and most just, utterly hidden and utterly present, most beautiful and most strong, abiding yet mysterious, suffering no change and changing all things: never new, never old, making all things new, *bringing age upon the proud and they know it not;* ever in action, ever at rest, gathering all things to Thee and needing none; sustaining and fulfilling and protecting, creating and nourishing and making perfect; ever seeking though lacking nothing. Thou lovest without subjection to passion, Thou art jealous but not with fear; Thou canst know repentance but not sorrow, be angry yet unperturbed by anger. Thou canst change the works Thou hast made but Thy mind stands changeless. Thou dost find and receive back what Thou didst never lose; art never in need but dost rejoice in Thy gains, art not greedy but dost exact interest manifold. Men pay Thee more than is of obligation to win return from Thee, yet who has anything that is not already Thine? Thou owest nothing yet dost pay as if in debt to Thy creature, forgivest what is owed to Thee yet dost not lose thereby. And with all this, what have I said, my God and my Life and my sacred Delight? What can anyone say when he speaks of Thee? Yet woe to them that speak not of Thee at all, since those who say most are but dumb.

V

Who shall grant me to rest in Thee? By whose gift shalt Thou enter into my heart and fill it so compellingly that I shall turn no more to my sins but embrace Thee, my only good? What art Thou to me? Have mercy, that I may tell. What rather am I to Thee, that Thou shouldst demand my love and if I do not love Thee be angry and threaten such great woes? Surely not to love Thee is already a great woe. For Thy mercies' sake, O Lord my God, tell me what Thou art to me. *Say unto my soul, I am Thy salvation.* So speak that I may hear, Lord, my heart is listening; open it that it may hear Thee say to my soul *I am Thy salvation.* Hearing that word, let me come in haste to lay hold upon Thee. Hide not Thy face from me. Let me see Thy face even if I die, lest I die with longing to see it.

The house of my soul is too small to receive Thee: let it be enlarged by Thee. It is all in ruins: do Thou repair it. There are things in it that must offend Thy gaze, I confess and know. But who shall cleanse it? or to what other besides Thee shall I cry out: *From my secret sins cleanse me, O Lord, and from those of others spare Thy servant? I believe, and therefore do I speak.* Lord Thou knowest, *Have I not confessed against myself my transgressions against Thee, and Thou, my God, hast forgiven the iniquities of my heart? I contend not in judgment with Thee,* who art the truth; and I have no will to deceive myself, *lest my iniquity lie unto itself.* Therefore I contend not in judgment with Thee, for *if Thou, O Lord, wilt mark iniquities, Lord, who shall endure it?*

### VI

Yet, though I am but dust and ashes, suffer me to utter my plea to Thy mercy; suffer me to speak since it is to God's mercy that I speak and not to man's scorn. From Thee too I might have scorn, but Thou wilt return and have compassion on me. What have I to say to Thee, God, save that I know not where I came from, when I came into this life-in-death—or should I call it death-in-life? I do not know. I only know that the gifts Your mercy had provided sustained me from the first moment: not that I remember it but so I have heard from the parents of my flesh, the father from whom, and the mother in whom, You fashioned me in time.

Thus for my sustenance and my delight I had woman's milk: yet it was not my mother or my nurses who stored their breasts for me: it was Yourself, using them to give me the food of my infancy, according to Your ordinance and the riches set by You at every level of creation. It was by Your gift that I desired what You gave and no more, by Your gift that those who suckled me willed to give me what You had given them: for it was by the love implanted in them by You that they gave so willingly that milk which by Your gift flowed in the breasts. It was a good for them that I received good from them, though I received it not *from* them but only through them: since all good things are from You, O God, and *from God is all my health*. But this I have learnt since: You have made it abundantly clear by all that I have seen You give, within me and about me. For at that time I knew how to suck, to lie quiet when I was content, to cry when I was in pain: and that was all I knew.

Later I added smiling to the things I could do, first in sleep, then awake. This again I have on the word of others, for naturally I do not remember; in any event, I believe it, for I have seen other infants do the same. And gradually I began to notice where I was, and the will grew in me to make my wants known to those who might satisfy them; but I could not, for my wants were within me and those others were outside: nor had they any faculty enabling them to enter into my mind. So I would fling my arms and legs about and utter sounds, making the few gestures in my power—these being as apt to express my wishes as I could make them: but they were not very apt. And when I did not get what I wanted, either because my wishes were not clear or the things not good for me, I was in a rage —with my parents as though I had a right to their submission, with free human beings as though they had been bound to serve me; and I took my revenge in screams. That infants are like this, I have learnt from watching other infants; and that I was like it myself I have learnt more clearly from these other infants, who did not know me, than from my nurses who did.

That infancy of mine died long since, yet I still live. But there is something I would enquire of You, Lord, because Your life is for ever and in You nothing dies: for before the beginning of time, before anything that can even be called "before," You are—and You are the God and Lord of all that You have created: and before Your face stand the causes of all things transient and the changeless principles of all things that change, and the eternal reasons of all the things of unreason and of time. Therefore, O God, tell me I beg, in pity to a creature who needs pity, whether my infancy followed upon some earlier age of my life that had passed away before it. Was the time I spent in my mother's womb such another age? I have heard something of [my mother's condition at] that time, and I have seen women big with child. And before that again, O God of my joy? Was I anywhere? Was I anyone? There is none to tell me—neither my parents, nor any man's experience, nor any memory of my own. Perhaps You laugh at me for seeking to know of such things since it is Your will that I adore You and praise You for what I do know. And I do truly, Lord of heaven and earth, adore You and praise You for my first being and the infancy of which I have now no memory: for You have left man to learn these things about himself from others, to accept much that touches him so closely on the word of his womenfolk.

Clearly then I had being and I had life: and toward the end of my infancy I tried hard to find ways of making my feelings known to others. Whence could such a living being come but from You, Lord? Could any man be his own maker? Or is there any other channel through which being and life should flow into us, save that we are made by You, Lord, to whom "being" and "being alive" are not two separate things, since infinite Being is identical with infinite Life? For You are infinite and in You is no change, nor does today pass away in You. Yet in another sense in You it does pass away, for in You are all such things—they could not

even have any being that could pass away unless You upheld
them in being. And because Your years do not pass, Your
years are today; and no matter how many our days and our
fathers' days have been, they have all passed in Your undying
day and from it have received such being and measures as
they had: and all the days to come shall similarly pass in
Your undying day and shall receive from it their being and
measures. But You are still the same. All our tomorrows to
the end of time You shall make to be in this Your day; and
all our yesterdays from the beginning of time You have
made to be in this Your day. What is it to me, if anyone does
not understand this? Let him rejoice as he asks: *What is this?*
Let him rejoice, and let him prefer to find You even if he
does not find this, rather than to find it and not You with it.

## VII

O God hear me! Woe unto men for their sins! When man
cries thus, You have mercy upon him, for You made man
but not the sin in him. Who shall remind me of the sins
of my infancy: *for in Thy sight there is none pure from
sin, not even the infant whose life is but a day upon the
earth.* But who is to inform me? Perhaps this or that tiny
child in whom I can see what I no longer remember of myself. [If he is to teach me] what then were my sins at that age?
That I wailed too fiercely for the breast? For if today I were
to make as gluttonously and as clamorously, not of course
for my mother's breasts, but for the food I now eat, I should
be ridiculed and quite properly condemned. This means
that what I did then was in fact reprehensible, although,
since I could not understand words of blame, neither custom
nor commonsense allowed me to be blamed. As we grow
older we root out such ways and cast them from us: [which
means that we hold them to be bad]—for no man engaged
in removing evil would knowingly cast out what is good.
Surely it was not good, even for that time of life, to scream
for things that would have been thoroughly bad for me;
to fly into hot rage because older persons—and free, not

slaves—were not obedient to me; to strike out as hard as I could, with sheer will to hurt, at my parents and other sensible folk for not yielding to demands which could only have been granted at my peril. Thus the innocence of children is in the helplessness of their bodies rather than any quality in their minds. I have myself seen a small baby jealous; it was too young to speak, but it was livid with anger as it watched another infant at the breast.

There is nothing unusual in this. Mothers and nurses will tell you that they have their own way of curing these fits of jealousy. But at any rate it is an odd kind of innocence when a baby cannot bear that another—in great need, since upon that one food his very life depends—should share the milk that flows in such abundance. These childish tempers are borne with lightly, not because they are not faults, or only small faults; but because they will pass with the years. This is clearly so: for though we bear with them now, the same things would not be tolerated in an older person.

You, O Lord my God, gave me in my infancy life and a body; and You supplied the body with senses, fitted it with limbs, gave it shape and proportion, and for its general well-being and security implanted in it all the instincts of a living being. And You, Lord, doer of all these things, command me to praise You in them, *to confess unto Thee and sing to Thy name, O most high;* because You are God, omnipotent and good, even if You had done these things alone: for none other can do them save You, the One, who are the exemplar of all things, the All-Beautiful, who form and set in order all things by Your law.

Thus, Lord, I do not remember living this age of my infancy; I must take the word of others about it and can only conjecture how I spent it—even if with a fair amount of certainty—from watching others now in the same stage. I am loth, indeed, to count it as part of the life I live in this world. For it is buried in the darkness of the forgotten as completely as the period earlier still that I spent in my mother's womb. But if *I was conceived in iniquity, and in sin my mother nourished me in the womb*, then where, my God, where, O Lord, where or when was I, Your servant, innocent? But I pass now from that time. For what concern have I now with a time of which I can recall no trace?

## VIII

From infancy I came to boyhood, or rather it came to me, taking the place of infancy. Yet infancy did not go: for where was it to go to? Simply it was no longer there. For now I was not an infant, without speech, but a boy, speaking. This I remember; and I have since discovered by observation how I learned to speak. I did not learn by elders teaching me words in any systematic way, as I was soon after taught to read and write. But of my own motion, using the mind which You, my God, gave me, I strove with cries and various sounds and much moving of my limbs to utter the feelings of my heart—all this in order to get my own way. Now I did not always manage to express the right meanings to the right people. So I began to reflect. [I observed that] my elders would make some particular sound, and as they made it would point at or move towards some particular thing: and from this I came to realize that the thing was called by the sound they made when they wished to draw my attention to it. That they intended this was clear from the motions of their body, by a kind of natural language common to all races which consists in facial expressions, glances of the eye, gestures, and the tones by which the voice expresses the mind's state—for example whether things are to be sought, kept, thrown away, or avoided. So, as I heard the same words again and again properly used in different phrases, I came gradually to grasp what things they signified; and forcing my mouth to the same sounds, I began to use them to express my own wishes. Thus I learnt to convey what I meant to those about me; and so took another long step along the stormy way of human life in society, while I was still subject to the authority of my parents and at the beck and call of my elders.

## IX

O God, my God, what emptiness and mockeries did I now experience: for it was impressed upon me as right and proper in a boy to obey those who taught me, that I might get on in the world and excel in the handling of words to gain honor among men and deceitful riches. I, poor wretch, could not see the use of the things I was sent to school to learn; but if I proved idle in learning, I was soundly beaten. For this procedure seemed wise to our ancestors: and many, passing the same way in days past, had built a sorrowful road by which we too must go, with multiplication of grief and toil upon the sons of Adam.

Yet, Lord, I observed men praying to You: and I learnt to do likewise, thinking of You (to the best of my understanding) as some great being who, though unseen, could hear and help me. As a boy I fell into the way of calling upon You, my Help and my Refuge; and in those prayers I broke the strings of my tongue—praying to You, small as I was but with no small energy, that I might not be beaten at school. And when You did not hear me (*not as giving me over to folly*), my elders and even my parents, who certainly wished me no harm, treated my stripes as a huge joke, which they were very far from being to me. Surely, Lord, there is no one so steeled in mind or cleaving to You so close—or even so insensitive, for that might have the same effect—as to make light of the racks and hooks and other torture instruments (from which in all lands men pray so fervently to be saved) while truly loving those who are in such bitter fear of them. Yet my parents seemed to be amused at the torments inflicted upon me as a boy by my masters, though I was no less afraid of my punishments or zealous in my prayers to You for deliverance. But in spite of my terrors I still did wrong, by writing or reading or studying less than my set tasks. It was not, Lord, that I lacked mind or memory, for You had given me as much of these as my age re-

quired; but the one thing I revelled in was play; and for
this I was punished by men who after all were doing exactly the same things themselves. But the idling of men is
called business; the idling of boys, though exactly like, is
punished by those same men: and no one pities either boys or
men. Perhaps an unbiased observer would hold that I was
rightly punished as a boy for playing with a ball: because this
hindered my progress in studies—studies which would give
me the opportunity as a man to play at things more degraded.
And what difference was there between me and the master
who flogged me? For if on some trifling point he had the
worst of the argument with some fellow-master, he was more
torn with angry vanity than I when I was beaten in a game
of ball.

X

Yet in acting against the commands of my parents and
schoolmasters, I did wrong, O Lord my God, Creator and
Ruler of all things, but of sin not Creator but Ruler only:
for I might later have made good use of those lessons that
they wanted me to learn, whatever may have been their
motive in wanting it. I disobeyed, not because I had chosen
better, but through sheer love of play: I loved the vanity
of victory, and I loved too to have my ears tickled with
the fictions of the theatre which set them to itching ever
more burningly: and in my eyes a similar curiosity burned
increasingly for the games and shows of my elders. Yet
those who put on such shows are held in high esteem.
And most people would be delighted to have their sons
grow up to give similar shows in their turn—and meanwhile
fully concur in the beatings those same sons get if these
shows hinder study: for study is the way to the prosperity
necessary for giving them! Look down in mercy, Lord, upon
such things; and set us free who now beseech Thee: and not
only us, but those also who have never besought Thee—
that they may turn to Thee and be made free.

## XI

Even as a boy, of course, I had heard of an eternal life promised because the Lord our God had come down in His humility upon our pride. And I was signed with the sign of His Cross and seasoned with His salt as I came new from the womb of my mother, who had great trust in You. When I was still a child, I fell gravely ill with some abdominal trouble and was close to death. You saw, Lord—for You were even then guarding me—with what earnest faith I besought the piety of my own mother, and of the Church which is the mother of us all, that I might receive the baptism of Your Christ, my Lord and my God. The mother of my flesh was in heavy anxiety, since with a heart chaste in Your faith she was ever in deep travail for my eternal salvation, and would have proceeded without delay to have me consecrated and washed clean by the Sacrament of salvation, while I confessed You, Lord Jesus, unto the remission of sins: but I made a sudden recovery. This caused my baptismal cleansing to be postponed: for it was argued that if I lived I should inevitably fall again into the filth of sin: and after baptism the guilt of sin's defilement would be in itself graver and put the soul in graver peril. I then believed, as did my mother and all our household, except my father: yet he did not prevail over the hold my mother's piety had upon me, to lead me not to believe in Christ because he did not as yet. She used all her endeavor, O God, that I should hold You for my father rather than him: and in this with Your aid she overcame her husband, in her greater virtue serving him because in serving him she served Your command likewise.

I ask You, my God—for I would know, if it is Your will to tell me—to what end was my baptism deferred? was it for my good that I was left to sin with a loose rein, or was the rein not truly loosed? Why do we constantly hear such phrases as: "Let him alone, let him keep on with what he is doing, he is not yet baptized"? In the matter of the body's health we do not say: "Let him be wounded worse, he

is not yet cured." It would have been far better had I
been made whole at once and had so used my own efforts
and the aid of my friends that the health brought to my soul
should be safe in Your keeping, by whose gift it was given
me. Far better, I say. But it was obvious that many mighty
waves of temptation threatened to break upon me as I grew
out of boyhood. So my mother knew: and she thought it
better to let them break upon the clay before it was moulded
to Christ's image rather than let the clay be moulded and
then assailed.

XII

But to continue with my boyhood, which was in less peril
of sin than my adolescence. I disliked learning and hated
to be forced to it. But I *was* forced to it, so that good was
done to me though it was not my doing. Short of being driven
to it, I certainly would not have learned. But no one does
well against his will, even if the thing he does is a good
thing to do. Nor did those who forced me do well: it was
by You, O God, that well was done. Those others had no
deeper vision of the use to which I might put all they
forced me to learn, but to sate the insatiable desire of man
for wealth that is but penury and glory that is but shame.
But You, Lord, *by Whom the very hairs of our head are
numbered,* used for my good the error of those who urged
me to study; but my own error, in that I had no will to
learn, you used for my punishment—a punishment richly
deserved by one so small a boy and so great a sinner. Thus,
You brought good for me out of those who did ill, and justly
punished me for the ill I did myself. So You have ordained
and so it is: that every disorder of the soul is its own
punishment.

XIII

To this day I do not quite see why I so hated the Greek
tongue that I was made to learn as a small boy. For I really
liked Latin—not the rudiments that we got from our first

teachers but the literature that we came to be taught later. For the rudiments—reading and writing and figuring—I found as hard and hateful as Greek. Yet this too could come only from sin and the vanity of life, because *I was flesh, and a wind that goes away and returns not.* For those first lessons were the surer. I acquired the power I still have to read what I find written and to write what I want to express; whereas in the studies that came later I was forced to memorise the wanderings of Aeneas—whoever *he* was—while forgetting my own wanderings; and to weep for the death of Dido who killed herself for love, while bearing dry-eyed my own pitiful state, in that among these studies I was becoming dead to You, O God, my life.

Nothing could be more pitiful than a pitiable creature who does not see to pity himself, and weeps for the death that Dido suffered through love of Aeneas and not for the death he suffers himself through not loving You, O God, Light of my heart, Bread of my soul, Power wedded to my mind and the depths of my thought. I did not love You and I went away from You in fornication: and all around me in my fornication echoed applauding cries "Well done! Well done!" *For the friendship of this world is fornication against Thee:* and the world cries "Well done" so loudly that one is ashamed of unmanliness not to do it. And for this I did not grieve; but I grieved for Dido, slain as she sought by the sword an end to her woe, while I too followed after the lowest of Your creatures, forsaking You, earth going unto earth. And if I were kept from reading, I grieved at not reading the tales that caused me such grief. This sort of folly is held nobler and richer than the studies by which we learn to read and write!

But now let my God cry aloud in my soul, and let Your truth assure me that it is not so: the earlier study is the better. I would more willingly forget the wanderings of Aeneas and all such things than how to write and read. Over the entrance of these grammar schools hangs a curtain: but this should be seen not as lending honor to the

mysteries, but as a cloak to the errors taught within. Let
not those masters—who have now lost their terrors for me
—cry out against me, because I confess to You, my God,
the desire of my soul, and find soul's rest in blaming my
evil ways that I may love Your holy ways. Let not the buyers
or sellers of book-learning cry out against me. If I ask
them whether it is true, as the poet says, that Aeneas ever
went to Carthage, the more ignorant will have to answer
that they do not know, the more scholarly that he certainly
did not. But if I ask with what letters the name Aeneas is
spelt, all whose schooling has gone so far will answer correctly, according to the convention men have agreed upon
for the use of letters. Or again, were I to ask which loss
would be more damaging to human life—the loss from
men's memory of reading and writing or the loss of these
poetic imaginings—there can be no question what anyone
would answer who had not lost his own memory. Therefore
as a boy I did wrong in liking the empty studies more than
the useful—or rather in loving the empty and hating the
useful. For one and one make two, two and two make four,
I found a loathsome refrain; but such empty unrealities as
the Wooden Horse with its armed men, and Troy on fire,
and Creusa's Ghost, were sheer delight.

XIV

But why did I hate Greek literature, which is filled with
similar tales? Homer is as skilled in the invention of such
things, and has the same charm and the same unreality:
yet as a boy I could not abide him. I suppose that Virgil
affects Greek boys when they are compelled to learn him as
Homer affected me. For the drudgery of learning a foreign
language sprinkled bitterness over all the sweetness of the
Greek tales. I did not know a word of the language: and I
was driven with threats and savage punishments to learn.
There had been a time of infancy when I knew no Latin
either. Yet I learnt it without threat or punishment merely
by keeping my eyes and ears open, amidst the flatterings of

nurses and the jesting and pleased laughter of elders leading me on. I learnt it without the painful pressure of compulsion, by the sole pressure of my own desire to express what was in my mind, which would have been impossible unless I had learnt words: and I learnt them not through people teaching me but simply through people speaking: to whom I was striving to utter my own feelings. All this goes to prove that free curiosity is of more value in learning than harsh discipline. But by Your ordinance, O God, discipline must control the free play of curiosity—for Your ordinance ranges from the master's cane to the torments suffered by the martyrs, and works that mingling of bitter with sweet which brings us back to You from the poison of pleasure that first drew us away from You.

## XV

Hear my prayer, O Lord; let not my soul fail under Thy discipline, nor let me fail in uttering to Thee Thy mercies: by them Thou hast drawn me out of all my most evil ways, that I should find more delight in Thee than in all the temptations I once ran after, and should love Thee more intensely, and lay hold upon Thy hand with all my heart's strength, and be delivered from every temptation unto the end.

O Lord, my King and my God: may whatever of value I learnt as a boy be used for Thy service, and what I now do in speaking and writing and reading and figuring. When I was learning vain things, Thou didst discipline me: and the sin of the delight I had in those vain things, Thou hast forgiven me. Among those studies, I learnt many a useful word, but these might have been learnt equally well in studies not vain: and that surely is the safe way for the young to tread.

## XVI

But [in this matter of classical studies] how woeful are you, O torrent of established custom. Who can resist you

or when will you run dry? How long will you continue to
roll the sons of Eve into that vast and terrible sea in which
even those who mount the cross scarcely escape drowning?
In you I read of Jove, both as the God of thunder and
as an adulterer. How could he be both? But so the story
goes: and so sham thunder is made to legitimize and play
pander to real adultery: yet these robed and gowned masters
are furious when Cicero, a man trained in their own school,
protests: "Homer invented these stories, ascribing things
human to the Gods: would that he had brought down things
divine to us." It would have been even truer to say that
Homer invented them, attributing divinity to the vilest of
men, with the result that crimes are held not to be crimes,
and those who do commit them are regarded as acting not
like abandoned men but like Gods from Olympus.

And still, O torrent from hell, the sons of men pay fees
to be hurled into you in order that they may learn such
things. And there is great interest when this sort of teaching
is carried on publicly in the forum under the very eye of laws
allotting salaries to the masters over and above the fees
paid by the pupils. And all the while the torrent lashes its
rocks and roars: "By these studies words are learned and the
eloquence acquired which is so necessary for persuasion and
exposition." Apparently the argument is that we should not
have come to know words like "golden," "shower," "lap,"
"deceive," "the temple of Heaven," and others of the sort,
unless Terence had brought a vicious youth upon the stage,
setting up Jove as a model for his own fornication, and all
the while gazing upon a picture on the wall of Jove deceiving
Danae by descending into her lap as a golden shower. Note
how the youth incites himself to lust as though commanded
from Heaven:
And what a God! [Jove] who shakes the temples of heaven
    with the roar of his thunder!
And I, a mere mortal, should I not do what he does? I have
    done it, and with joy.

The words are not learned one whit more easily because

of all this vileness: but the vileness is committed all the more boldly because of the words. I make no accusation against the words, which in themselves are choice and precious vessels, but against the wine of error that is in them, and is poured out to us by teachers already drunken with it. And we, unless we drank, were flogged and had no right of appeal to any sober judge. And I, my God, in Whose sight I can now recall these things without peril, learnt them willingly, and sinfully delighted in them, and so was regarded as a youth of much promise.

### XVII

Give me leave, O my God, to speak of my mind, Your gift, and of the follies in which I wasted it. It chanced that a task was set me, a task which I did not like but had to do. There was the promise of glory if I won, the fear of ignominy, and a flogging as well, if I lost. It was to declaim the words uttered by Juno in her rage and grief when she could not keep the Trojan prince from coming to Italy. I had learnt that Juno had never said these words, but we were compelled to err in the footsteps of the poet who had invented them: and it was our duty to paraphrase in prose what he had said in verse. In this exercise that boy won most applause in whom the passions of grief and rage were expressed most powerfully and in the language most adequate to the majesty of the personage represented.

What could all this mean to me, O My true Life, My God? Why was there more applause for the performance I gave than for so many classmates of my own age? Was not the whole business so much smoke and wind? Surely some other matter could have been found to exercise mind and tongue. Thy praises, Lord, might have upheld the fresh young shoot of my heart, so that it might not have been whirled away by empty trifles, defiled, a prey to the spirits of the air. For there is more than one way of sacrificing to the fallen angels.

## XVIII

Yet it was no wonder that I fell away into vanity and went
so far from Thee, My God, seeing that men were held up
as models for my imitation who were covered with shame
if, in relating some act of theirs in no way evil, they fell
into some barbarism or grammatical solecism: yet were
praised, and delighted to be praised, when they told of their
lusts, provided they did so in correct words correctly arranged. All these things Thou seest, O Lord, and art silent:
for Thou art patient and plenteous in mercy and truth. But
wilt Thou always stay silent? Even now Thou dost draw out
of this pit of horror the soul that seeks Thee and thirsts
for Thy joys, *the heart that says to Thee I have sought
Thy face: Thy face, Lord, will I still seek:* for to be darkened in heart is to be far from Thy face. It is not on
our feet or by movement in space that we go from Thee or
return to Thee: Thy prodigal son did not charter horses or
chariots or ships, or fly with wings or journey on his two
feet to that far country where he wasted in luxurious living
what Thou as a loving father hadst given him on his departure—loving when Thou didst give, more loving still to Thy
son when he returned, all poor and stripped. To be lustful,
that is darkened, in heart, is to be far from Thy face.

Behold, O Lord My God, and, seeing, see patiently, with
what anxious care the sons of men observe the rules of letters and syllables taught by the speakers of our tongue before us, while they neglect the eternal rules of everlasting
salvation taught by You. The learner or teacher of the established rules of pronunciation is held more contemptible if
he drops an 'h' and speaks of a 'uman being*—thus breaking a law of language—than if he hates a human being—
thus breaking a law of God. It is strange that we should not
realise that no enemy could be more dangerous to us than
the hatred with which we hate him, and that by our efforts

* Thus neatly does Dr. Pusey represent the man who for "hominem" says
"ominem."

against him we do less damage to our enemy than is wrought in our own heart. Obviously the knowledge of letters is not more deeply engraved in us than the law of conscience against doing to another what one would not bear if done to oneself. How hidden art Thou, O God the only great, dwelling in silence in the high places, and by Thy untiring law sending blindness as the punishment for unlawful lusts. A man seeking the fame of eloquence—before a judge who is also a man, with a multitude of men standing about —inveighs against his adversary with inhuman hatred. Such a man will be most vigilantly on guard lest by a slip of the tongue he drop an 'h' and murder the word "human": yet worries not at all that by the fury of his mind he may murder a real human.

### XIX

These were the ways of the world upon whose threshold I stood as a boy, and such was the arena for which I was train-ing—more concerned to avoid committing a grammatical error than to be void of envy in case I did commit one and another did not. This I say and confess to Thee, O My God: and in this I was praised by those whom my one idea of success was to please. I did not see the whirl of vileness into which I had been cast away from Thy eyes: for what was more unclean than I, seeing that I did not win the ap-proval even of my own kind: I told endless lies to my tutors, my masters and my parents: all for the love of games, the craving for stage shows, and a restlessness to do what I saw done in these shows.

I stole from my parents' cellar and table, sometimes be-cause I was gluttonous myself, sometimes to have something to give other boys in exchange for implements of play which they were prepared to sell although they loved them as much as I. Even in games, when I was clearly outplayed I tried to win by cheating, from the vain desire for first place. At the same time I was indignant and argued furiously when I caught anyone doing the very things that I had done to others. When I was caught myself, I would fly into a rage rather than give way.

Is this boyhood innocence? It is not, Lord. I cry Thy mercy, O My God. Yet as we leave behind tutors and masters and nuts and balls and birds and come to deal with prefects and kings and the getting of gold and estates and slaves, these are the qualities which pass on with us, one stage of life taking the place of another as the greater punishments of the law take the place of the schoolmaster's cane. Therefore, O God our King, when you said "of such is the Kingdom of Heaven," it could only have been humility as symbolised by the low stature of childhood that you were commending.

XX

Yet, Lord, I should have owed thanks to You, My God and the most excellent Creator and Ruler of the Universe, even if it had been Your will that I should not live beyond boyhood. For even then I was; I lived: I felt: even so early I had an instinct for the care of my own being, a trace in me of that most profound Unity whence my being was derived; in my interior sense I kept guard over the integrity of my outward sense perception, and in my small thoughts upon small matters I had come to delight in the truth. I hated to be wrong, had a vigorous memory, was well trained in speech, delighted in friendship, shunned pain, meanness and ignorance. In so small a creature was not all this admirable and reason for praise? Yet all these were the gifts of my God, for I did not give them to myself. All these were good and all these were I. Therefore He Who made me is good and He is my Good: and in Him I shall exult for all the good qualities that even as a boy I had. But in this lay my sin: that I sought pleasure, nobility, and truth not in God but in the beings He had created, myself and others. Thus I fell into sorrow and confusion and error. Thanks be to Thee, my Joy and my Glory and my Hope and my God: thanks be to Thee for Thy gifts: but do Thou preserve them in me.

Thus Thou wilt preserve me, and the things Thou hast given me will increase and be made perfect, and I shall be with Thee: because even that I exist is Thy gift.

# BOOK TWO

## THE SIXTEENTH YEAR

I PROPOSE now to set down my past wickedness and the carnal corruptions of my soul, not for love of them but that I may love Thee, O my God. I do it for love of Thy love, passing again in the bitterness of remembrance over my most evil ways that Thou mayest thereby grow ever lovelier to me, O Loveliness that dost not deceive, Loveliness happy and abiding: and I collect my self out of that broken state in which my very being was torn asunder because I was turned away from Thee, the One, and wasted myself upon the many.

Arrived now at adolescence I burned for all the satisfactions of hell, and I sank to the animal in a succession of dark lusts: *my beauty consumed away,* and I stank in Thine eyes, yet was pleasing in my own and anxious to please the eyes of men.

My one delight was to love and to be loved. But in this I did not keep the measure of mind to mind, which is the luminous line of friendship; but from the muddy concupiscence of the flesh and the hot imagination of puberty mists steamed up to becloud and darken my heart so that I could not distinguish the white light of love from the fog of lust. Both love and lust boiled within me, and swept my youthful immaturity over the precipice of evil desires to leave me half drowned in a whirlpool of abominable sins Your wrath had grown mighty against me and I knew it not. I had grown deaf from the clanking of the chain of my mortality, the punishment for the pride of my soul: and I departed further from You, and You left me to myself: and I was tossed about and wasted and poured out and boiling over in my fornications: and You were silent, O my late-won Joy. You were silent, and I, arrogant and depressed, weary and restless, wandered further and further from You into more and more sins which could bear no fruit save sorrows.

If only there had been some one then to bring relief to the wretchedness of my state, and turn to account the fleeting beauties of these new temptations and bring within bounds their attractions for me: so that the tides of my youth might have driven in upon the shore of marriage: for then they might have been brought to calm with the having of children as Your law prescribes, O Lord, for in this way You form the offspring of this our death, able with gentle hand to blunt the thorns that You would not have in Your paradise. For Your omnipotence is not far from us, even when we are far from You. Or, on the other hand, I might well have listened more heedfully to the voice from the clouds: *"Nevertheless such [as marry] shall have tribulation of the flesh; but I spare you"*; and *"It is good for a man not to touch a woman"*; and *"He that is without a wife is solicitous for the things that belong to the Lord, how he may please God: but he that is with a wife is solicitous for the things of the world, how he may please his wife."* I should have listened more closely to these words and made myself a eunuch for the kingdom of heaven; and so in all tranquillity awaited Your embraces. Instead I foamed in my wickedness, following the rushing of my own tide, leaving You and going beyond all Your laws. Nor did I escape Your scourges. No mortal can. You were always by me, mercifully hard upon me, and besprinkling all my illicit pleasures with certain elements of bitterness, to draw me on to seek for pleasures in which no bitterness should be. And where was I to find such pleasures save in You O Lord, You who use sorrow to teach, and wound us to heal, and kill us lest we die to You. Where then was I, and how far from the delights of Your house, in that sixteenth year of my life in this world, when the madness of lust—needing no licence from human shamelessness, receiving no licence from Your laws—took complete control of me, and I surrendered wholly to it? My family took no care to save me from this moral destruction by marriage: their only concern was that I should learn to make as fine and persuasive speeches as possible.

III

In that year my studies were interrupted. I had come back from Madaura, a neighbouring city to which I had been sent to study grammar and rhetoric, and the money was being got together for the longer journey to Carthage, where I was to go because my father was set upon it—not that he was rich, for he was only a poor citizen of Tagaste. But to whom am I telling this? Not to Thee, O My God, but in Thy presence I am telling it to my own kind, to the race of men, or rather to that small part of the human race that may come upon these writings. And to what purpose do I tell it? Simply that I and any other who may read may realise out of what depths we must cry to Thee. For nothing is more surely heard by Thee than a heart that confesses Thee and a life in Thy faith.

Everyone of course praised my father because, although his means did not allow it, he had somehow provided the wherewithal for his son to travel so far for the sake of his studies. Many a very much richer citizen did no such thing for his children. Yet this same father never bothered about how I was growing towards You or how chaste or unchaste I might be, so long as I grew in eloquence, however much I might lack of Your cultivation O God, who are the one true and good Lord of Your field, my heart.

But during that sixteenth year between Madaura and Carthage, owing to the narrowness of the family fortunes I did not go to school, but lived idly at home with my parents. The briars of unclean lusts grew so that they towered over my head, and there was no hand to root them out. On the contrary my father saw me one day in the public baths, now obviously growing towards manhood and showing the turbulent signs of adolescence. The effect upon him was that he already began to look forward to grandchildren, and went home in happy excitement to tell my mother. He rejoiced, indeed, through that intoxication in which the world forgets You its Creator and loves what You have created instead of You, the intoxication of the invisible wine of a will perverted and turned towards baseness. But in my mother's breast You had already laid the foundation of Your temple and begun Your holy habitation: whereas my father was still only a catechumen, and a new catechumen at that. So that she was stricken with a holy fear. And though I was not as yet baptised, she was in terror of my walking in the crooked ways of those who walk with their backs towards You and not their faces.

I have dared to say that You were silent, my God, when I went afar from You. But was it truly so? Whose but Yours were the words You dinned into my ears through the voice of my mother, Your faithful servant? Not that at that time any of it sank into my heart to make me do it. I still remember her anxiety and how earnestly she urged upon me not to sin with women, above all not with any man's wife. All this sounded to me womanish and I should have blushed to obey. Yet it was from You, though I did not know it and thought that You were silent and she speaking: whereas You were speaking to me through her, and in ignoring her I was ignoring You: I, her son, the son of Your handmaid, Your servant. But I realised none of this and went headlong on my course, so blinded that I was ashamed among the other youths that my viciousness was less than theirs; I heard them boasting of their exploits, and the viler the exploits the louder the boasting; and I set about the same exploits not only for the pleasure of the act but for the pleasure of the boasting.

Nothing is utterly condemnable save vice: yet I grew in vice through desire of praise; and when I lacked opportunity to equal others in vice, I invented things I had not done, lest I might be held cowardly for being innocent, or contemptible for being chaste. With the basest companions I walked the streets of Babylon [the city of this World as opposed to the

city of God] and wallowed in its filth as if it had been a bed
of spices and precious ointments. To make me cleave closer
to that city's very center, the invisible Enemy trod me down
and seduced me, for I was easy to seduce. My mother had
by now fled out of the center of Babylon, but she still
lingered in its outskirts. She had urged me to chastity but she
did not follow up what my father had told her of me: and
though she saw my sexual passions as most evil now and full
of peril for the future, she did not consider that if they could
not be pared down to the quick, they had better be brought
under control within the bounds of married love. She did not
want me married because she feared that a wife might be a
hindrance to my prospects—not those hopes of the world to
come which my mother had in You, O God, but my prospects
as a student. Both my parents were unduly set upon the
success of my studies, my father because he had practically
no thought of You and only vain ambition for me, my
mother because she thought that the usual course of studies
would be not only no hindrance to my coming to You but
an actual help. Recalling the past as well as I can, that is
how I read my parents' characters. Anyhow, I was left to do
pretty well as I liked, and go after pleasure not only beyond
the limit of reasonable discipline but to sheer dissoluteness
in many kinds of evil. And in all this, O God, a mist hung
between my eyes and the brightness of Your truth: *and mine
iniquity had come forth as it were from fatness.*

IV

Your law, O Lord, punishes theft; and this law is so
written in the hearts of men that not even the breaking of
it blots it out: for no thief bears calmly being stolen from—
not even if he is rich and the other steals through want.
Yet I chose to steal, and not because want drove me to it—
unless a want of justice and contempt for it and an excess
for iniquity. For I stole things which I already had in plenty
and of better quality. Nor had I any desire to enjoy the
things I stole, but only the stealing of them and the sin.

There was a pear tree near our vineyard, heavy with fruit,
but fruit that was not particularly tempting either to look at
or to taste. A group of young blackguards, and I among them,
went out to knock down the pears and carry them off late
one night, for it was our bad habit to carry on our games in
the streets till very late. We carried off an immense load of
pears, not to eat—for we barely tasted them before throwing
them to the hogs. Our only pleasure in doing it was that it
was forbidden. Such was my heart, O God, such was my
heart: yet in the depth of the abyss You had pity on it.
Let that heart now tell You what it sought when I was thus
evil for no object, having no cause for wrongdoing save my
wrongness. The malice of the act was base and I loved it—
that is to say I loved my own undoing, I loved the evil in
me—not the thing for which I did the evil, simply the evil:
my soul was depraved, and hurled itself down from security
in You into utter destruction, seeking no profit from wickedness but only to be wicked.

## v

There is an appeal to the eye in beautiful things, in
gold and silver and all such; the sense of touch has its own
powerful pleasures; and the other senses find qualities in
things suited to them. Worldly success has its glory, and
the power to command and to overcome: and from this
springs the thirst for revenge. But in our quest of all these
things, we must not depart from You, Lord, or deviate from
Your Law. This life we live here below has its own attractive-
ness, grounded in the measure of beauty it has and its harmony with the beauty of all lesser things. The bond of human
friendship is admirable, holding many souls as one. Yet
in the enjoyment of all such things we commit sin if through
immoderate inclination to them—for though they are good,
they are of the lowest order of good—things higher and better are forgotten, even You, O Lord our God, and Your
Truth and Your Law. These lower things have their delights but not such as my God has, for He made them all:

*and in Him doth the righteous delight, and He is the joy of*
*the upright of heart.*

Now when we ask why this or that particular evil act was
done, it is normal to assume that it could not have been done
save through the desire of gaining or the fear of losing some
one of these lower goods. For they have their own charm and
their own beauty, though compared with the higher values
of heaven they are poor and mean enough. Such a man has
committed a murder. Why? He wanted the other man's wife
or his property; or he had chosen robbery as a means of livelihood; or he feared to lose this or that through his victim's
act; or he had been wronged and was aflame for vengeance.
Would any man commit a murder for no cause, for the sheer
delight of murdering? The thing would be incredible. There
is of course the case of the man [Catiline] who was said to be
so stupidly and savagely cruel that he practised cruelty and
evil even when he had nothing to gain by them. But even
there a cause was stated—he did it, he said, lest through
idleness his hand or his resolution should grow slack. And
why did he want to prevent that? So that one day by the multiplication of his crimes the city should be his, and he would
have gained honors and authority and riches, and would
no longer be in fear of the law or in the difficulties that
want of money and the awareness of his crimes had brought
him. So that not even Catiline loved his crimes as crimes:
he loved some other thing which was his reason for committing them.

### VI

What was it then that in my wretched folly I loved in you,
O theft of mine, deed wrought in that dark night when I was
sixteen? For you were not lovely: you were a theft. Or are
you anything at all, that I should talk with you? The pears
that we stole were beautiful for they were created by Thee,
Thou most Beautiful of all, Creator of all, Thou good God,
my Sovereign and true Good. The pears were beautiful but it
was not pears that my empty soul desired. For I had any num-

ber of better pears of my own, and plucked those only that I might steal. For once I had gathered them I threw them away, tasting only my own sin and savouring that with delight; for if I took so much as a bite of any one of those pears, it was the sin that sweetened it. And now, Lord my God, I ask what was it that attracted me in that theft, for there was no beauty in it to attract. I do not mean merely that it lacked the beauty that there is in justice and prudence, or in the mind of man or his senses and vegetative life: or even so much as the beauty and glory of the stars in the heavens, or of earth and sea with their oncoming of new life to replace the generations that pass. It had not even that false show or shadow of beauty by which sin tempts us.

[For there *is* a certain show of beauty in sin.] Thus pride wears the mask of loftiness of spirit, although You alone, O God, are high over all. Ambition seeks honor and glory, although You alone are to be honored before all and glorious forever. By cruelty the great seek to be feared, yet who is to be feared but God alone: from His power what can be wrested away, or when or where or how or by whom? The caresses by which the lustful seduce are a seeking for love: but nothing is more caressing than Your charity, nor is anything more healthfully loved than Your supremely lovely, supremely luminous Truth. Curiosity may be regarded as a desire for knowledge, whereas You supremely know all things. Ignorance and sheer stupidity hide under the names of simplicity and innocence: yet no being has simplicity like to Yours: and none is more innocent than You, for it is their own deeds that harm the wicked. Sloth pretends that it wants quietude: but what sure rest is there save the Lord? Luxuriousness would be called abundance and completeness; but You are the fullness and inexhaustible abundance of incorruptible delight. Wastefulness is a parody of generosity: but You are the infinitely generous giver of all good. Avarice wants to possess overmuch: but You possess all. Enviousness claims that it strives to excel: but what can excel before You? Anger clamors for just vengeance: but whose vengeance is so just as Yours? Fear is the recoil from a new and sudden threat to something one holds dear, and a cautious regard for one's own safety: but nothing new or sudden can happen to You, nothing can threaten Your hold upon things loved, and where is safety secure save in You? Grief pines at the loss of things in which desire delighted: for it wills to be like to You from whom nothing can be taken away.

Thus the soul is guilty of fornication when she turns from You and seeks from any other source what she will nowhere find pure and without taint unless she returns to You. Thus even those who go from You and stand up against You are still perversely imitating You. But by the mere fact of their imitation, they declare that You are the creator of all that is, and that there is nowhere for them to go where You are not.

So once again what did I enjoy in that theft of mine? Of what excellence of my Lord was I making perverse and vicious imitation? Perhaps it was the thrill of acting against Your law—at least in appearance, since I had no power to do so in fact, the delight a prisoner might have in making some small gesture of liberty—getting a deceptive sense of omnipotence from doing something forbidden without immediate punishment. I was that slave, who fled from his Lord and pursued his Lord's shadow. O rottenness, O monstrousness of life and abyss of death! Could you find pleasure only in what was forbidden, and only because it was forbidden?

VII

*What shall I render unto the Lord,* that I can recall these things and yet not be afraid! *I shall love Thee, Lord, and shall give thanks to Thee and confess Thy name,* because Thou hast forgiven me such great sins and evil deeds. I know that it is only by Thy grace and mercy that Thou hast melted away the ice of my sins. And the evil I have not done, that also I know is by Thy grace: for what might I not have done, seeing that I loved evil solely because it was evil? I confess that Thou hast forgiven all alike—the sins I committed of my own motion, the sins I would have committed but for Thy grace.

Would any man, considering his own weakness, dare to attribute his chastity or his innocence to his own powers and so love Thee less—as if he did not need the same mercy as those who return to Thee after sin. If any man has heard Thy voice and followed it and done none of the things he finds me here recording and confessing, still he must not scorn me: for I am healed by the same doctor who preserved him from falling into sickness, or at least into such grievous sickness. But let him love Thee even more: seeing me rescued out of such sickness of sin, and himself saved from falling into such sickness of sin, by the one same Saviour.

### VIII

*What fruit therefore had I* (in my vileness) *in those things of which I am now ashamed?* Especially in that piece of thieving, in which I loved nothing except the thievery—though that in itself was no *thing* and I only the more wretched for it. Now—as I think back on the state of my mind then—I am altogether certain that I would not have done it alone. Perhaps then what I really loved was the companionship of those with whom I did it. If so, can I still say that I loved nothing over and above the thievery? Surely I can; that companionship was nothing over and above, because it was nothing. What is the truth of it? Who shall show me, unless He that illumines my heart and brings light into its dark places? What is the thing that I am trying to get at in all this discussion? If I had liked the pears that I stole and wanted to enjoy eating them, I might have committed the offence alone, if that had been sufficient, to get me the pleasure I wanted; I should not have needed to inflame the itch of my desires by rubbing against accomplices. But since the pleasure I got was not in the pears, it must have been in the crime itself, and put there by the companionship of others sinning with me.

## IX

What was my feeling in all this? Depraved, undoubt-
edly, and woe is me that I had it. But what exactly was it?
*Who can understand sins?* We laughed together as if our
hearts were tickled to be playing a trick upon the owners,
who had no notion of what we were doing and would very
strongly have objected. But what delight did I find in that,
which I should not equally have found if I had done it alone?
Because we are not much given to laughing when we are
alone? Not much given, perhaps, but laughter does sometimes overcome a man when no one else is about, if
something especially ridiculous is seen or heard or floats into
the mind. Yet I would not have done this by myself: quite
definitely I would not have done it by myself.

Here, then, O God, is the memory still vivid in my mind.
I would not have committed that theft alone: my pleasure
in it was not what I stole but that I stole: yet I would not
have enjoyed doing it, I would not have done it, alone. O
friendship unfriendly, unanalysable attraction for the mind,
greediness to do damage for the mere sport and jest of it, desire for another's loss with no gain to oneself or vengeance to
be satisfied! Someone cries "Come on, let's do it"—and we
would be ashamed to be ashamed!

## X

Who can unravel that complex twisted knottedness? It
is unclean, I hate to think of it or look at it. I long for Thee,
O Justice and Innocence, Joy and Beauty of the clear of
sight, I long for Thee with unquenchable longing. There is
sure repose in Thee and life untroubled. He that enters into
Thee, enters into the joy of his Lord and shall not fear and
shall be well in Him who is the Best. I went away from Thee,
my God, in my youth I strayed too far from Thy sustaining
power, and I became to myself a barren land.

# BOOK THREE

## FROM SIXTEEN TO EIGHTEEN

I CAME to Carthage, where a cauldron of illicit loves leapt and boiled about me. I was not yet in love, but I was in love with love, and from the very depth of my need hated myself for not more keenly feeling the need. I sought some object to love, since I was thus in love with loving; and I hated security and a life with no snares for my feet. For within I was hungry, all for the want of that spiritual food which is Thyself, my God; yet [though I was hungry for want of it] I did not hunger for it: I had no desire whatever for incorruptible food, not because I had it in abundance but the emptier I was, the more I hated the thought of it. Because of all this my soul was sick, and broke out in sores, whose itch I agonized to scratch with the rub of carnal things—carnal, yet if there were no soul in them, they would not be objects of love. My longing then was to love and to be loved, but most when I obtained the enjoyment of the body of the person who loved me.

Thus I polluted the stream of friendship with the filth of unclean desire and sullied its limpidity with the hell of lust. And vile and unclean as I was, so great was my vanity that I was bent upon passing for clean and courtly. And I did fall in love, simply from wanting to. O my God, my Mercy, with how much bitterness didst Thou in Thy goodness sprinkle the delights of that time! I was loved, and our love came to the bond of consummation: I wore my chains with bliss but with torment too, for I was scourged with the red hot rods of jealousy, with suspicions and fears and tempers and quarrels.

II

I developed a passion for stage plays, with the mirror they held up to my own miseries and the fuel they poured on my flame. How is it that a man wants to be made sad by the sight of tragic sufferings that he could not bear in his own person? Yet the spectator does want to feel sorrow, and it is actually his feeling of sorrow that he enjoys. Surely this is the most wretched lunacy? For the more a man feels such sufferings in himself, the more he is moved by the sight of them on the stage. Now when a man suffers himself, it is called misery; when he suffers in the suffering of another, it is called pity. But how can the unreal sufferings of the stage possibly move pity? The spectator is not moved to aid the sufferer but merely to be sorry for him; and the more the author of these fictions makes the audience grieve, the better they like him. If the tragic sorrows of the characters—whether historical or entirely fictitious—be so poorly represented that the spectator is not moved to tears, he leaves the theatre unsatisfied and full of complaints; if he *is* moved to tears, he stays to the end, fascinated and revelling in it. So that tears and sorrow, it would seem, are things to be sought. Yet surely every man prefers to be joyful. May it be that whereas no one wants to be miserable, there is real pleasure in pitying others—and we love their sorrows because without them we should have nothing to pity?

All this takes its rise in that stream of friendship [of which we have been speaking]. But where does that stream go to? What is the direction of its flow? Why must it run into—and lose itself in—that torrent of pitch which boils out in great waves of vile lust? For by some inclination in itself friendship is twisted and torn away from its heavenly cleanness.

Is compassion, feeling for others, therefore to be shunned? By no means. The sorrows of others must move our love. But beware of uncleanness, O my soul, under the protection of my God, the God of our fathers who is to be praised and exalted above all forever; beware of uncleanness. I can still feel for others. But in those days when I went to the theatres I was glad with lovers when they sinfully enjoyed each other —although the whole thing was merely fictitious and part of a stage play—and when they lost each other I was sad for them; but either way I enjoyed the play. But today I have more pity for the sinner getting enjoyment from his sin than when he suffers torment from the loss of pleasure which is ultimately destructive, and the loss of happiness which is only misery. This clearly is the truer compassion, but the sorrow I feel for him gives me no pleasure. Although he that grieves with the grief-stricken is to be commended for his work of charity, yet the man who is fraternally compassionate would prefer to find nothing in others to need his compassion. Only in the impossible event of good-will being malevolent, could a man who is truly and sincerely filled with pity desire that there should be miserable people for him to pity. There is a kind of compassionate sorrow that is good, but there is no kind that we should rejoice to feel. And thus do you act, Lord God, for You love souls with a greater and deeper purity than we can, and are more incorruptibly compassionate because no sorrow can reach to wound You. *And who is sufficient for these things?*

But to return to that time. In my wretchedness I loved to be made sad and sought for things to be sad about: and in the misery of others—though fictitious and only on the stage—the more my tears were set to flowing, the more pleasure did I get from the drama and the more powerfully did it hold me. There I was, a wretched sheep strayed from Your fold and impatient of the Shepherd: what wonder that I became infected with a foul disease? That is why I loved those sorrows—not that I wanted them to bite too deep (for I had no wish to suffer the sorrows I loved to look upon), but simply to scratch the surface of my heart as I saw them on the stage: yet, as if they had been fingernails, their scratching was followed by swelling and inflammation and sores with pus flowing. Such was my life; but was that a life, my God?

### III

Yet from afar off Your faithful mercy hovered over me. I wasted myself in baseness, pursuing a sacrilegious curiosity

which led me once I had deserted You to the uttermost trea-
son and the deceiving service of devils, to whom I made
offering of my vile deeds. And in all this You chastised me
with Your scourges. For I dared so far one day within the
walls of Your church and during the very celebration of
Your mysteries to desire and carry out an act worthy of the
fruits of death. For this You lashed me with the heaviest
punishments, yet the punishments were as nothing to the
guilt of my act, O my God, my exceeding great Mercy, my
Refuge from the fierce dangers among which I wandered in
my arrogance, going ever further from You, loving my way
and not Your ways, in love with my runaway liberty.

Those of my occupations at that time which were held as
reputable were directed towards the study of the law, in
which I meant to excel—and the less honest I was, the more
famous I should be. The very limit of human blindness is to
glory in being blind. By this time I was a leader in the School
of Rhetoric and I enjoyed this high station and was arrogant
and swollen with importance: though You know, O Lord,
that I was far quieter in my behaviour and had no share
in the riotousness of the *eversores*—the Overturners—for
this blackguardly diabolical name they wore as the very
badge of sophistication. Yet I was much in their company
and much ashamed of the sense of shame that kept me from
being like them. I was with them and I did for the most part
enjoy their companionship, though I abominated the acts
that were their specialty—as when they made a butt of some
hapless newcomer, assailing him with really cruel mockery
for no reason whatever, save the malicious pleasure they got
from it. There was something very like the action of devils
in their behaviour. They were rightly called Overturners,
since they had themselves been first overturned and perverted, tricked by those same devils who were secretly
mocking them in the very acts by which they amused themselves in mocking and making fools of others.

IV

With these men as companions of my immaturity, I was studying the books of eloquence; for in eloquence it was my ambition to shine, all from a damnable vaingloriousness and for the satisfaction of human vanity. Following the normal order of study I had come to a book of one Cicero, whose tongue practically everyone admires, though not his heart. That particular book is called *Hortensius* and contains an exhortation to philosophy. Quite definitely it changed the direction of my mind, altered my prayers to You, O Lord, and gave me a new purpose and ambition. Suddenly all the vanity I had hoped in I saw as worthless, and with an incredible intensity of desire I longed after immortal wisdom. I had begun that journey upwards by which I was to return to You. My father was now dead two years; I was eighteen and was receiving money from my mother for the continuance of my study of eloquence. But I used that book not for the sharpening of my tongue; what won me in it was what it said, not the excellence of its phrasing.

How did I then burn, my God, how did I burn to wing upwards from earthly delights to You. But I had no notion what You were to do with me. For with You is wisdom. Now love of wisdom is what is meant by the Greek word philosophy, and it was to philosophy that that book set me so ardently. There are those who seduce men's minds by philosophy, colouring and covering their errors with its great and fine and honourable name: almost all who in Cicero's own time and earlier had been of that sort are listed in his book and shown for what they are. Indeed it illustrates the wholesome advice given by the Spirit through Your good and loving servant: *Beware lest any man cheat you by philosophy, and vain deceits; according to the tradition of men, according to the elements of the world, and not according to Christ: for in Him dwelleth all the fulness of the Godhead corporeally.* At that time, You know, O Light of my heart, those writings of the Apostle were not yet known to me. But the one thing that delighted me in Cicero's exhortation was that I should love, and seek, and win, and hold, and embrace, not this or that philosophical school but Wisdom itself, whatever it might be. The book excited and inflamed me; in my ardour the only thing I found lacking was that the name of Christ was not there. For with my mother's milk my infant heart had drunk in, and still held deep down in it, that name according to Your mercy, O Lord, the name of Your Son, my Saviour; and whatever lacked that name, no matter how learned and excellently written and true, could not win me wholly.

V

So I resolved to make some study of the Sacred Scriptures and find what kind of books they were. But what I came upon was something not grasped by the proud, not revealed either to children, something utterly humble in the hearing but sublime in the doing, and shrouded deep in mystery. And I was not of the nature to enter into it or bend my neck to follow it. When I first read those Scriptures, I did not feel in the least what I have just said; they seemed to me unworthy to be compared with the majesty of Cicero. My conceit was repelled by their simplicity, and I had not the mind to penetrate into their depths. They were indeed of a nature to grow in Your little ones. But I could not bear to be a little one; I was only swollen with pride, but to myself I seemed a very big man.

VI

I fell in with a sect of men [the Manicheans] talking high-sounding nonsense, carnal and wordy men. The snares of the devil were in their mouths, to trap souls with an arrangement of the syllables of the names of God the Father and of the Lord Jesus Christ and of the Paraclete, the Holy Ghost, our Comforter. These names were always on their lips, but only as sounds and tongue noises; for their heart was empty of the true meaning. They cried out "Truth, truth;" they were forever uttering the word to me, but the thing was nowhere in them; indeed they spoke falsehood not only of You, who are truly Truth, but also of the elements of this world, Your creatures. Concerning these I ought to have passed beyond even the philosophers who spoke truly, for love of You, O my supreme and good Father, Beauty of all things beautiful. O Truth, Truth, how inwardly did the very marrow of my soul pant for You when time and again I heard them sound Your name. But it was all words—words spoken, words written in many huge tomes. In these dishes—while I hungered for You— they served me up the sun and the moon, beautiful works of Yours, but works of Yours all the same and not Yourself: not even Your mightiest works. For Your spiritual creation is greater than these material things, brilliantly as they shine in the sky.

Yet not even for the noblest of Your works did I hunger and thirst but for Yourself, the Truth, *with whom there is no change nor shadow of alteration.* And still in those poor dishes they set before me splendid fantasies: it would indeed have been better to love the sun, which is at least true to the eyes, than those falsities which deceive the mind through the eyes. All the same, I swallowed them because I thought that they were Yourself: yet I did not swallow them with much appetite, because You did not taste in my mouth as You are—for after all You were not those empty falsehoods—and I was not nourished by them, but utterly dried up. Food in dreams is exactly like real food, yet what we eat in our dreams does not nourish: for we are dreaming. But those fantasies of theirs were not in any way like You, as You have since spoken to me; for they were material images, false shows of bodies. The true bodies that we see with our bodily vision, whether in the sky or on the earth, are truer than they: we see them as beasts and birds do, and they are more certain than our images of them. And again these images have more reality than the grandiose infinite bodies we deduced from them, which have no being at all. On such emptiness did I then feed and was not fed.

But You, God of my Love, for whom I long that I may find strength, are not those bodies which we see, though it is in the heavens that we see them; nor are You those bodies which we do not see in the heavens, because You have created them too, nor do You hold them among Your mightiest works. How far then is the reality of You from those empty imaginings of mine, imaginings of bodies which had no being whatever. The images of those bodies which do have being are more certain than they, and the bodies themselves more certain than the images. Yet even these You are not. You are not even the soul, which is the life of bodies—and therefore obviously better and more certain than the bodies it vivifies: but You are the Life of souls, the Life of lives, Livingness itself, and You shall not change, O Life of my soul.

Where then were You and how far from me? I had indeed straggled far from You, not even being allowed to eat the husks of the swine whom I was feeding with husks. How much better were the sheer fables of the poets and literary men than all the traps [that Manes set for souls]. Verses, and poems, and Medea flying, were less harmful than the Five Elements, variously transformed in strife with the five Dens of Darkness, which have no being whatsoever and are death to the soul that believes them. It is possible to get real food for the mind out of verses and poems; and though I sang of Medea flying, I did not think it was true; and when I heard it sung I did not believe it. But these fantasies of the Manichees I did believe. Alas, by what stages was I brought down to the deepest depths of the pit, giving myself needless labour and turmoil of spirit for want of the truth: in that I sought You my God—to You I confess it, for You had pity on me even when I had not yet confessed—in that I sought You not according to the understanding of the mind by which You have set us above the beasts, but according to the sense of the flesh. Yet all the time You were more inward than the most inward place of my heart and loftier than the highest. But I had come upon the woman of Solomon's parable, the shameless woman, knowing nothing, who sits on a seat at the door of her house and says: *Eat ye the bread of secrecies willingly, and drink ye stolen waters which are sweet.* She seduced me because she found me dwelling externally in the eye of my flesh, and ruminating within myself upon such food as, through the body's eye, the mind had swallowed.

### VII

But I did not know that other reality which truly is; and through my own sharpness that I let myself be taken in by fools, who deceived me with such questions as: Whence comes evil? And is God bounded by a bodily shape and has he hair and nails? And are those [patriarchs] to be esteemed righteous who had many wives at the same time and slew men and offered sacrifices of living animals? By all this my ignorance was much troubled, and it seemed to me that I was coming to the truth when I was in fact going away from it. I did not know that evil has no being of its own but is only an absence of good, so that it simply is not. How indeed should I see this, when the sight of my eyes saw no deeper than bodies and the sight of my soul no deeper than images of bodies? I did not even know that God is a spirit, having no parts extended in length and breadth, to whose being bulk does not belong: for bulk is less in its part than in its whole: and if it be infinite, it is less in the part circumscribed by a certain space than in its infinity: and so could not be wholly itself in every place, as a spirit is, as God is. And I was further ignorant what is the principle in us by which we are; and what Scripture meant by saying that we are made to the image of God.

Nor did I know that true and inward righteousness which judges not according to custom but according to the most righteous law of Almighty God. By that law the ways of conduct of different places and times are shaped as is best for those places and times, though the law itself is always and everywhere the same, not different in different places or changing with the ages. By this righteousness, Abraham and Isaac and Jacob and Moses and David and all those others praised by God were righteous, although they are judged not so by ignorant men who apply the tests of their human minds, and measure all the conduct of the human race by the measure of their own custom. They are like a man handling armour and not knowing what piece is meant for what part of the body and so putting a greave on his head and a helmet on his feet and complaining that they do not fit; or as if on a given day on which it was illegal to do business in the afternoon, a man should grumble because he was not allowed to go on selling in the afternoon, though he had been in the morning; or as if in a given house he should see something handled by one servant but not allowed to the one who has to pour the wine; or that something were done behind the stable which is forbidden in the dining room: as if, in short, he should be angry because in the one dwelling house and the one family the same things are not allowed to every member of the household and in all parts of the house. Such are those who are scandalized when they hear that something was permitted to righteous men in one age, and not permitted in another; and that God gave one man this command, another that, as the difference of the age required, yet both alike served the same righteousness: just as in one man and in one day and in one house different things are held fitting for different members, and a particular act is lawful now but not lawful an hour hence, and something is allowed or indeed commanded in one corner which is forbidden and punished in another. Does this mean that justice is unstable and changeable? No, but the times over which justice presides are not alike, for they are times. Men, because their life upon earth is short, are unable of their own observation to compare the conditions of past ages and foreign nations which they have not experienced with those which they have experienced. In the matter of

one body or day or house, they can readily see what is fitting
for this or that member, this or that moment, this or that
part of the house or rank in the household; they accept such
differences [because they fall within their experience]: yet
remain scandalised at the differences shown in Scripture.

But all this I did not then know or realise; it was beating
in on me the whole time and I had not eyes to see. Thus
when I composed verses, I was not free to put any foot where
I pleased, but in different places according to the metre I
was using; and in one line I could not use the same foot
in every position: none the less the art I was practising,
the art of poetry, did not have a different law for different
places, but the same law throughout. Yet I failed to see that
the justice obeyed by these good and holy men was all the
more excellent and admirable because while it contained all
its precepts in one and never varied: yet it did not order
and decree all things alike but to each age what was proper
to each. Thus in my blindness I blamed those holy patriarchs
who not only used things present as God commanded and
inspired them, but also foretold the future as God revealed
it to them.

VIII

In no time or place could it be wrong for a man to love
God with his whole heart and his whole soul and his whole
mind, and his neighbor as himself. Therefore those sins
which are against nature, like those of the men of Sodom,
are in all times and places to be detested and punished.
Even if all nations committed such sins, they should all
alike be held guilty by God's law which did not make
men so that they should use each other thus. The friendship which should be between God and us is violated when
that nature—whose author He is—is polluted by so perverted a lust. Actions which are against the customs of human societies are to be avoided according to the variety of
such customs; so that that which is agreed upon by the custom, or decreed by the law, of state or people, is not to be

violated at the mere pleasure whether of citizen or alien. For
every part is defective that is not in harmony with the whole.

But when God orders something against the custom
or covenant of a state, though it never had been done
it must be done; and if it was [once done but] allowed to
lapse, it must be restored; and if it was not a law before, it
must be made a law now. In a state it is lawful for the
reigning monarch to command something which none had
ever commanded before him and he himself had never commanded before; and obedience in this event is not against
the fellowship of that state: indeed disobedience would be
against the fellowship, for it is the general agreement of all
societies of men to obey their kings. How much more then
may God so act, the ruler of all Creation, whose commands
are to be obeyed without hesitation. For as among the powers
of human society the greater power has a right to the obedience of the lesser, so God to the obedience of all.

In sins where there is a real will to harm another, it
may be either by calumny or injury; and, whichever of these
two it is, the sin is committed either for the sake of revenge (as when one enemy attacks another); or to gain something that another has (as when a bandit sets upon a travel-
ler); or to escape some danger (as when one man is afraid of
another); or through envy (as when a man in poverty attacks
one more prosperous, or one who has prospered attacks
another whom he fears as likely to equal him or hates for
having already equalled him); or for mere pleasure in another's suffering (like the spectators at gladiatorial shows,
or people who are always mocking and deriding their neighbors). These are the main heads of sin, which swarm forth
from the lust for holding the first place, or the lust of the
eye, or the lust of the senses, or from any one or two of
them, or from all together. By these we live evilly against the
three and the seven, the ten-stringed harp, the Ten Commandments given by You, O God Most High and Most
Gracious.

But how are sins of the first sort against You, who can

suffer no corruption; or how are sins of the second sort against You, who can suffer no harm? You punish the sins men commit against themselves, because though their sin is against You, they are wronging their own souls and their iniquity gives itself the lie. Either they corrupt and pervert their own nature, which You have created and set in order —by making wrong use of the things You have permitted, or by burning towards a use of things not permitted which is against nature; or their guilt lies in raging against You in thought and word and kicking against the prick; or else, in complete contempt of the existing order of society, they go their own insolent way with private agreements or private feuds according to their personal likes or dislikes.

And all this happens, O Fountain of Life, the only and the true Creator and Ruler of the universe, whenever You are forsaken, and out of the pride of the individual a part is loved as though it were the whole. Therefore by lowly love of You must we return to You: and You cleanse us from evil habit, and You are merciful to the sins of those who confess to You, and You hear the groans of those chained in sin and You loose us from the fetters we have made for ourselves—all this You do unless we raise against You the arrogance of a sham liberty, and through the greedy desire to have more (at the risk of losing all) love our own private good more than You, who are the common good of all.

## IX

But amongst these vices and crimes and countless iniquities are the sins into which men fall although they are in general on the right way. By those who judge rightly, these sins are blamed according to the rule of perfection, but the persons themselves may still be praised for the hope of a better harvest, as the blade gives hope of the growing corn. And there are some actions again that are very much like sins and yet are not sins, since they neither offend You, our Lord God, nor the bond of society: thus when certain things are set aside to meet the requirements of life or some given circumstance, and it is not clear whether this is done through a mere liking to hoard; or certain actions are punished by a person in authority for the sake of correcting the wrong-doer, and it is not clear whether he may not have done it through a mere desire to cause pain. Thus many actions that to men seem blameworthy, are approved in Your sight; and many that are praised by men are condemned by You, O God—all because often the appearance of the act may be quite different from the mind of the doer or because there is some unrealized element in the situation. But when on a sudden You order something unusual and improbable, even if You had formerly forbidden it, it must obviously be done—though You may conceal the cause of Your command for the time and though it may be against the ordinance of this or that society of men: a society of men is just, only if it obeys You. But happy are they who know that it was You who commanded. For by those that serve You all things are done either to supply what is needful for the present moment or to foreshadow things to come.

## X

But I knew nothing of all this and so I derided those Your holy servants and prophets. And I gained nothing by mocking them, except that I should myself be mocked by You. Gradually and inevitably I was drawn to accept every kind of nonsense—as that a fig weeps when it is plucked and its mother tree sheds tears of sap. But provided the fig had been plucked by another man's sin and not his own, some Manichean saint might eat it, digest it in his stomach and groaning and sighing in prayer breathe out from it angels: nay more, he might breathe out certain particles of the Godhead; and these particles of the true and supreme God would have remained in bondage in the fruit unless set free by the teeth and belly of some holy Elect one. And I believed, poor wretch, that more mercy was to be shown to the fruits of the earth than to men, for whose use they were created. For if any man, being hungry—and not being a Manichean—should ask for some, I should have held it worthy of the punishment of death to give him even a mouthful.

XI

And You *sent Your hand from above*, and raised my soul out of that depth of darkness, because my mother, Your faithful one, wept to You for me more bitterly than mothers weep for the bodily deaths of their children. For by the faith and the spirit which she had from You, she saw me as dead; and You heard her, Lord. You heard her and did not despise her tears when they flowed down and watered the earth against which she pressed her face wherever she prayed. You heard her. What else could have been the cause of that dream by which You so comforted her that she consented to live with me and to eat at the same table in the house: which previously she had refused to do, because she shunned and detested the blasphemies of my error. In her dream she saw herself standing on a wooden rule and a youth all radiant coming to her cheerful and smiling upon her, whereas she was grieving and heavy with her grief. He asked her—not to learn from her but, as is the way of visions, to teach her—the causes of her sorrow and the tears she daily shed. She replied that she was mourning for the loss of my soul. He commanded her to be at peace and told her to observe carefully and she would see that where she was, there was I also. She looked, and saw me standing alongside her on the same rule. How should she have had this dream unless Your ears had heard her heart, O Good Omnipotent, You who have such care for each one of us as if You had care for him alone, and such care for all as if we were all but one person?

And the same must have been the reason for this too: that when she had told me her vision and I tried to interpret it to mean that she must not despair of one day being as I was, she answered without an instant's hesitation: "No. For it was not said to me where he is, you are, but where you are, he is." I confess to You, O Lord, that if I remember aright—and I have often spoken of it since—I was more deeply moved by that answer which You gave through my mother—in that she was not disturbed by the false plausibility of my interpretation and so quickly saw what was to be seen (which I certainly had not seen until she said it)—than by the dream itself: by which the joy that was to come to that holy woman so long after was foretold so long before for the relief of her present anguish. Nine years were to follow in which I lay tossing in the mud of that deep pit and the darkness of its falsity, though I often tried to rise and only fell the more heavily. All that time this chaste, god-fearing and sober widow—for such You love— was all the more cheered up with hope. Yet she did not relax her weeping and mourning. She did not cease to pray at every hour and bewail me to You, and her prayers found entry into Your sight. But for all that You allowed me still to toss helplessly in that darkness.

## XII

One other answer I remember You gave her in that time. Many such things I pass over, because I am hastening on to the matters which I am more urgently pressed to confess to You, and many I have simply forgotten. But You gave her another assurance by the mouth of Your priest, a certain bishop reared up in the Church and well grounded in Your Scriptures. My mother asked him in his kindness to have some discussion with me, to refute my errors, to unteach me what was evil and teach me what was good, for he often did this when he found such people as it might profit. He refused, rightly as I have realized since. He told her that I was as yet not ripe for teaching because I was all puffed up with the newness of my heresy and had already upset a number of insufficiently skilled people with certain questions—as she had, in fact, told him. "But," said he, "let him alone. Only pray to the Lord for him: he will himself discover by reading what his error is and how great his impiety."

The bishop went on to tell her that his mother had been seduced by the Manichees so that as a small child he had been given over to them; and he had not only read practically all their books but had also copied them out; and had found out for himself, with no need for anyone to argue or convince him, that he must leave the sect. And he had left it. When he had told her this, my mother would not be satisfied but urged him with repeated entreaties and floods of tears to see me and discuss with me. He, losing patience, said: "Go your way; as sure as you live, it is impossible that the son of these tears should perish." In the conversations we had afterwards, she often said that she had accepted this answer as if it had sounded from heaven.

# BOOK FOUR

## FROM EIGHTEEN TO TWENTY-SEVEN

THROUGHOUT that nine-year period, from my nineteenth year to my twenty-eighth, I was astray myself and led others astray, was deceived and deceived others in various forms of self-assertion, publicly by the teaching of what are called the liberal arts, privately under the false name of religion; in the one proud, in the other superstitious, in both vain. On the one side of my life I pursued the emptiness of popular glory and the applause of spectators, with competition for prize poems and strife for garlands of straw and the vanity of stage shows and untempered lusts; on the other side I was striving to be made clean of all this same filth, by bearing food to those who were called elect and holy, that in the factory of their own stomachs they should turn it into angels and deities by whom I was to be set free. And I followed out this line of conduct; and so did my friends who were deceived by me and with me. Let the proud of heart deride me now and all who have never been brought low and broken by Thee unto salvation, O my God: it is only for Thy glory that I confess to Thee all my ingloriousness. Grant me, I beseech Thee, to retraverse now in memory the past ways of my error and to *offer Thee a sacrifice of rejoicing*. For without Thee, what am I but a guide to my own destruction? Or at my best what am I but an infant suckled on Thy milk and feeding upon Thee, O Food incorruptible? What indeed is any man, seeing that he is but a man? Let the strong in their own power mock on, I in my weakness and neediness will confess unto Thee.

II

In those years I taught the art of Rhetoric. Overcome myself by the desire of money, I offered for sale skill in speech to overcome others by. But You know, O Lord, I preferred to have honest scholars as honesty is nowadays reckoned: and without guile I taught them guilefulness, that they might use it not against the life of an innocent man, but for the life of a guilty man. And You, O God, saw me far from You stumbling in that slippery way, showing amidst much smoke some small spark of honour: for in my schoolmastership I honestly did my best for men who loved vanity and sought after lying: and in truth I was one with them. In those years I took one woman, not joined to me in lawful marriage, but one whom wandering lust and no particular judgement had brought my way. Yet I had but that one woman, and I was faithful to her. And with her I learnt by my own experience what a gulf there is between the restraint of the marriage-covenant entered into for the sake of children and the mere bargain of a lustful love, where if children come they come unwanted—though when they are born, they compel our love.

I remember once, when I had made up my mind to enter a contest for a poem to be recited on the stage, some magician, I have forgotten his name, demanded how much I would be willing to give him to be certain of victory. I loathed and abominated the filthy rites they practiced, and I told him that if the wreath were of gold, and immortal at that, I would not allow a fly to be slain that I might win it. For it seems that he was to slay certain living creatures in his rites, and by such compliments to persuade the devils to favor me. Yet, O God of my heart, it was not from any purity towards You that I rejected this evil thing. I did not know how to love You, since in its thinking upon You my mind did not rise above a sort of material resplendence. A soul that pants after such idle imaginations simply commits fornication against You, and trusts in shadows, and feeds the winds. I would not have him offer sacrifice on my behalf to devils, and all the while I was myself offering them sacrifice by the superstition I was in. For surely to feed them—that is by our error to become their sport and their derision—is to feed the winds.

### III

For the impostors who were called mathematicians [astrologers] I did not scruple to consult, because they offered no sacrifice, and directed no prayers to any spirit to aid their divination. Yet true Christian piety necessarily rejects and condemns their art. For *it is good to confess unto Thee, Lord* and say, *Be merciful to me, heal my soul, for I have sinned against Thee;* and not to misuse Thy mercy as a license to sin but to remember the words of our Lord: *Behold, Thou art made whole: sin no more, lest some worse thing happen to thee.* All this saving truth the astrologers strive to destroy, when they teach that the inevitable cause of sin is in the heavens, that it is the doing of Venus or Saturn or Mars: in other words that man, flesh and blood and proud corruption, is guiltless, and that the guilt lies with the Creator and Ruler of heaven and the stars of heaven. And He is none other than our God, very Loveliness and Well-spring of Justice, *who shall render to every man according to his works:* and *a broken and a contrite heart wilt Thou not despise.*

The proconsul at that time was a man of much wisdom, skilled in medicine and famed for his skill. He set upon my distempered head the wreath I won in the contest: but not as a healer of my distemper. For that disease You alone cure who *resist the proud and give grace to the humble.* Yet You did not fail to aid me through that old man and to use him for the healing of my soul. I came to know him better and pay the closest attention to his words, for without particular pretence, his talk was at once grave and gay from the sheer vitality of his thought. When I told him that I was much given to the books of the horoscope-casters, with much fatherly kindness he advised me to throw them away and not waste upon such nonsense time and trouble that could be put to better use. He told me that in his earlier years he had had some idea of studying that same art and indeed of making it his profession; obviously, since he had understood Hippocrates, he was quite able to understand this other kind of learning as well. But he had given it up and concentrated upon the study of medicine simply because he had found it false, and as an honest man had no desire to make his living by cheating people. "But you," he said, "have the profession of rhetoric to support yourself by, and are pursuing this astrological nonsense voluntarily and not through financial necessity. Therefore you ought all the more to trust me in the matter, for when I sought to attain sufficient skill in it, it was because I meant to make it my sole means of livelihood."

I asked him how he explained the fact that many things were foretold truly by it. He answered, very reasonably, that it was due to the force of chance, which is always to be allowed for in the order of things. Thus if one happened to consult the pages of some poet, who was singing (and thinking) of quite other matters, the eye often fell on a verse quite extraordinarily relevant to the matter in one's own mind; and, he said, it was not more extraordinary if from the mind of man—by some higher but quite blind instinct, not by art but merely by chance—things should sometimes emerge that should seem to have a bearing upon the affairs and actions of the inquirer.

Surely it was You who from him or through him procured this for me and gave my memory the hint of the answer that I was later to arrive at for myself. But at the time neither he nor my close friend Nebridius—a young man of great worth and high moral character, who laughed at the whole business of divination—could persuade me to give up these studies: the authority of the writers of the books still had the greater power with me and I had not yet found the certain proof I sought that would settle beyond doubt that the truths they foretold came by chance or luck, and not by the art of the star-gazers.

IV

During the period in which I first began to teach in the town of my birth, I had found a very dear friend, who was pursuing similar studies. He was about my own age, and was now coming, as I was, to the very flowering-time of young manhood. He had indeed grown up with me as a child and we had gone to school together and played together. Neither in those earlier days nor indeed in the later time of which I now speak was he a friend in the truest meaning of friendship: for there is no true friendship unless You weld it between souls that cleave together through that charity which is shed in our hearts by the Holy Ghost who is given to us. Yet it had become a friendship very dear to us, made the warmer by the ardor of studies pursued together. I had turned him from the true faith—in which being little more than a boy he was not deeply grounded—towards those superstitious and soul-destroying errors that my mother bewailed in me. With me he went astray in error, and my soul could not be without him. But You are ever close upon the heels of those who flee from You, for You are at once God of Vengeance and Fount of Mercy, and You turn us to Yourself by ways most wonderful. You took this man from the life of earth when he had completed scarcely a year in a friendship that had grown sweeter to me than all the sweetness of the life I knew.

What man could recount all Your praises for the things he has experienced in his own single person? What was it, O my God, that You accomplished then and how unsearchable is the abyss of Your judgements! For he was in a high fever and when he had for a long time lain unconscious in a deathly sweat so that his life was despaired of, he was baptized. Naturally he knew nothing of it, and I paid little heed, since I took for granted that his mind would retain what he had learned from me and not what was done upon his body while he was unconscious. But it turned out very differently. The fever left him and he recovered. As soon as I could speak to him—which was as soon as he could speak to me, for I had not left him and indeed we depended too much upon each other—I began to mock, assuming that he would join me in mocking, the baptism which he had received when he had neither sense nor feeling. For by now he had been told of it. But he looked at me as if I had been his deadly enemy, and in a burst of independence that startled me warned me that if I wished to continue his friend I must cease that kind of talk. I was stupefied and deeply perturbed. I postponed telling him of my feelings until he should be well again, and thus in such condition of health and strength that I could discuss what was in my mind. But he was snatched from the reach of my folly, that he might be safe with You for my future consolation. Within a few days he relapsed into his fever and died. And I was not there.

My heart was black with grief. Whatever I looked upon had the air of death. My native place was a prison-house and my home a strange unhappiness. The things we had done together became sheer torment without him. My eyes were restless looking for him, but he was not there. I hated all places because he was not in them. They could not say "He will come soon," as they would in his life when he was absent. I became a great enigma to myself and I was forever asking my soul why it was sad and why it disquieted me so sorely. And my soul knew not what to answer me. If I said "Trust in God" my soul did not obey—naturally, because the man whom she had loved and lost was nobler and more real than the imagined deity in whom I was bidding her trust. I had no delight but in tears, for tears had taken the place my friend had held in the love of my heart.

**v**

But now, Lord, all that has passed and time has dulled the ache of the wound. May I learn from You who are Truth, may I make the ear of my heart attentive to the word of Your mouth, that You may tell me why tears are so sweet to the sorrowful. Have You, for all that You are everywhere, cast our misery from You? You abide in Yourself, we are tossed from trial to trial: yet if we might not utter our sorrow to Your ears, nothing should remain for our

hope. How does it come then that from the bitterness of life
we can pluck fruit so sweet as is in mourning and weeping
and sighing and the utterance of our woe? Are all these things
such relief to our misery because of our hope that You hear
them? Obviously this is so of our prayers, because they are
uttered with the sole aim of reaching You. But is it so also
of the sorrow and grief for a thing lost, in which I was then
overwhelmed? I had no hope of bringing him back to life,
nor for all my tears did I ask for this: simply I grieved
and wept. For I was in misery and had lost my joy. Or is
weeping really a bitter thing, pleasing to us only from a
distaste for the things we once enjoyed and only while the
distaste remains keen?

## VI

But why do I speak of these things? I should not be asking
questions but making my confession to You. I was wretched,
and every soul is wretched that is bound in affection of
mortal things: it is tormented to lose them, and in their loss
becomes aware of the wretchedness which in reality it had
even before it lost them. Such was I at that time. And I
wept most bitterly and in that bitterness found my only
repose. I was wretched, yet I held my wretched life dearer
than the friend for whose loss I was wretched. For although
I would have liked to change the unhappiness of my life,
yet I was more unwilling to lose my life itself than I had
been to lose my friend; and I doubt if I would have been
willing to lose it even to be with him—as the tradition is,
whether true or false, of Orestes and Pylades, who wanted
to die for each other and both together, because for either
life without the other was worse than death. But in me
there was an odd kind of feeling, the exact opposite of theirs,
for I was at once utterly weary of life and in great fear of
death. It may be that the more I loved him the more I hated
and feared, as the cruellest enemy, that death which had
taken him from me; and I was filled with the thought that
it might snatch away any man as suddenly as it had snatched

him. That this was then my mind, I still remember. Behold
my heart, O my God, look deep within it; see how I remember, O my Hope, You who cleanse me from all the uncleanness of such affections *directing my eyes towards You
and plucking my feet out of the snare.* I wondered that other
mortals should live when he was dead whom I had loved
as if he would never die; and I marvelled still more that
he should be dead and I his other self living still. Rightly
has a friend been called "the half of my soul." For I
thought of my soul and his soul as one soul in two bodies;
and my life was a horror to me because I would not live
halved. And it may be that I feared to die lest thereby he
should die wholly whom I had loved so deeply.

### VII

O madness that knows not how to love men as men! O
foolish man to bear the lot of man so rebelliously! I had
both the madness and the folly. I raged and sighed and
wept and was in torment, unable to rest, unable to think. I
bore my soul all broken and bleeding and loathing to be
borne by me; and I could find nowhere to set it down to
rest. Not in shady groves, nor in mirth and music, nor in
perfumed gardens, nor in formal banquets, nor in the delights of bedroom and bed, not in books nor in poetry could
it find peace. I hated all things, hated the very light itself;
and all that was not he was painful and wearisome, save
only my tears: for in them alone did I find a little peace.
When my soul gave over weeping, it was still crushed under
the great burden of a misery which only by You, Lord,
could be lightened and lifted. This I knew; but I had neither
the will nor the strength—and what made it more impossible
was that when I thought of You it was not as of something
firm and solid. For my God was not yet You but the error
and vain fantasy I held. When I tried to rest my burden upon
that, it fell as through emptiness and was once more heavy
upon me; and I remained to myself a place of unhappiness,
in which I could not abide, yet from which I could not

depart. For where was my heart to flee for refuge from my heart? Whither was I to fly from myself? To what place should I not follow myself? Yet leave my native place I did. For my eyes would look for him less where they had not been accustomed to see him. I left the town of **Tagaste** and came to **Carthage**.

### VIII

Time takes no holiday. It does not roll idly by, but through our senses works its own wonders in the mind. Time came and went from one day to the next; in its coming and its passing it brought me other hopes and other memories, and little by little patched me up again with the kind of delights which had once been mine, and which in my grief I had abandoned. The place of that great grief was slowly taken, not perhaps by new griefs, but by the seeds from which new griefs should spring. For that first grief had pierced so easily and so deep only because I had spilt out my soul upon the sand, in loving a mortal man as if he were never to die. At any rate the comfort I found in other friends—and the pleasure I had with them in things of earth—did much to repair and remake me. And it was all one huge fable, one long lie; and by its adulterous caressing, my soul, which lay itching in my ears, was utterly corrupted. For my folly did not die whenever one of my friends died.

All kinds of things rejoiced my soul in their company —to talk and laugh and do each other kindnesses; read pleasant books together, pass from lightest jesting to talk of the deepest things and back again; differ without rancour, as a man might differ with himself, and when most rarely dissension arose find our normal agreement all the sweeter for it; teach each other or learn from each other; be impatient for the return of the absent, and welcome them with joy on their home-coming; these and such like things, proceeding from our hearts as we gave affection and received it back, and shown by face, by voice, by the eyes, and a thousand other pleasing ways, kindled a flame which fused our very souls and of many made us one.

## IX

This is what men value in friends, and value so much that their conscience judges them guilty if they do not meet friendship with friendship, expecting nothing from their friend save such evidences of his affection. This is the root of our grief when a friend dies, and the blackness of our sorrow, and the steeping of the heart in tears for the joy that has turned to bitterness, and the feeling as though we were dead because he is dead. Blessed is the man that loves Thee, O God, and his friend in Thee, and his enemy for Thee. For he alone loses no one that is dear to him, if all are dear in God, who is never lost. And who is that God but our God, the God who made heaven and earth, who fills them because it is by filling them with Himself that he has made them? No man loses Thee, unless he goes from Thee; and in going from Thee, where does he go or where does he flee save from Thee to Thee—from God well-pleased to God angered? For where shall he not find Thy law fulfilled in his punishment? Thy law is truth and truth is Thou.

## X

*Convert us, O God of hosts, and show us Thy face, and we shall be saved.* Wherever the soul of man turns, unless towards God, it cleaves to sorrow, even though the things outside God and outside itself to which it cleaves may be things of beauty. For these lovely things would be nothing at all unless they were from Him. They rise and set: in their rising they begin to be, and they grow towards perfection, and once come to perfection they grow old, and they die: not all grow old but all die. Therefore when they rise and tend toward being, the more haste they make toward fullness of being, the more haste they make towards ceasing to be. That is their law. You have given them to be parts of

a whole: they are not all existent at once, but in their de-
partures and successions constitute the whole of which
they are parts. Our own speech, which we utter by making
sounds signifying meanings, follows the same principles.
For there never could be a whole sentence unless one word
ceased to be when its syllables had sounded and another
took its place. In all such things let my soul praise You, O
God, Creator of all things, but let it not cleave too close in
love to them through the senses of the body. For they go
their way and are no more; and they rend the soul with
desires that can destroy it, for it longs to be one with the
things it loves and to repose in them. But in them is no
place of repose, because they do not abide. They pass, and
who can follow them with any bodily sense? Or who can
grasp them firm even while they are still here?

Our fleshly sense is slow because it is fleshly sense: and
that is the limit of its being. It can do what it was made to do;
but it has no power to hold things transient as they run
their course from their due beginning to their due end. For
in Your word, by which they are created, they hear their
law: "From this point: not beyond that."

XI

Be not foolish, my soul, nor let the ear of your heart be
deafened with the clamor of your folly. Listen. The Word
Himself calls to you to return, and with Him is the place of
peace that shall not be broken, where your love will not be
forsaken unless it first forsake. Things pass that other things
may come in their place and this material universe be established in all its parts. "But do I depart anywhere?" says
the Word of God. Fix your dwelling in Him, commit to
God whatsoever you have: for it is from God. O my soul,
wearied at last with emptiness, commit to Truth's keeping
whatever Truth has given you, and you shall not lose any; and
what is decayed in you shall be made clean, and what is sick
shall be made well, and what is transient shall be reshaped
and made new and established in you in firmness; and they

shall not set you down where they themselves go, but shall stand and abide and you with them, before God who stands and abides forever.

Why, O perverse soul of mine, will you go on following your flesh? Rather turn, and let it follow you. Whatever things you perceive by fleshly sense you perceive only in part, not knowing the whole of which those things are but parts and yet they delight you so much. For if fleshly sense had been capable of grasping the whole—and had not for your punishment received part only of the whole as its just limit—you would wish that whatever exists in the present might pass on, that the whole might be perceived by you for your delight. What we speak, you hear by a bodily sense: and certainly you do not wish the same syllable to go on sounding but to pass away that other syllables may come and you may hear the whole speech. It is always so with all things that go to make up one whole: all that goes to make up the whole does not exist at one moment. If all could be perceived in one act of perception, it would obviously give more delight than any of the individual parts. But far better than all is He who made all; and He is our God. He does not pass away and there is none to take His place.

### XII

If material things please you then praise God for them, but turn back your love upon Him who made them: lest in the things that please you, you displease Him. If souls please you, then love them in God because they are mutable in themselves but in Him firmly established: without Him they would pass and perish. Love them, I say, in Him, and draw as many souls with you to Him as you can, saying to them: "Him let us love: He made this world and is not far from it." For He did not simply make it and leave it: but as it is from Him so it is in Him. See where He is, wherever there is a savour of truth: He is in the most secret place of the heart, yet the heart has strayed from Him.

O sinners, return to your own heart and abide in Him that made you. Stand with Him and you shall stand, rest in Him and you shall be at peace. Where are you going, to what bleak places? Where are you going? The good that you love is from Him: and insofar as it is likewise *for* Him it is good and lovely; but it will rightly be turned into bitterness, if it is unrightly loved and He deserted by whom it is. What goal are you making for, wandering around and about by ways so hard and laborious? Rest is not where you seek it. Seek what you seek, but it is not where you seek it. You seek happiness of life in the land of death, and it is not there. For how shall there be happiness of life where there is no life?

But our Life came down to this our earth and took away our death, slew death with the abundance of His own life: and He thundered, calling to us to return to Him into that secret place from which He came forth to us—coming first into the Virgin's womb, where humanity was wedded to Him, our mortal flesh, though not always to be mortal; and thence *like a bridegroom coming out of his bride chamber, rejoicing as a giant to run his course.* For He did not delay but rushed on, calling to us by what He said and what He did, calling to us by His death, life, descent, and ascension to return to Him. And He withdrew from our eyes, that we might return to our own heart and find Him. For He went away and behold He is still here. He would not be with us long, yet He did not leave us. He went back to that place which He had never left, for the world was made by Him. And He was in this world, and He came into this world to save sinners. Unto Him my soul confesses and He hears it, for it has sinned against Him. O ye sons of men, how long will ye be so slow of heart? Even now when Life has come down to you, will you not ascend and live? But to what high place shall you climb, since you are in a high place and have *set your mouth against the heavens?* First descend that you may ascend, ascend to God. For in mounting up *against* God you fell. Tell the souls of men to weep in this valley of tears, and so bear them up with you to God, because it is by His Spirit that you are speaking this to them, if in your speaking you are on fire with the fire of charity.

### XIII

But these things I did not at that time know, and I was in love with those lower beauties. I was sinking into the very depths and I said to my friends: "Do we love anything save what is beautiful? What then is beautiful? and what is beauty? What is it that allures us and delights us in the things we love? Unless there were grace and beauty in them they could not possibly draw us to them." Looking deeper I saw that in things themselves we must distinguish between the beauty which belongs to the whole in itself, and the becomingness which results from right relation to some other thing, as a part of the body to the whole body, or a shoe to the foot, and such like. This thought surged up into my mind from the very depths of my heart and I composed certain books *De Pulchro et Apto*—on the Beautiful and the Fitting—two books or three, I fancy; You know, O God, for I do not remember. I no longer have them. Somehow or other they have been lost.

### XIV

What was it, O Lord my God, that moved me to dedicate these books to Hiereus, an Orator of Rome? I had never seen him, but I was won to him for the fame of his learning, which was indeed very notable, and I had heard things he had said which seemed to me admirable. But he pleased me mainly because he pleased others; they praised him highly, amazed that a Syrian, brought up on Greek, should afterwards prove so wonderful a speaker in the Latin tongue, amazed too at his great learning in the field of philosophy. Thus a man is praised and we love him though we have in fact never seen him. Does such a love pass from the lips of the one who praises into the heart of the one who hears the praise? Not at all. Simply one lover is inflamed by another. That is why we are won to a man we hear praised only if we believe that the praise comes from a sincere heart, that is when the praise is uttered by one who truly loves.

Thus I then loved men upon the judgement of men, but not upon Your judgement, my God, in whom no man is deceived. But yet it is to be noted that the feeling I had for such men was not like the feeling I had for some great charioteer, say, or fighter with beasts, whose popularity was so great with the crowd. I admired *them* far differently and for more serious reasons, admired them indeed as I would myself wish to have been admired. I certainly had no desire to be praised and liked as actors are, though I myself both liked them and praised them. For myself I would have chosen to remain utterly unknown rather than so known, and to be hated rather than so loved. How are the balances of these varied and diverse loves so distributed within one soul? How is it that I admire a quality in an-other and yet seem to hate it too, since I should detest and despise it in myself. After all, he and I are both men. It is not as a man might admire a good horse and yet have no desire to be a horse, even if he could manage it. The matter of myself and the actor is different, for he and I share the same nature. How then do I admire a man for being what I should hate to be, although I too am a man? Man is a great deep, Lord. You number his very hairs and they are not lost in Your sight: but the hairs of his head are easier to number than his affections and the movements of his heart.

But that orator whom I so admired was the kind of man that I should have wished myself to be; and I erred through swollen pride, and I was blown about by every wind, and You steered my course for me too hiddenly. And I know now and with sure confidence confess to You that I loved the man more for the love of those who praised him than for the qualities for which he was praised: if those same people had not praised but abused him, and had described the very same qualities in him abusively and with scorn,

I should not have been kindled towards him nor brought to admire him. Yet obviously the qualities would have been the same and the man himself not different: only the attitude of the speakers would have been different. Thus the soul is prostrate and helpless, when it does not adhere to the stability of truth. According as the winds of speech blow from the lungs of those who think they know, so is the soul twisted and turned, and twisted and turned again, and the light shines not for it and it cannot see the truth. Yet the truth is right before it. I thought I should be very much the gainer if my style and my ideas might come to the knowledge of so famous a man. If he thought well of them, I should be still more on fire for him; but if he thought ill, my vain heart, all void of Your stability, would have been wounded deep. All the same I enjoyed setting my meditation to work upon the theme of the Beautiful and the Fitting which I dedicated to him; and with no one else to admire it, I admired it myself.

## xv

But I had not yet seen that this great matter [of the Beautiful and the Fitting] turns upon Your workmanship, O Almighty by whom alone things marvellous are done; and my mind considered only corporeal forms. I defined and distinguished the Beautiful as that which is so of itself, the Fitting as that which is excellent in its relation of fitness to some other thing; and it was by corporeal examples that I supported my argument. I did consider the nature of the soul, but again the false view I had of spiritual things would not let me get at the truth—although by its sheer force the truth was staring me in the face. I turned my throbbing mind away from the incorporeal to line and colour and bulk, and because I did not see these things in my mind, I concluded that I could not see my mind. Further, loving the peace I saw in virtue and hating the discord in vice, I noted the unity of the one and the dividedness of the other; and it seemed to me that in the unity lay the rational mind and the nature of truth and the supreme Good: but in the dividedness I thought I saw some substance of irrational life, and the nature of a supreme Evil. This Evil I saw not only as substance but even as life: and yet, poor wretch, I held that it was not from You, my God, from Whom all things are. I called the first a Monad seeing it as a mind without sex, and the other I called a Dyad—the anger I saw in deeds of violence, the lust I saw in deeds of impurity: but I was talking blindly. For I did not as yet know, I had not been taught, that evil was not any substance, nor was this soul of ours the supreme and immutable good.

Just as we have sins against others if our emotion, in which lies the impetus to act, is vicious and thrusts forward arrogantly and without measure, and damage to self if that affection of the soul whence carnal desires rise is ungoverned: similarly errors and false opinions contaminate life if the rational soul itself is corrupted. So was my soul at that time, for I did not realise that it had to be illumined by another light, if it was to be a partaker of truth, because it is not itself the essence of truth. For *Thou lightest my lamp, O Lord; O my God, enlighten my darkness:* and *of Thy fullness we all have received.* For *Thou art the true Light which enlighteneth every man that cometh into this world:* because *in Thee there is neither change nor shadow of alteration.*

But I was at once striving towards You and thrust back from You, so that I knew the taste of death: for You resist the proud. What could be worse pride than the incredible folly in which I asserted that I was by nature what You are? Since I was not myself immutable—as was clear enough from the fact of my desire to become wise and change from worse to better—I chose rather to think You mutable than to think I was not as You are. Thus I was thrust back: You resisted my windy pride. So that I went on imagining corporeal forms: and being flesh I accused the flesh, and being a wayfaring spirit I did not return to You but in my drifting was borne on towards imaginings which have no reality either in You or in me or in the body, and were not created for me by Your truth but were invented by my own folly playing upon matter. And I spoke much to the little ones of Your flock—my own fellow citizens from whom I was in exile, though I did not know it,—and like the argumentative fool that I was I put to them the question: "Why does the soul err if God created it?" But I would not have any one ask me: "Why then does God err?" And I preferred to maintain that Your immutable substance had been constrained to suffer error, rather than admit that my own mutable substance had gone astray through its own fault and fallen into error for its punishment.

I was around twenty-six or twenty-seven when I wrote these books, revolving within my mind the corporeal imaginings whose clamour filled the ears of my heart, while I was straining them, O Loveliness of Truth, to catch Your inner melody, meditating upon the Beautiful and the Fitting, and yearning that I might stand and hearken to You and rejoice with joy for the voice of the Bridegroom. But for this I had not the strength. I was drawn out of myself by the voices of my error and went falling ever lower through the sheer weight of my own pride. You did not *make me to hear joy and gladness,* nor *did the bones exult which were not yet humbled.*

## XVI

And what did it profit me that when I was barely twenty years old there came into my hands, and I read and understood, alone and unaided, the book of Aristotle's Ten Categories—a book I had longed for as for some great and divine work because the master who taught me Rhetoric at Carthage, and others held learned, mouthed its name with such evident pride? I compared notes with others, who admitted that they had scarcely managed to understand the book even with the most learned masters not merely lecturing upon it but making many diagrams in the dust: and they could not tell me anything of it that I had not discovered in reading it for myself. For it seemed to me clear enough what the book had to say of substances, like man, and of the accidents that are in substances, like the figure of a man, what sort of man he is, and of his stature, how many feet high, and of his family relation-ships, whose brother he is, or where he is placed, or when he was born, or whether he is standing or sitting or has his shoes on or is armed, or whether he is doing something or having something done to him—and all the other countless things that are to be put either in these nine categories of which I have given examples, or in the chief category of substance.

Not only did all this not profit me, it actually did me harm, in that I tried to understand You, my God, marvellous in Your simplicity and immutability, while imagining that whatsoever had being was to be found within these ten categories—as if You were a substance in which inhered Your own greatness or beauty, as they might inhere in a body. In fact Your greatness and Your beauty are Your-self: whereas a body is not large and beautiful merely by being a body, because it would still be a body even if it were less large and less beautiful. The idea I had of You was falsehood and not truth, a fiction of my own littleness, not the solid ground of Your beatitude. For it was Your com-mand, and so it came to pass in me, that *the earth should bring forth thorns and thistles* for me and that *in the sweat of my brow I should eat my bread.*

And what did it profit me that I read and understood for myself all the books of what are called the Liberal Arts that I was able to get hold of, since I remained the vile slave of evil desires? I enjoyed the books, while not knowing Him from whom came whatever was true or certain in them. For I had my back to the light and my face to the things upon which the light falls: so that my eyes, by which I looked upon tne things in the light, were not themselves illumined. What-ever was written either of the art of rhetoric or of logic, of the dimensions of figures or music or arithmetic I understood with no great difficulty and no need of an instructor: this You know, Lord my God, because swiftness of understand-ing and keenness of perceiving are Your gift. But none of this did I offer in sacrifice to You. Therefore it was not for my profit but rather for my harm, that I laboured so to have so great a part of my substance in my own power, and preserved my strength but not for You, going from You into a far country to waste my substance upon loves that were only harlots. For what did it profit me to have good ability since I did not use it well? I did not discover that these matters were very difficult even for the studious and intelligent to grasp, until I tried to teach them to others—and that pupil was regarded as the most excellent who could follow my exposition least laggingly.

But what did all this profit me while I held that You, Lord God of truth, were a luminous immeasurable body and I a kind of particle broken from that body? It was an extreme of perverseness, but so I then was: and I do not now blush to confess to You the mercies You have shown me, O My God, and to call upon You, any more than I then blushed to profess my blasphemies before men and to bark at You. Of what use to me then was my intelligence, swift to run clear through those sciences, of what use were all those knotty books I unravelled without the aid of any human teacher, when in the doctrine of love of You I erred so far and so foully and so sacrilegeously? Or what great harm to Your little ones was their far slower intelligence: since they strayed not far from You and so could fledge their wings in safety in the nest of Your church, and nourish the wings of charity with the food of solid faith?

O Lord our God let us hope in the protecting shadow of Thy wings. Guard us and bear us up. Bear us up Thou wilt, as tiny infants and on to our gray hairs: for when Thou art our strength, it is strength indeed, but when our strength is our own it is only weakness. With Thee our good ever lives, and when we are averted from Thee we are perverted. Let us now return to Thee, O Lord, that we may not be overturned, for with Thee lives without any defect our good which is Thyself. We have no fear that there should be no place of return, merely because by our own act we fell from it: our absence does not cause our home to fall, which is Thy Eternity.

# BOOK FIVE

## AGED TWENTY-EIGHT

R ECEIVE the sacrifice of my Confessions offered by my tongue, which Thou didst form and hast moved to confess unto Thy name. *Heal Thou all my bones* and *they shall say: Lord, who is like to Thee?* A man who makes confession to Thee does not thereby give Thee any information as to what is happening within him. The closed heart does not close out Thy eye, nor the heart's hardness resist Thy hand. For Thou dost open it at Thy pleasure whether for mercy or for justice, and *there is nothing that can hide itself from Thy heat.* But let my soul praise Thee that it may love Thee, and let it tell Thee Thy mercies that it may praise Thee. Without ceasing Thy whole creation speaks Thy praise—the spirit of every man by the words that his mouth directs to Thee, animals and lifeless matter by the mouth of those who look upon them: that so our soul rises out of its mortal weariness unto Thee, helped upward by the things Thou hast made and passing beyond them unto Thee who hast wonderfully made them: and there refreshment is and strength unfailing.

Let the wicked in their restlessness go from Thee and flee away. Yet Thou dost see them, cleaving through their darkness. And all the universe is beautiful about them, but they are vile. What harm have they done Thee? Or have they brought dishonour upon Thy government, which from the heavens unto the latest things of earth is just and perfect? Where indeed did they flee to when they fled from Thy face? Or where dost Thou not find them? The truth is that they fled, that they might not see Thee who sawest them. And so with eyes blinded they stumbled against Thee—for Thou dost not desert any of the things that Thou hast made—they stumbled against Thee in their injustice and justly suffered, since they had withdrawn from Thy mercy and stumbled against Thy justice and fallen headlong upon Thy wrath. Plainly they do not know that Thou art everywhere whom no place compasses in, and that Thou alone art ever present even to those that go furthest from Thee. Let them therefore turn back and seek Thee because Thou hast not deserted Thy creatures as they have deserted their Creator. Let them turn back, and behold Thou art there in their hearts, in the hearts of those that confess to Thee and cast themselves upon Thee and weep on Thy breast as they return from ways of anguish. Gently Thou dost wipe away their tears and they weep the more and are consoled in their weeping: because Thou, Lord, and not any man that is only flesh and blood, Thou, Lord who hast made them, dost remake them and give them comfort. But where was I when I sought after Thee? Thou wert there before me, but I had gone away from myself and I could not even find myself, much less Thee.

### III

I now set before the face of my God the twenty-ninth year of my age. There had just come to Carthage one Faustus, a bishop of the Manichees. He was a great snare of the devil and many were caught in the snare through the charm of his speech. In fact I found this admirable myself, but I was coming to distinguish between it and the truth for which I was then so hungry. I was concerned not with the dish, but with such knowledge as this Faustus, of whom they thought so highly, might set before me to feed upon. Report had already told me great things of him, as a man learned in all profitable learning and especially learned in the liberal sciences.

Now I had read many works of the philosophers and retained a great deal in my memory, and I compared certain of these things with the long-winded fables of the Manichees. What the philosophers taught seemed to me the more probable, though their power was limited to making judgment of this world and they could not pierce through to its Lord. For *the Lord is high and looks on the low: and the proud He knows afar off.* Nor do You draw near, Lord, to any save the contrite of heart; the proud cannot find You, not even if they have skill beyond the natural to number the stars and the grains of sand, and measure out the places of the constellations and plot the courses of the planets. For with the mind and understanding that Thou hast given them they investigate such things: and indeed they have discovered much, and foretold many years in advance eclipses of the sun and the moon, the day, the hour and what part should be in eclipse, and their calculations proved right. It happened as they had foretold; and they put in writing the rules they had arrived at, and these may be read to-day: and by these rules can be foretold the year and the month of the year and the day of the month and the hour of the day and the part of its light that sun or moon is to suffer eclipse: and it will happen as foretold. And men who do not know this art marvel and are amazed, and those that know it boast and are made much of, in their evil pride turning from You and losing Your light: an eclipse of the sun they see so long before it happens, yet they fail to see their own eclipse actually present. They do not religiously enquire what is the source of that gift of understanding by which they enquire these lesser things: and if they find that it is You that have made them, they do not give themselves to You that You should preserve what You have made: nor do they slay in sacrifice to You what they have made themselves to be: for they do not slaughter their self-conceits like birds, nor the curiosities—by which they voyage through the secret ways of the abyss—like the fish of the sea, nor their carnal lusts like the beasts of the field: that You, O God, You the consuming fire, should burn up those dead cares and renew the men themselves to immortal life.

They do not know that way which is Your Word, by which You have made not only the things that they number but also themselves who do the numbering, and the bodily sense by which they see what they number, and the mind from which their numbering comes: *and of Thy wisdom there is no number*. But the Only-Begotten was Himself *made unto us Wisdom and Justice and Sanctification,* and was numbered amongst us and *paid tribute to Caesar*. They do not know the way by which they should descend from themselves to Him, and by Him ascend to Him. They do not know this way, and they fancy themselves raised on high and shining with the stars, whereas they fall upon the earth and *their foolish heart is darkened*.

Much that they say of the created universe is true, but they do not religiously seek the Truth, the architect of the created universe; so that they either do not find Him, or if they find Him and know Him to be God, they do not honour him as God or give Him thanks, but become vain in their imaginings and profess themselves to be wise, attributing to themselves what is Yours and at the same time in a kind of perverse blindness attributing their own qualities to You —so that they load with their falsehoods You who are the Truth, and *changing the glory of the incorruptible God into the likeness of the image of a corruptible man, and of birds, and of four-footed beasts, and of creeping things, and changing the truth of God into a lie, they worship and serve the creature rather than the creator.*

All the same I remembered many truths that they had spoken of the created world itself, and I saw their theories justified by numbers and the order of time and the visible evidence of the stars. I compared all this with what Manes had said, for he wrote at great length upon such matters and quite wildly: but I did not find in him any explanation of the solstices or the equinoxes or the eclipses of sun and moon; nor any of such things as I had learnt in the books of worldly philosophy. I was commanded to believe [what Manes wrote], yet it did not harmonize with the principles I had arrived at by mathematics and indeed by my own eyes, but was far otherwise.

IV

Yet, Lord God of truth, is any man pleasing to You for knowing such things? Surely a man is unhappy even if he knows all these things but does not know You; and that man is happy who knows You even though he knows nothing of them. And the man who knows both You and them is not the happier for them but only on account of You: if knowing You he glorifies You as You are and gives thanks and does not become vain in his thoughts. For just as he is better who knows he possesses a tree and gives thanks to You for the use it is to him, although he does not know how many cubits high it is or the width of its spread, than another man who can measure it and number its branches but neither possesses it nor knows and loves Him who created it; so it would be absurd to doubt that a true Christian—who in some sense possesses all this world of riches and who having nothing yet possesses all things by cleaving unto You whom all things serve—is better though he does not even know the circles of the Great Bear than one who can measure the heavens and number the stars and balance the elements, if in all this he neglects You who have *ordered all things in measure and number and weight.*

V

Who then asked this Manes to write of such things, when piety can be acquired without knowledge of them? For You have said unto man: *Behold the fear of the Lord, that is wisdom.* Manes might very well have been totally without wisdom even though he knew these things perfectly: but in that he had the impudence to presume to teach them when he did not know them, he obviously could not know fear of the Lord. For it is vanity to profess these worldly matters even when one knows them, but piety to confess unto You. Thus he had gone astray and had spoken much of these things: to the sole end that he might be convicted of ignorance by those who had learned them aright, and so his com-

petence upon other more abstruse matters could be readily judged. He did not want to be thought little of, but
tried to persuade men that the Holy Ghost, the Comforter
and Enricher of Your faithful, was resident in himself personally, with plenary authority. Therefore when he was
caught out in error about the sky and the stars and the movements of sun and moon, though these things do not pertain to
religious doctrine, yet his sacrilegious auda ity was apparent
in that he said things not only unknown to him but plainly
false: and in the swollen madness of his pride would have
them credited to himself as to a divine person.

Now when I see some brother Christian, any brother Christian, ignorant of these things and confusing one thing with
another, I can look patiently upon such a man as he utters
his opinion; and I do not see how it can hurt him to be
ignorant of the place or condition of material things provided he does not hold any belief unworthy of You, O Lord,
Creator of all. But it does hurt him if he thinks that this
pertains to the essence of pious doctrine and dares to uphold
too obstinately things he does not know. Even this weakness
in the first beginnings of a man's faith is borne patiently by
Charity, our mother, while the new man is rising unto a
perfect man, so as not to be carried away with every wind
of doctrine. But Manes had dared to set himself up as
teacher, source, guide, and leader of all whom he could convince in these matters, so that those who followed him believed that they were following no mere man but Your Holy
Spirit: once he was caught out in error, surely such madness
could be seen only as detestable and utterly to be rejected?
But I had not as yet clearly discovered whether the changes
in the length of days and nights, and the alternation of night
and day, and the eclipses of sun and moon, and other things
of which I read in the books of the astronomers, could be
explained along his lines: for if they could, even though
it might still remain unproven whether the things were so
or not, yet I was prepared to trust rather in his authority on
account of his reputation for sanctity.

VI

And for almost all those nine years in which without a settled mind I listened to the Manichees, I had looked forward with unbounded desire to the coming of this Faustus. For the others whom I had met, when they failed to find answers to the questions of this sort I posed, promised me Faustus: on his arrival and by conference with him these things would be most lucidly explained, together with any more important questions I might ask. When at last he came I found him a pleasant man of pleasant speech, who rolled off the same kind of things that the others had said with a great deal more charm.

But for my thirst of what use were the most attractive cup-bearer and the most precious cups? My ears had already had their fill of such stuff; it seemed to me no better merely because it was expressed better, nor true because eloquent. Nor did I feel that the soul must be wise because the face was attractive and the speech becoming. Obviously those who had promised him to me were not good judges of reality; and they thought him wise simply because they liked his speaking.

As it happens I have met just the opposite kind of man, who is suspicious of truth and unwilling to accept it if it is uttered in rich and ordered language. But You, O my God, had taught me in secret and marvellous ways. That it was You who taught me, I believe: for it is the truth, and there is no other teacher of truth save You, no matter where or when it may happen to shine. From You then I learned that a thing was not bound to be true because uttered eloquently, nor false because the utterance of the lips is ill-arranged; but that on the other hand a thing is not necessarily true because badly uttered, nor false because spoken magnificently. For it is with wisdom and folly as with wholesome and unwholesome food: just as either kind of food can be served equally well in rich dishes or simple, so plain or beautiful language may clothe either wisdom or folly indifferently.

Therefore the eagerness with which I had so long awaited the man was well repaid by his action and attitude in disputation, and by the apt and fluent language in which he clothed his ideas. I was pleased, and I praised and extolled him along with many another, indeed, more loudly than most. But I was disappointed that, with his flock thronging round him, I was not allowed to address him and put him the questions that troubled me and discuss them as man to man and with comment back and forth. At last I was able to find opportunity, and with some of my friends I sought his attention at a time when we could properly exchange ideas. I mentioned certain questions that concerned me and I found at once that the man was not learned in any of the liberal sciences save literature, and not especially learned even in that. He had read some of Cicero's speeches and a very few books of Seneca, some of the poets and such writings of his own sect as had been written in Latin and were not difficult; over and above that he had daily practice in oratory; and these combined to furnish his eloquence, which was rendered more pleasing and persuasive by the guidance of a good intelligence and a kind of grace that was natural to him. Is it not thus, as I remember it, Lord my God, Judge of my conscience? My heart and my memory are open before You, who were then acting in me by the hidden secret of Your Providence, and bringing my shameful errors before my face, that I might see them and hate them.

## VII

For when I realized that he was unlearned in those matters in which I had thought he excelled, I began to despair of his being able to clarify and solve for me the questions that troubled me—though as I now realize he might have been able to hold the truth of piety even though he was a man of no learning, if he had not been a Manichean. For their books are packed with long-winded nonsense about the sky and the stars and the sun and the moon; and I now saw that he could not with any profundity show me, as I desired, as against the mathematical explanations I had read elsewhere, if the reality was still as the books of Manes stated it, or if at least some explanation equally good could be drawn from them. When I set these questions out for consideration and discussion, he was too modest to presume to undertake the task. He knew that he did not know these things, and he was not ashamed to admit it; he was not one of those talkative people—of whom I had suffered many—who would undertake to teach me, and say nothing. For he had a heart, which though it was not right towards God, was reasonably cautious in the matter of himself. He was not entirely ignorant of his own ignorance, and he did not want rashly to get caught up in a dispute which he could not hope to win and from which he could not gracefully retire. Even for this I liked him better: the modesty of a mind admitting incapacity is a finer thing than the knowledge I was in search of. And thus I found him upon all more difficult and abstruse questions.

The keenness with which I had studied the writings of Manes was thus somewhat blunted; and I was the more hopeless about their other doctors, now that, upon many matters which troubled me, the famous Faustus had shown so ill. But I began to see a good deal of him because of the very keen interest he had in literature, which at that time as professor of Rhetoric I was teaching young students at Carthage; we read either books he wanted (because he had heard of them), or such as I thought suitable to his intelligence. But all my effort and determination to make progress in the sect simply fell away through my coming to know this man. Not that I separated myself from them entirely; but simply, not finding anything better than the course upon which I had somehow or other stumbled, I decided to look no further for the time unless something more desirable should chance to appear. Thus Faustus, who had been a snare that brought death to many, did without his knowledge or will begin to unbind the snare that held me. For Thy hand, O my God, in the secret of Thy Providence did not desert my soul; from the blood of my mother's heart, sacrifice for me was offered Thee day and night by her tears, and Thou didst act with me in marvellous ways. For it was Thou, my God, who didst do it. For *with the Lord shall the steps of a man be directed* and *he shall like well his way.* How shall we attain salvation unless by Thy hand Thou dost remake what Thou didst make?

### VIII

It was by Your action upon me that I was moved to go to Rome and teach there what I had taught in Carthage. How I was persuaded to this, I shall not omit to confess to You, because therein Your most profound depths and Your mercy ever present towards us are to be meditated upon and uttered forth. My reason for going to Rome was not the greater earnings and higher dignity promised by the friends who urged me to go—though at that time, these considerations certainly influenced my mind: the principal and practically conclusive reason, was that I had heard that youths there pursued their studies more quietly and were kept within a stricter limit of discipline. For instance, they were not allowed to come rushing insolently and at will into the school of one who was not their own master, nor indeed to enter it at all unless he permitted.

At Carthage the licence of the students is gross and beyond all measure. They break in impudently and like a pack of madmen play havoc with the order which the master has established for the good of his pupils. They commit many outrages, extraordinarily stupid acts, deserving the punishment of the law if custom did not protect them. Their state is the more hopeless because what they do is supposed to be sanctioned, though by Your eternal law it could never be sanctioned; and they think they do these things unpunished, when the very blindness in which they do them is their punishment, so that they suffer things incomparably worse than they do. When I was a student I would not have such habits in myself, but when I became a teacher I had to endure them in others; and so I decided to go to a place where, as I had been told by all who knew, such things were not done. But You, O my Hope and my Portion in the land of the living, forced me to change countries for my soul's salvation: You pricked me with such goads at Carthage as drove me out of it, and You set before me certain attractions by which I might be drawn to Rome—in either case using men who loved this life of death, one set doing lunatic things, the other promising vain things: and to reform my ways You secretly used their perversity and my own. For those who had disturbed my peace were blind in the frenzy of their viciousness, and those who urged me to go elsewhere savoured of earth. While I, detesting my real misery in the one place, hoped for an unreal happiness in the other.

Why I left the one country and went to the other, You Knew, O God, but You did not tell either me or my mother. She indeed was in dreadful grief at my going and followed me right to the seacoast. There she clung to me passionately, determined that I should either go back home with her or take her to Rome with me, but I deceived her with the pretence that I had a friend whom I did not want to leave until he had sailed off with a fair wind. Thus I lied to my mother, and such a mother; and so got away from her. But this also You have mercifully forgiven me, bringing me from the waters of that sea, filled as I was with execrable uncleanness, unto the water of Your grace; so that when I was washed clean, the floods that poured from my mother's eyes, the tears with which daily she watered the ground towards which she bent her face in prayer for me, should cease to flow. She would not return home without me, but I managed with some difficulty to persuade her to spend the night in a place near the ship where there was an oratory in memory of St. Cyprian. That night I stole away without her: she remained praying and weeping. And what was she praying for, O my God, with all those tears but that You should not allow me to sail! But You saw deeper and granted the essential of her prayer: You did not do what she was at that moment asking, that You might do the thing she was always asking. The wind blew and filled our sails and the shore dropped from our sight. And the next morning she was frantic with grief and filled Your ears with her moaning and complaints because You seemed to treat her tears so lightly, when in fact You were using my own desires to snatch me away for the healing of those desires, and were justly punishing her own too earthly affection for me with the scourge of grief. For she loved to have me with her, as is the way of mothers but far more than most mothers; and she did not realize what joys you would bring her from my going away. She did not realize it, and so she wept and lamented, and by the torments she suffered showed the heritage of Eve in her, seeking with sorrow what in sorrow she had brought forth. But when she had poured out all her accusation at my cruel deception, she turned once more to prayer to You for me. She went home and I to Rome.

IX

Rome welcomed me with the scourge of bodily illness, and I very nearly went to hell bearing all the weight of deadly sins which I had committed against You and myself and other men, over and above the bond of original sin whereby we all die in Adam. For You had not yet forgiven any of my sins in Christ, nor had He yet by His cross healed the enmity which I had contracted towards You by them. How, indeed, could they be healed by the cross of a phantom, which at that time I thought Him? The death of my own soul was as real, as the death of His body seemed to me false; and the life of my soul was as false—since on this matter it was in error—as the death of His body was real. My fever grew worse and I was very close to going off to perdition. For where should I have gone if I had departed then save to fire and torments such as my deeds deserved in the justice of Your ordinance? My mother was far away and knew nothing of my illness, but she prayed on for me. You who are present everywhere heard her where she was and had compassion on me where I was, so that I recovered the health of my body, though still far from health in my sacrilegious heart. For great as that peril had been I did not ask for Your baptism; and I was better as a boy in that I had begged it of my mother's piety, as I have already related and confessed. But I had grown rooted into my shame; and new in folly scorned Your healing precepts, who had saved me from double death in my sins. Had my mother's heart been pierced by *that* wound, it would never have been made whole. I have no words to express the love she had for me, and with how much more anguish she was now in spiritual travail of me than when she had borne me in the flesh. I cannot see how she could have been healed if my death in sin had come to pierce the deepest heart of her love. And where would then have been those urgent and ceaselessly repeated prayers? Nowhere but with You. But would You, O God of mercy, despise the contrite and humble heart of that chaste and pious widow, so generous in alms-giving, so ready in the service of Your saints, who let no day pass without attending the sacrifice at Your altar, and came twice a day with never an exception, morning and evening, to Your church, not to listen to idle tales and the gossip of the women but that she might hear You in Your discourses, and You her in her prayers? You could not despise and withhold Your help from the tears with which she begged of You not gold and silver nor any changing fleeting good, but the salvation of my soul—for it was by Your gift that she was what she was. Rather, Lord, You were ever at hand to hear her and do all in the order that You had predestinated. It could not be that You should deceive her in those visions and answers, those I have mentioned and others I have not mentioned. She laid them up in her faithful heart and again and again reminded You of them in her prayers, as of things written with Your own hand. Because Your mercy endures forever, You deign, when You forgive any soul all its debts, to become Yourself a debtor by Your promises.

X

Thus You brought me out of that sickness and healed the son of Your handmaid in his body, that he might live on to receive a better and surer way of health. At Rome I again associated with those deceived and deceiving Holy Ones: not only with the Hearers, like the man in whose house I had fallen sick and recovered, but also with those whom they call the Elect. For I still held the view that it was not we that sinned, but some other nature sinning in us; and it pleased my pride to be beyond fault, and when I did any evil not to confess that I had done it, that You might heal my soul because it had sinned against You: I very much preferred to excuse myself and accuse some other thing that was in me but was not I. But in truth I was wholly I, it was my impiety that had divided me against myself. My sin was all the more incurable because I thought I was not a sinner; and my iniquity was most execrable in that I would rather have You, God Almighty, vanquished in me to my destruction than myself vanquished by You for my salvation.

You had not then as yet *set a watch before my mouth and a door round about my lips,* that *my heart might not incline to evil words, to make excuses in sins, with men that work iniquity:* and therefore was I still united with their Elect.

All the same because I despaired of finding any profit in that false doctrine, I began to hold slackly and carelessly even the ideas with which I had decided to rest content while I could find nothing better.

The notion began to grow in me that the philosophers whom they call Academics were wiser than the rest, because they held that everything should be treated as matter of doubt and affirmed that no truth can be understood by men. For so it seemed clear to me that they thought—and so they are commonly held to teach—though I did not yet understand their real meaning. And I did not neglect to dissuade my host from the excessive confidence that I saw he had in the fables with which the books of Manes are packed. All the same I was much more in their company than in the company of others who were not of their heresy. I did not defend it with my earlier keenness, yet the friendship of these men, of whom Rome shelters a great number, made me slower to seek any other: especially since I had no hope of being able to find the truth in Your church, O Lord of heaven and earth, Creator of all things visible and invisible. For they had turned me against it: and it seemed to me degrading to believe that You had the shape of our human flesh and were circumscribed within the bodily outlines of our limbs. When I desired to think of my God, I could not think of Him save as a bodily magnitude—for it seemed to me that what was not such was nothing at all: this indeed was the principal and practically the sole cause of my inevitable error.

Because of this I thought that the substance of evil was in some sense similar, and had its own hideous and formless bulk, either gross which they called earth, or thin and tenuous like the air: for they imagine it to be some malignant mind creeping over the earth. And because such poor piety as I had constrained me to hold that the good God could not have created any nature evil, I supposed that there were two opposing powers, each infinite, yet the evil one lesser and the good one greater; and from this abominable foundation other sacrilegious notions followed.

When my mind tried to find help in the Catholic faith, it was beaten back because the Catholic faith is not what I thought it was. It seemed to me more reverent, O my God, whom Your mercies in me glorify, to hold You infinite in all other parts even if I must confess You finite in that part where the power of evil was set against You, than to imagine You finitely contained in all Your parts in the shape of a human body. And it seemed better to believe that You had never created evil, than to believe that anything of the nature that I thought evil was should be from You: in my ignorance I thought of evil not simply as some kind of substance, but actually as bodily substance, because I had not learned to think of mind save as a more subtle body, extended in space [as bodies are]. I thought of our Saviour Himself, Your only-begotten Son, as brought forth for our salvation from the mass of Your most luminous substance: and I could believe nothing of him unless I could picture it in my own vain imagination. I argued that such a nature could not possibly be born of the virgin Mary, unless it were mingled with her flesh. And I could not see how that which I had thus figured to myself could be mingled and not defiled. Thus I feared to believe the Word made flesh lest I be forced to believe the Word defiled by flesh. I have no doubt that Your spiritual ones will smile at me, though kindly and lovingly, to read these confusions of my thought. But such I then was.

XI

Furthermore I thought it quite impossible to defend certain things which the Manichees had criticized in Your Scriptures: but I did by now quite honestly desire to discuss these things one by one with someone learned in Scripture and find out what he made of them. For the speech of one Elpidius, who had spoken and disputed face to face against the Manichees, had already begun to affect me at Carthage, when he produced arguments from Scripture which were not easy to answer. And the answer they gave seemed to me feeble—indeed they preferred not to give it in public but only among ourselves in private—the answer being that the Scriptures of the New Testament had been corrupted by some persons unknown who wished to graft the law of the Jews upon the Christian faith; yet the Manicheans made no effort to produce uncorrupted copies. But I was held captive and stifled by these bodily masses, for I still thought corporeally; I panted under their weight for the clear pure air of Your truth, but still I could not breathe it.

XII

I began diligently to set about that for which I had come to Rome, namely the teaching of Rhetoric. First I gathered some few at my home, and by them I began to become known. And then I learned that Rome had its drawbacks which I had not had to suffer in Africa. For it is true that the riotous incursions of blackguardly youngsters did not happen here: but, so I was warned, "at a given moment a number of students plan together to cheat their master of his fees, and go off to some other master; for they are utterly faithless and hold justice cheap, compared with love of money." My heart hated them, and not with righteous hatred: for pretty surely I hated them more because of what I myself had to suffer from them than for the wrong they did to teachers generally. Such students are indeed depraved: they fornicate against You, O God, in loving the fleeting temptations of time and the filthy cash which soils the hand that holds it, and in embracing this passing world to the scorn of You who abide and ever call them, pardoning the adulterous soul of man when it returns to You. I still hate such vicious and perverse creatures; but I love them as subjects for amendment, souls who might be brought to love the lessons they learn more than money, and You, God, the Truth and Fullness of assured Good and most chaste Peace, more than the lessons. But at that time I disliked them for the harm they did me more than I wished them to become good for Your sake.

XIII

When therefore a message from Milan came to Rome, to the prefect, asking for a professor of Rhetoric for that city and arranging for public funds to cover his journey, I applied for the post with support from men far gone in the follies of the Manichees—the purpose of my journey being to be quit of them, though neither they nor I realized it. The prefect Symmachus approved of a public oration I delivered for the occasion, and sent me. So I came to Milan, to the bishop and devout servant of God, Ambrose, famed among the best men of the whole world, whose eloquence did then most powerfully minister to *Thy people the fatness of Thy wheat and the joy of Thy oil and the sober intoxication of Thy wine.* All unknowing I was brought by God to him, that knowing I should be brought by him to God. That man of God received me as a father, and as bishop welcomed my coming. I came to love him, not at first as a teacher of the truth, which I had utterly despaired of finding in Your church, but for his kindness towards me. I attended carefully when he preached to the people, not with the right intention, but only to judge whether his eloquence was equal to his fame or whether it flowed higher or lower than had been told me. His words I listened to with the greatest care; his matter I held quite unworthy of attention. I enjoyed the charm of his speaking, though for all his learning it was not so pleasing and captivating as that of Faustus: I refer of course only to the actual speaking: for the rest there was no comparison at all. Faustus was simply straying about among the fallacies of the Manichees, Ambrose taught the doctrine of salvation most profitably. But salvation is far from sinners, of the sort that I then was. Yet little by little I was drawing closer, though I did not yet realize it.

XIV

Thus I did not take great heed to learn what he was saying but only to hear how he said it: that empty interest was all I now had since I despaired of man's finding the way to You. Yet along with the words, which I admired, there also came into my mind the subject-matter, to which I attached no importance. I could not separate them. And while I was opening my heart to learn how eloquently he spoke, I came to feel, though only gradually, how truly he spoke. First I began to realize that there was a case for the things themselves, and I began to see that the Catholic faith, for which I had thought nothing could be said in the face of the Manichean objections, could be maintained on reasonable grounds: this especially after I had heard explained figuratively several passages of the Old Testament which had been a cause of death for me when taken literally. Many passages of these books were expounded in a spiritual sense and I came to blame my own hopeless folly in believing that the law and the prophets could not stand against those who hated and mocked at them. I did not yet feel that the Catholic way was to be followed, merely because it might have some learned men to maintain it and answer objections adequately and not absurdly; nor did I think that what I had so far held was to be condemned because both views were equally defensible. In fact the Catholic side was clearly not vanquished, yet it was not clearly victorious. I then bent my mind to see if I could by any clear proofs convict the Manicheans of error. If only I had been able to conceive of a substance that was spiritual, all their strong points would have been broken down and cast forth from my mind. But I could not.

Concerning the body of this world, and the whole of that nature which our bodily senses can attain to, I thought again and again and made many comparisons; and I still judged that the views of so many of the philosophers were more probable. So in what I thought to be the manner of the Academics—that is to say, doubting of all things and wavering between one and another—I decided that I must leave the Manichees; for in that time of doubt, I did not think I could remain in a sect to which I now preferred certain of the philosophers. Yet I absolutely refused to entrust the care of my sick soul to the philosophers, because they were without the saving name of Christ. I determined, then, to go on as a catechumen in the Catholic Church—the church of my parents—and to remain in that state until some certain light should appear by which I might steer my course.

# BOOK SIX

## AGED TWENTY-NINE

O God, my hope from my youth, where were You all this time, where had You gone? For was it not You who created me and distinguished me from the beasts of the field and made me wiser than the birds of the air? Yet I walked through dark and slippery places, and I went out of myself in the search for You and did not find the God of my heart. I had come into the depths of the sea and I had lost faith and all hope of discovering the truth. By this time my mother had come to me, following me over sea and land with the courage of piety and relying upon You in all perils. For they were in danger from a storm, and she reassured even the sailors—by whom travellers newly ventured upon the deep are ordinarily reassured—promising them safe arrival because thus You had promised her in a vision. She found me in a perilous state through my deep despair of ever discovering the truth. But even when I told her that if I was not yet a Catholic Christian, I was no longer a Manichean, she was not greatly exultant as at some unlooked-for good news, because she had already received assurance upon that part of my misery; she bewailed me as one dead certainly, but certainly to be raised again by You, offering me in her mind as one stretched out dead, that You might say to the widow's son: *"Young man, I say to thee arise":* and he should sit up and begin to speak and You should give him to his mother. So her heart was not shaken with any tumult of exultation at hearing that what daily she had begged of You with tears had in so large part happened: for I was at least rescued from heresy, even if I had not yet attained the truth. In fact, because she was certain that You would give her what remained since You had promised her all, she answered me serenely and with a heart full of confidence that in Christ she believed that she would see me a faithful Catholic before she died. So much she said to me. But to You, O fount of mercy, she multiplied her prayers and her tears that You should hasten Your help and enlighten my darkness: and she hastened to church more zealously than ever and drank in the words of Ambrose as a fountain of water springing up into life everlasting. She loved that man as an angel of God because she had learned that it was by him that I had been brought so far as to the wavering state I was now in; through which she took it for granted that I had to pass on my way from sickness to health, with some graver peril yet to come, analagous to what doctors call the crisis.

## II

My mother had brought meal and bread and wine to certain oratories built to the memory of saints, as was her custom in Africa. But the sacristan prevented her. When she learned that the bishop himself had forbidden the practice, she received the prohibition so devoutly and obediently that I wondered at the ease with which she turned into a critic of her own former custom rather than of the present prohibition. For her soul was not a slave to wine-drinking, nor had she any love of wine to provoke her to hatred of the truth, like so many of both sexes who are as much sickened by a hymn of sobriety as drunkards would be if one poured water into their wine. But when my mother brought her basket with those accustomed dainties—of which she meant to eat a little and give away the rest—she never allowed herself more than one small cup diluted to her sober palate, and from this she would sip no more than was fitting. And if there were many oratories of departed saints to be honoured in that way, she took round with her the same cup to be used in each place: and this, not only diluted with water but by now lukewarm, she would share with others present in small sips, for her concern was with piety and not with the pleasure of the wine.

But when she found that the custom was forbidden by so

famous a preacher and so pious a bishop even to those who
used it soberly, lest it might be an occasion of gluttony to
the heavier drinkers; and because in any event these funeral
feasts in honour of our parents in the faith were too much
like the superstitions of the heathens, she abandoned the
practice quite willingly. In place of her basket filled with
the fruits of the earth, she learned to offer at the shrines of
the martyrs a breast full of prayers purer than any such gifts.
Thus she was able to give what she could to the needy; and
the communion of the Lord's Body was celebrated where the
martyrs had been immolated and crowned in the likeness
of His Passion.

But yet, O Lord my God, it does seem to me—and upon
this matter my heart is in Your sight—that my mother might
not so easily have borne the breaking of her custom if it had
been forbidden by some other whom she did not love as she
loved Ambrose. For on account of my salvation she loved
him dearly; and he loved her on account of her most religious
way of life, for she was fervent in spirit and ever doing good,
and she haunted the church. So that when he saw me he
often broke out in her praises, congratulating me that I had
such a mother, and not realizing what sort of a son she had:
for I doubted all these things and did not believe that the
way of life could be discovered.

### III

Nor did I then groan in prayer for Your help. My mind
was intent upon inquiry and unquiet for argumentation.
I regarded Ambrose as a lucky man by worldly standards
to be held in honour by such important people: only his
celibacy seemed to me a heavy burden. I had no means
of guessing, and no experience of my own to learn from,
what hope he bore within him, what struggles he might
have against the temptations that went with his high place,
what was his consolation in adversity, and on what joys of
Your bread the hidden mouth of his heart fed. Nor did he
know how I was inflamed nor the depth of my peril. I

could not ask of him what I wished as I wished, for I was kept from any face to face conversation with him by the throng of men with their own troubles, whose infirmities he served. The very little time he was not with these he was refreshing either his body with necessary food or his mind with reading. When he read, his eyes travelled across the page and his heart sought into the sense, but voice and tongue were silent. No one was forbidden to approach him nor was it his custom to require that visitors should be announced: but when we came into him we often saw him reading and always to himself; and after we had sat long in silence, unwilling to interrupt a work on which he was so intent, we would depart again. We guessed that in the small time he could find for the refreshment of his mind, he would wish to be free from the distraction of other men's affairs and not called away from what he was doing. Perhaps he was on his guard lest [if he read aloud] someone listening should be troubled and want an explanation if the author he was reading expressed some idea over obscurely, and it might be necessary to expound or discuss some of the more difficult questions. And if he had to spend time on this, he would get through less reading than he wished. Or it may be that his real reason for reading to himself was to preserve his voice, which did in fact readily grow tired. But whatever his reason for doing it, that man certainly had a good reason.

Anyhow I was given no opportunity of putting such questions as I desired to that holy oracle of Yours, his breast, unless they were of a sort to be heard briefly. But the agitation working in me required that he should be fully at leisure if I were to pour it out before him; and I never found him so. Still I heard him every Sunday preaching the word of truth to his congregation; and I became more and more certain that all those knots of cunning and calumny, which those who deceived me had tangled up against the holy books, could be untangled. I learned that the phrase "man created by You in Your own image" was not taken by

Your spiritual children, whom of our Catholic mother You have made to be born anew by grace, to mean that You are bounded within the shape of a human body. And although I had not the vaguest or most shadowy notion how a spiritual substance could be, yet I was filled with shame—but joyful too—that I had been barking all these years not against the Catholic faith but against mere figments of carnal imaginations. I had been rash and impious in that I had spoken in condemnation of things which I should have learned more truly of by inquiry. For You, O highest and nearest, most hidden and most present, have not parts greater and smaller; You are wholly everywhere, yet nowhere limited within space, nor are You of any bodily form. And yet You have made man in Your own image, and man is in space from head to foot.

IV

Thus I was ignorant how this image of Yours could be; but I should have knocked at the door and proposed the question how it was to be believed, and not jeeringly opposed it as if it were believed in this or that particular way. The anxiety as to what I should hold as sure gnawed at my heart all the more keenly, as my shame increased at having been so long tricked and deceived by the promise of certainty, and at having with a rashness of error worthy of a child gone on spouting forth so many uncertainties as confidently as if I had known them for sure. That they were false, I saw clearly only later. Yet already I was certain that they were at least uncertain, and that I had taken them for certain, when in the blindness of my opposition I attacked Your Catholic church. I did not yet know that she was teaching the truth, but I had found that she did not teach the things of which I had so strongly accused her. So I was first confounded and then enlightened. And I rejoiced, O my God, that Your only church, the Body of Your only Son, in which the name of Christ had been put upon me while I was still an infant, had no taste for such puerile nonsense; nor in her sound doctrine had she the notion of somehow packing You, the Creator of all things, into any space—however mighty and ample yet bounded upon all sides—in the shape of a human body.

I was glad also that the old scriptures of the Law and the Prophets were set before me now, no longer in that light in which they had formerly seemed absurd, when I criticised Your holy ones for thinking this or that which in plain fact they did not think. And it was a joy to hear Ambrose who often repeated to his congregation, as if it were a rule he was most strongly urging upon them, the text: *the letter killeth, but the spirit giveth life.* And he would go on to draw aside the veil of mystery and lay open the spiritual meaning of things which taken literally would have seemed to teach falsehood. Nothing of what he said struck me as false, although I did not as yet know whether what he said was true. I held back my heart from accepting anything, fearing that I might fall once more, whereas in fact the hanging in suspense was more deadly. I wanted to be as certain of things unseen as that seven and three make ten. For I had not reached the point of madness which denies that even this can be known; but I wanted to know other things as clearly as this, either such material things as were not present to my senses, or spiritual things which I did not know how to conceive save corporeally. By believing I might have been cured; for then the eye of my mind would have been clearer and so might in some way have been directed towards Your truth which abides for ever and knows no defect. But as usually happens, the man who has tried a bad doctor is afraid to trust even a good one: so it was with the health of my soul, which could not be healed save by believing, and refused to be healed that way for fear of believing falsehood. Thus I was resisting Your hands, for You first prepared for us the medicine of faith and then applied it to the diseases of the world and gave it such great power.

V

From this time on I found myself preferring the Catholic doctrine, realising that it acted more modestly and honestly in requiring things to be believed which could not be proved—whether they were in themselves provable though not by this or that person, or were not provable at all—than the Manichees who derided credulity and made impossible promises of certain knowledge, and then called upon men to believe so many utterly fabulous and absurd things because they could not be demonstrated. Next, Lord, with gentle and most merciful hand You worked upon my heart and rectified it. I began to consider the countless things I believed which I had not seen, or which had happened with me not there—so many things in the history of nations, so many facts about places and cities which I had never seen, so many things told me by friends, by doctors, by this man, by that man: and unless we accepted these things, we should do nothing at all in this life. Most strongly of all it struck me how firmly and unshakeably I believed that I was born of a particular father and mother, which I could not possibly know unless I believed it upon the word of others. Thus You brought me to see that those who believed Your Bible, which You have established among almost all peoples with such authority, were not to be censured, but rather those who did not believe it, and that I must give no heed to any who might say to me: "How do you know that those Scriptures were given to mankind by the Spirit of the One true and most true God?" For this point above all was to be believed; because no assault of fallacious questions which I had read in such multitude in the philosophers—who in any event contradicted each other—could constrain me not to believe both that You are, though what might be Your nature I did not know, and that the government of human affairs belongs to You.

But though I held these truths sometimes more strongly sometimes less, yet I always believed both that You are and that You have a care of us: even if I did not know what I must hold as to Your substance, or what way leads to You—or leads back to You. Thus, since men had not the strength to discover the truth by pure reason and therefore we needed the authority of Holy Writ, I was coming to believe that You would certainly not have bestowed such eminent authority upon those Scriptures throughout the world, unless it had been Your will that by them men should believe in You and in them seek You.

Now that I heard them expounded so convincingly, I saw that many passages in these books which had at one time struck me as absurdities, must be referred to the profundity of mystery. Indeed the authority of Scripture seemed to be more to be revered and more worthy of devoted faith in that it was at once a book that all could read and read easily, and yet preserved the majesty of its mystery in the deepest part of its meaning: for it offers itself to all in the plainest words and the simplest expressions, yet demands the closest attention of the most serious minds. Thus it receives all within its welcoming arms, and at the same time brings a few direct to You by narrow ways: yet these few would be fewer still but for this twofold quality by which it stands so lofty in authority yet draws the multitude to its bosom by its holy lowliness. So I dwelt upon these things and You were near me, I sighed and You heard me, I was wavering uncertainly and You guided me, I was going the broad way of the world and You did not forsake me.

VI

I was all hot for honours, money, marriage: and You made mock of my hotness. In my pursuit of these, I suffered most bitter disappointments, but in this You were good to me since I was thus prevented from taking delight in anything not Yourself. Look now into my heart, Lord, by whose will I remember all this and confess it to You. Let my soul cleave to You now that You have freed it from the tenacious hold of death. At that time my soul was in misery, and You pricked the soreness of its wound, that leaving all things it might turn to You, who are over all and without whom all would return to nothing, that it might turn to You and be healed. I was in utter misery and there was one day especially on which You acted to bring home to me the realisation of my misery. I was preparing an oration in praise of the Emperor in which I was to utter any number of lies to win the applause of people who knew they were lies. My heart was much wrought upon by the shame of this and inflamed with the fever of the thoughts that consumed it. I was passing along a certain street in Milan when I noticed a beggar. He was jesting and laughing and I imagine more than a little drunk. I fell into gloom and spoke to the friends who were with me about the endless sorrows that our own insanity brings us: for here was I striving away, dragging the load of my unhappiness under the spurring of my desires, and making it worse by dragging it: and with all our striving, our one aim was to arrive at some sort of happiness without care: the beggar had reached the same goal before us, and we might quite well never reach it at all. The very thing that he had attained by means of a few pennies begged from passers-by—namely the pleasure of a temporary happiness—I was plotting for with so many a weary twist and turn.

Certainly his joy was no true joy; but the joy I sought in my ambition was emptier still. In any event he was cheerful and I worried, he had no cares and I nothing but cares. Now if anyone had asked me whether I would rather be cheerful or fearful, I would answer: "Cheerful": but if he had gone on to ask whether I would rather be like that beggar or as I actually was, I would certainly have chosen my own state though so troubled and anxious. Now this was surely absurd. It could not be for any true reason. I ought not to have preferred my own state rather than his merely because I was the more learned, since I got no joy from my learning, but sought only to please men by it—not even to teach them, only to please them. Therefore did You break my bones with the rod of Your discipline.

Let my soul pay no heed to those who would say: "It makes a difference what one is happy about. The beggar found joy in his drunkenness, you sought joy in glory." But what glory, Lord? A glory not in You. For my glory was no truer than his joy, and it turned my head even more. That very night he would sleep off his drunkenness: but how often and often I had gone to bed with mine and woken up with it, and would in the future go to bed with it and wake up with it. It does indeed make a difference what one is happy about: I know it, and I know that the happiness of a sure hope is incomparably beyond all such vanity. And there was indeed a difference between him and me—for he was much the happier man: not only because he was soaked in his merriment while I was eaten up with cares, but also because he by wishing luck to all comers had at least got wine, while I by lying was aiming only to get empty praise.

I spoke much to this effect to the friends that were with me: and I often observed that it was with them as it was with me, and I found it very ill with me. So I worried and by worrying doubled the ill. And when by chance prosperity smiled in my direction, I lacked the spirit to seize it, for it fled away almost before I could get my hand upon it.

## VII

We were gloomy together with such thoughts, I and those who were closest to me. I discussed the problem especially with Alypius and Nebridius. Alypius was born in the same town as I. His parents were of high rank there. He was younger than I, indeed he had studied under me both when I began my teaching in our native town and afterwards at Carthage. He was much attached to me because he thought me kindly and learned, and I to him because of the great bent towards virtue that was so marked in him so young. But at Carthage the maelstrom of ill morals—and especially

the passion for idle spectacles—had sucked him in, his special madness being for gladiatorial shows. When he first
came into the grip of this wretched craving, I had set up a
school for the public and was teaching rhetoric. He had not
come to me as a pupil because of some difference that had
arisen between his father and me. I discovered that he was
quite fatally devoted to the Games, and I was much worried
because it seemed to me that so much promise was to be
thrown away, or had already been thrown away. But I had
no way of advising him or forcibly restraining him, neither
the goodwill of a friend nor the right of a master. For I
took for granted that he would feel about me as his father
did. In fact he did not. He took his own line in the matter
rather than his father's, and fell into the way of greeting
me when we met and of coming sometimes into my school
to listen awhile and be off again.

But it had passed from my mind that I could do anything to
prevent the waste of so good a mind in the blind and ruin-
ous pursuit of the empty pastimes he was in. But You, Lord,
who hold the helm of all that You have created, had not forgotten him—and indeed he was one day to be numbered
amongst Your children as a high priest of Your sacrament.
That his amendment might be obviously due to You,
You brought it about through me, and without my being
aware of it. For one day when I was sitting in my usual place
with my students in front of me, he came in, greeted me, sat
down and gave his attention to what was being discussed. I
had in hand a passage that I was expounding: and it suddenly
struck me that it could be very well illustrated by a comparison taken from the Games—a comparison which would
make the point I was establishing clearer and more amusing,
and which involved biting mockery of those who were slaves
to that particular insanity. You know, O my God and his, that
I was not thinking of Alypius or his need to be cured of
that disease. But he applied it instantly to himself and
thought I had said it solely on his account. Another might
have taken it as a reason for being angry with me, but the

youth was honest enough to take it as a reason for being angry with himself and for warmer attachment to me. You said long ago and caused it to be written in Your Book: *Rebuke a wise man and he will love you.*

As a matter of fact I had not been rebuking him, but You use all men with or without their knowledge for a purpose known to Yourself—and that purpose is just. Thus of my heart and tongue You made burning coals, to cauterize and heal a mind of such promise though it lay sick. Let him praise You not who does not realize Your mercies, which my soul's depths confess to You. As a result of what he had heard me say, he wrenched himself up out of the deep pit in which he had chosen to be plunged and in the darkness of whose pleasures he had been so woefully blinded. He braced his mind and shook it till all the filth of the Games fell away from it and he went no more.

Then he prevailed upon his unwilling father to let him be one of my students. His father did at last yield. Alypius began to take lessons from me again and so came to be involved with me in the same superstitions. He loved especially the pretence the Manichees made of continence, which he took to be quite genuine. But in fact it was a senseless and misleading continence, which seduced precious souls not yet able to reach the profound depth of virtue and easily deceived with the surface appearance of what was only an unreal counterfeit of virtue.

### VIII

In pursuit of the worldly career whose necessity his parents were always dinning into his ears, he had gone before me to Rome to study Law: and there incredibly he had been carried away again by an incredible passion for gladiatorial shows. He had turned from such things and utterly detested them. But it happened one day that he met some friends and fellow-students coming from dinner: and though he flatly refused and vigorously resisted, they used friendly violence and forced him along with them to the amphitheater on a

day of these cruel and murderous Games. He protested
"Even if you drag my body to the place, can you force me to
turn my mind and my eyes on the show? Though there, I
shall not be there, and so I shall defeat both you and it."

Hearing this his companions led him on all the faster,
wishing to discover whether he could do as he had said. When
they had reached the Arena and had got such seats as they
could, the whole place was in a frenzy of hideous delight.
He closed up the door of his eyes and forbade his mind
to pay attention to things so evil. If only he could have
stopped his ears too! For at a certain critical point in the
fight, the vast roar of the whole audience beat upon him.
His curiosity got the better of him, and thinking that he
would be able to treat the sight with scorn—whatever the
sight might be—he opened his eyes and was stricken with a
deeper wound in the soul than the man whom he had
opened his eyes to see got in the body. He fell more miserably than the gladiator whose fall had set the crowd to that
roar—a roar which had entered his ears and unlocked his
eyes, so that his soul was stricken and beaten down. But in
truth the reason was that its courage had so far been only
audaciousness, and it was weak because it had relied upon
itself when it should have trusted only in You. Seeing the
blood he drank deep of the savagery. He did not turn away
but fixed his gaze upon the sight. He drank in all the frenzy,
with no thought of what had happened to him, revelled in
the wickedness of the contest and was drunk with lust for
blood. He was no longer the man who had come there but
one of the crowd to which he had come, a fit companion
for those who had brought him.

What more need I say? He continued to gaze, shouted,
grew hot, and when he departed took with him a madness
by which he was to be goaded to come back again, not only
with those who at first took him there, but even more than
they and leading on others. Yet out of all this You drew
him with strong and merciful hand, teaching him to have
confidence in You, not in himself. But this was long after.

## IX

For the time, the matter was only laid up in his memory for his future healing. So also was an incident which had happened earlier while he was still a student in my school at Carthage. He was in the market-place at noon one day going over in his mind something that he had to say by heart (as students usually have to do) when You allowed him to be arrested as a thief by the officers in charge of the market. I imagine that You allowed this, O our God, for no other cause than that one who was to be so great should learn thus early that in judging cases man must not too easily be condemned by man through rash credulity. As he was walking by himself before the judgment-seat with his tablets and his pen, the real thief, a young man who was also a student, came along with an axe concealed under his clothes and quite unseen by Alypius went up to the leaden gratings which are over the silversmiths' shops and began to cut away the lead. When they heard the sound of the axe the silversmiths underneath began to call out and sent men to seize whomever they might find. The thief heard their voices and ran away leaving his axe behind for fear that he might be caught with it.

Now Alypius who had not seen the man arrive saw him depart, observed the speed of his departure, and wondering what it was all about went up to the place. He found the axe and stood looking at it with surprise. At this moment those who had been sent found him alone and carrying the weapon whose noise had startled them and brought them there. They seized him, dragged him off, and gathering the neighbouring shopkeepers made a great boast of having caught the thief in the act. They took him off to hand him over to the officers of the law. But his lesson stopped there. For at that point, Lord, You came to the aid of his innocence, of which indeed You were the only witness. For as he was being led off to imprisonment or torture, they were met by a certain architect, who had the principal charge of public buildings. They were particularly pleased to meet him just then, because they were themselves under suspicion of stealing the goods that were lost out of the market-place, and they felt that at last he would know who had done the stealing. But this man had often seen Alypius at the house of a certain Senator whom he himself frequently visited. He knew him at once and taking him by the hand drew him away from the crowd and enquired the cause of all the trouble. He heard what had happened and commanded the rabble who thronged about raging and threatening Alypius to come with him. They came to the house of the young man who had done the deed. There was a boy outside the door who was quite ready to tell the whole thing, being too young to fear that any harm would come to his master from what he said: for he had gone with him to the market place. Alypius remembered seeing the boy and told the architect, who showed the hatchet to the boy and asked him whose it was. "Ours" replied the boy immediately. He was questioned further and disclosed everything. Thus the guilt was transferred to the man who lived in that house, to the great confusion of the crowd which had been hurling its taunts at Alypius. Alypius indeed, who was later to be a dispenser of Your word and to investigate many cases in Your Church, went off very much wiser for the experience.

x

I found him at Rome when I came there and he became my close friend. He went with me to Milan, so that he might be still with me, and might at the same time practice the Law he had studied, but this rather to please his parents than of his own wish. He had already sat three times as an Assessor, displaying an integrity that caused others to marvel—whereas he marvelled that any should prefer money to honesty. His character was tested further, not only by the temptation of bribery but also by the threat of danger to himself. At Rome he had been Assessor to the Chancellor of the Italian Treasury. There was at the time a very powerful Senator, to whom many were bound by favours received, while many stood in fear of him. He wanted to have permission granted him for something forbidden by the law. Ordinarily so powerful a man would have got it as a matter of course. But Alypius refused. A bribe was offered: he treated it with complete contempt. He was threatened and treated the threats likewise. Everyone was amazed at so rare a spirit, in that he neither courted the friendship nor feared the enmity of a man so important and so well known for the innumerable means at his disposal for advancing or damaging others. The Judge himself to whom Alypius acted as Assessor, did not want to grant the permit, but would not openly refuse it: he put the blame upon Alypius, claiming that Alypius would not let him do it: and in truth if he had tried, Alypius would have left the court.

The only thing that did tempt him was his love of study: he thought of having books copied for him at the reduced rates allowed to Praetors. But considering the equity of the matter he came to a better decision, holding justice which forbade it more valuable than the power to do it. All that I have so far said is small: yet *he that is faithful in that which is least, is faithful also in that which is greater;* nor is that word void which proceeded from the mouth of Your Truth: *If then you have not been faithful in the unjust Mammon, who will trust you with that which is the true? and if you have not been faithful in that which is another's who will give you that which is your own?* Such then was the man who was so close a friend, and shared my wavering as to the course of life we should adopt.

I have mentioned Nebridius. He had left his native place near Carthage: he had left Carthage itself where he had mainly lived, had left his rich family estate and his house and his mother, for she would not come with him. All these things he had left and had come to Milan for no other reason than to be with me: for with a real passion for truth and wisdom, he was in the same anguish as I and the same uncertain wavering; and he continued his ardent search for the way of happiness and his close investigation of the most difficult questions. Thus there were together the mouths of three needy souls, bitterly confessing to one another their spiritual poverty and waiting upon You that You *might give them their food in due season*. And amidst the bitter disappointments which through Your mercy followed all our worldly affairs, darkness clouded our souls as we tried to see why we suffered these things. And we turned away in deepest gloom saying: *"How long shall these things be?"* This question was ever on our lips, but for all that we did not give up our worldly ways, because we still saw no certitude which it was worth changing our way of life to grasp.

XI

I was much exercised in mind as I remembered how long it was since that nineteenth year of my age in which I first felt the passion for true knowledge and resolved that when I found it I would give up all the empty hopes and lying follies of vain desires. And here I was going on for thirty, still sticking in the same mire, greedy for the enjoyment of things present though they ever eluded me and wasted my soul: and at every moment saying: "To-morrow I shall find it: it will be all quite clear and I shall grasp it. Faustus will come and explain everything. And those mighty Academics—is it true that nothing can be grasped with certainty for the directing of life? No: we must search the more closely and not despair. For now the things in the Scriptures which used to seem absurd are no longer absurd, but can be quite properly understood in another sense. I shall set my foot upon that step on which my parents placed me as a child, until I clearly find the truth. But where shall I search? When shall I search? Ambrose is busy. I am myself too busy to read. And in any event where can I find the books? Who has them, or when can I procure them? Can I borrow them from anyone? I must appoint set times, set apart certain hours for the health of my soul. A great hope has dawned: the Catholic faith does not teach the things I

thought and vainly accused it of. Catholic scholars hold it
blasphemy to believe God limited within the shape of a
human body. Do I hesitate to knock, that other truths may
be opened? My pupils occupy the morning hours, but what
do I do with the rest? Why not do this? But if I do, when
shall I have time to visit the powerful friends of whose influence I stand in need, or when prepare the lessons I sell
to my pupils, or when refresh myself by relaxing my
mind from too close pre-occupation with my heavy con-
cerns?

"But perish all this. Let me dismiss this vanity and emptiness and give myself wholly to the search for truth. Life
is a poor thing, death may come at any time: if it were to
come upon me suddenly, in what state should I depart this
life? And where am I to learn the things I have neglected?
Or must I not rather suffer the punishment of my negli-
gence? Or does death perhaps cut off and end all care along
with our bodily sense? This too must be settled. But God
forbid that it should be so. It is not for nothing or any mere
emptiness that the magnificence of the authority of the Christian Faith is spread over all the world. Such great and wonderful things would never have been wrought for us by God,
if the life of the soul were ended by the death of the body.
Why then do I delay to drop my hopes of this world and
give myself wholly to the search for God and true happiness?

"Yet stay a moment. After all, these worldly things are
pleasant, they have their own charm and it is no small charm.
The mind is not easily cut off from them merely because it
would be base to go back to them. Again, it would not be too
difficult to win some post of honour: and what more should
I have to wish for? I have a body of powerful friends:
even if I press on to nothing more ambitious, I could at
least get a governorship. And then I could marry a wife,
with some little money of her own, so that she would not
increase my expenditure. And so I should have reached
the limit of ambition. Many great men, well worthy of our

imitation, have given themselves to the pursuit of wisdom even though they had wives."

These things went through my mind, and the wind blew one way and then another, and tossed my heart this way and that. Time was passing and I delayed to turn to the Lord. From day to day I postponed life in You, but I did not postpone the death that daily I was dying in myself. I was in love with the idea of happiness, yet I feared it where it was, and fled away from it in my search for it. The plain truth is that I thought I should be impossibly miserable if I had to forego the embraces of a woman: and I did not think of Your mercy as a healing medicine for that weakness, because I had never tried it. I thought that continency was a matter of our own strength, and I knew that I had not the strength: for in my utter foolishness I did not know the word of Your Scripture that none can be continent unless You give it. And truly You would have given it if with groaning of spirit I had assailed Your ears and with settled faith had cast my care upon You.

### XII

It was Alypius indeed who kept me from marrying, with his unvarying argument that if I did we could not possibly live together with untroubled leisure in the pursuit of wisdom, as we had so long desired. For on that side of things he was quite extraordinarily chaste. Early in adolescence he had had the experience of sexual intercourse, but it took no hold upon him. Indeed he regretted having done it and despised it and from then on lived in complete continence. I brought up the example of those who had pursued wisdom in the married state, and served God faithfully, and faithfully kept and cherished their friends. But indeed I was far enough from their greatness of spirit. I was bound by this need of the flesh, and dragged with me the chain of its poisonous delight, fearing to be set free: and I rejected his words of wise counsel, pushing away the hand that would set me free as though it were hurting a sore place.

Moreover, through me the serpent began to speak to Aly-pius himself. By my tongue the devil wove fascinating snares and scattered them in his path for the entangling of his hither-to untrammeled feet. For he marvelled to see me, of whom he thought so much, stuck so fast in the grip of that particular lust as to affirm whenever we talked of it that I could not possibly lead a single life. I urged on my side, when I saw how puzzled he was, that there was a great difference between the snatched and furtive experience of sex which he had had as a boy—and now scarcely remembered and could therefore brush aside with no particular trouble—and the enjoyment of my permanent state. It only needed the honorable name of marriage, and he would have had no cause to wonder why I could not give up that way of life. The result was that he began to desire marriage himself, not through any lust for the pleasure of it but solely through curiosity: for as he ex-plained, he wanted to discover what the thing was without which my life—which to him seemed so pleasing—would have seemed to me no life at all but torment. For his mind, itself free from the chain, marvelled at my enslave-ment; and from marvelling he came to a desire to try it. Thus he might well have entered upon the same experience and so fallen into the enslavement which at present he found so incomprehensible: for he was willing to make a covenant with death, and *he that loves danger shall fall into it.* Such honour as there is in marriage from the duty of well-ordered life together and the having of children, had very small influence with either of us. What held me so fiercely bound was principally the sheer habit of sating a lust that could never be satisfied, and what drew him who was not yet bound was curiosity about me. Thus we stood until You, O most High, not forsaking our dust but pitying our piti-fulness, helped us by secret and wonderful ways.

## XIII

Great effort was made to get me married. I proposed, the girl was promised me. My mother played a great part in the

matter for she wanted to have me married and then cleansed
with the saving waters of baptism, rejoicing to see me grow
every day more fitted for baptism and feeling that her prayers
and Your promises were to be fulfilled in my faith. By my
request and her own desire she begged You daily with the
uttermost intensity of her heart to show her in a vision something of my future marriage, but You would never do it. She
did indeed see certain vain fantasies, under the pressure
of her mind's preoccupation with the matter; and she
told them to me, not, however, with the confidence she
always had when You had shown things to her, but as if she
set small store by them; for she said that there was a certain
unanalysable savor, not to be expressed in words, by which
she could distinguish between what You revealed and the
dreams of her own spirit. Still she pushed on with the matter
of my marriage, and the girl was asked for. She was still
two years short of the age for marriage but I liked her and
agreed to wait.

## XIV

There was a group of us friends who had much serious
discussion together, concerning the cares and troubles of
human life which we found so hard to endure. We had almost
decided to seek a life of peace, away from the throng of men.
This peace we hoped to attain by putting together whatever
we could manage to get, and making one common household for all of us: so that in the clear trust of friendship,
things should not belong to this or that individual, but one
thing should be made of all our possessions, and belong
wholly to each one of us, and everybody own everything.
It seemed that there might be perhaps ten men in this fellowship. Among us there were some very rich men, especially
Romanianus, our fellow townsman, who had been a close
friend of mine from childhood and had been brought to the
court in Milan by the press of some very urgent business.
He was strongest of all for the idea and he had considerable
influence in persuasion because his wealth was much greater

than anyone else's. We agreed that two officers should be chosen every year to handle the details of our life together, leaving the rest undisturbed. But then we began to wonder whether our wives would agree, for some of us already had wives and I meant to have one. So the whole plan, which we had built up so neatly, fell to pieces in our hands and was simply dropped. We returned to our old sighing and groaning and treading of this world's broad and beaten ways: for many thoughts were in our hearts, but *Thy counsel standeth forever*. And out of Thy counsel didst Thou deride ours and didst prepare Thine own things for us, meaning to *give us meat in due season* and *to open Thy hands and fill our souls with Thy blessing*.

## XV

Meanwhile my sins were multiplied. She with whom I had lived so long was torn from my side as a hindrance to my forthcoming marriage. My heart which had held her very dear was broken and wounded and shed blood. She went back to Africa, swearing that she would never know another man, and left with me the natural son I had had of her. But I in my unhappiness could not, for all my manhood, imitate her resolve. I was unable to bear the delay of two years which must pass before I was to get the girl I had asked for in marriage. In fact it was not really marriage that I wanted. I was simply a slave to lust. So I took another woman, not of course as a wife; and thus my soul's disease was nourished and kept alive as vigorously as ever, indeed worse than ever, that it might reach the realm of matrimony in the company of its ancient habit. Nor was the wound healed that had been made by the cutting off of my former mistress. For there was first burning and bitter grief; and after that it festered, and as the pain grew duller it only grew more hopeless.

## XVI

Praise be to Thee, glory to Thee, O fountain of mercies. I became more wretched and Thou more close to me. Thy right hand was ready to pluck me from the mire and wash me clean, though I knew it not. So far nothing called me back from the depth of the gulf of carnal pleasure save fear of death and of the judgment to come, which, through all the fluctuations of my opinions, never left my mind. I discussed with my friends Alypius and Nebridius concerning the nature of good and evil, and Epicurus would certainly have won the palm in my judgment if I had not believed that after death there remained life for the soul and treatment according to its deserts, which Epicurus did not hold. And I put the question, supposing we were immortals and could live in perpetual enjoyment of the body without any fear of loss, why we should not then be happy, or what else should we seek. I did not realize that it belonged to the very heart of my wretchedness to be so drowned and blinded in it that I could not conceive that light of honor, and of beauty loved for its own sake, which the eye of the flesh does not see but only the innermost soul. I was so blind that I never came to ask myself what was the source of the pleasure I found in discussing these ideas (worthless as they were) with friends, and of my inability to be happy without friends, even in the sense of happiness which I then held, no matter how great the abundance of carnal pleasure. For truly I loved my friends. for their own sake, and I knew that I was in turn so loved by them. O, tortuous ways! Woe to my soul with its rash hope of finding something better if it forsook Thee! My soul turned and turned again, on back and sides and belly, and the bed was always hard. For Thou alone art her rest. And behold Thou art close at hand to deliver us from the wretchedness of error and establish us in thy way, and console us with Thy word: "Run, I shall bear you up and bring you and carry you to the end."

# BOOK SEVEN

## AGED THIRTY

## 1

Now my evil sinful youth was over and I had come on into young manhood; but the older in years, the baser was my vanity, in that I could not conceive any other kind of substance than what these eyes are accustomed to see. I did not indeed, O God, think of You under the figure of a human body. From the moment I began to know anything of philosophy, I had rejected that idea; and I rejoiced to find the same rejection in the faith of our spiritual mother, Your Catholic Church. But what else to think You I did not know.

As a man, though so poor a man, I set myself to think of You as the supreme and sole and true God; and with all my heart I believed You incorruptible and inviolable and immutable, for though I did not see whence or how, yet I saw with utter certainty that what can be corrupted is lower than what cannot be corrupted, that the inviolable is beyond question better than the violable, and that what can suffer no change is better than what can be changed. My heart cried out passionately against all my imaginings; and I tried with this one truth to beat away all that circling host of uncleannesses from the eyes of my mind. But they were scarce gone for the space of a single glance. They came again close packed upon me, pressed upon my gaze and so clouded it that though I did not even then think of You under the shape of a human body, yet I could not but think of You as some corporeal substance, occupying all space, whether infused in the world, or else diffused through infinite space beyond the world. Yet even at this I thought of You as incorruptible and inviolable and immutable, and I still saw those as better than corruptible and violable and mutable. But whatever I tried to see as not in space seemed to me to be nothing, absolutely nothing, not even a void: for if a body were taken out of its place and the place remained without any body, whether of earth or water or air or sky, it would still be an empty place, a space-occupying nothingness.

Thus I was so gross of mind—not seeing even myself clearly—that whatever was not extended in space, either diffused or massed together or swollen out or having some such qualities or at least capable of having them, I thought must be nothing whatsoever. My mind was in search of such images as the forms my eye was accustomed to see; and I did not realize that the mental act by which I formed these images, was not itself a bodily image: yet it could not have formed them, unless it were something and something great. I conceived of You, Life of my life, as mighty everywhere and throughout infinite space, piercing through the whole mass of the world, and spread measureless and limitless every way beyond the world, so that the earth should have You and the sky should have You and all things should have You, and that they should be bounded in You but You nowhere bounded. For as the body of the air, which is above the earth, does not hinder the sun's light from passing through it, and that light penetrates it, yet does not break it or cut it but fills it wholly: so I thought that the body not only of the sky and air and sea but of the earth also was penetrable by You and easily to be pierced in all its parts, great and small, for the receiving of Your presence, while Your secret inspiration governed inwardly and outwardly all the things You had created.

This I held because I could think of nothing else. But it was false. For if it were so, a greater part of the earth would have contained a greater part of You, and a lesser a lesser; and all things should be filled with You in such a way that the body of an elephant should contain more of You than the body of a sparrow simply because it is larger and takes up so much more room; and so You would make Your parts present in the parts of the world piece by piece, little pieces in the little pieces, great masses in the great masses.

That of course is not the truth of it. But You had not as yet
enlightened my darkness.

## II

But against the Manichees who deceived others because
they were deceived themselves, and whose speech was dumb-
ness because Your word did not sound from them, that argument was sufficient which long before, as far back as our
Carthage days, had been proposed by Nebridius. I remember
that when we heard it we were all powerfully struck by it.
What would that imaginary brood of Darkness, which the
Manichees were wont to set up as an opposing substance,
have done against You if You had refused to fight with it.
For if the answer was that it would have done You some
damage, that would have been to make You violable and subject to corruption. But if the answer was that it could in no
way have harmed You, then they would show no reason for
Your fighting with it. But it was precisely the result of
Your fighting that some part or member of You, some
offspring of Your substance, was mingled with those contrary
powers, those natures not created by You; and was so far
corrupted by them and changed for the worse as to be turned
from beatitude into misery and to need assistance to deliver it and make it clean. This was the human soul.
It was enslaved, contaminated and corrupted; and to its aid
came Your Word in its freedom and purity and integrity. But
that Word was itself corruptible, because it was from one
and the same substance [as the soul]. Thus if they affirmed
You, whatever You are—that is Your substance by which
You are—to be incorruptible, all these ideas of theirs must
be false and execrable; but if they affirm You corruptible,
that would on the face of it be false and to be abominated.
Therefore this argument of Nebridius was sufficient against
these men, and I should utterly have vomited them up
from my overcharged breast, because they had no way of
escape, without horrible sacrilege of heart and tongue, from
what they held and said of You.

But though I said and firmly held that the Lord God was incorruptible and unalterable and in no way changeable, the true God who made not only our souls but our bodies also, and not only our souls and bodies but all things whatsoever, as yet I did not see, clear and unravelled, what was the cause of Evil. Whatever that cause might be, I saw that no explanation would do which would force me to believe the immutable God mutable; for if I did that I should have been the very thing I was trying to find [namely a cause of evil]. From now it was with no anxiety that I sought it, for I was sure that what the Manichees said was not true. With all my heart I rejected them, because I saw that while they inquired as to the source of evil, they were full of evil themselves, in that they preferred rather to hold that Your substance suffered evil than that their own substance committed it.

So I set myself to examine an idea I had heard—namely that our free-will is the cause of our doing evil, and Your just judgment the cause of our suffering evil. I could not clearly discern this. I endeavoured to draw the eye of my mind from the pit, but I was again plunged into it; and as often as I tried, so often was I plunged back. But it raised me a little towards Your light that I now was as much aware that I had a will as that I had a life. And when I willed to do or not do anything, I was quite certain that it was myself and no other who willed, and I came to see that the cause of my sin lay there.

But what I did unwillingly, it still seemed to me that I rather suffered than did, and I judged it to be not my fault but my punishment: though as I held You most just, I was quite ready to admit that I was being justly punished.

But I asked further: "Who made me? Was it not my God, who is not only Good but Goodness itself? What root reason is there for my willing evil and failing to will good, which would make it just for me to be punished? Who was it that set and ingrafted in me this root of bitterness, since I was wholly made by my most loving God? If the devil is the author, where does the devil come from? And if by his own perverse will he was turned from a good angel into a devil, what was the origin in him of the perverse will by which he became a devil, since by the all-good Creator he was made wholly angel?" By such thoughts I was cast down again and almost stifled; yet I was not brought down so far as the hell of that error, where no man confesses unto You, the error which holds rather that You suffer evil than that man does it.

## IV

I now tried to discover other truths, as I had already come to realise that incorruptible is better than corruptible, so that You must be incorruptible, whatever might be Your nature. For no soul ever has been able to conceive or ever will be able to conceive anything better than You, the supreme and perfect Good. Therefore since the incorruptible is unquestionably to be held greater than the corruptible—and I so held it—I could now draw the conclusion that unless You were incorruptible there was something better than my God. But seeing the superiority of the incorruptible, I should have looked for You in that truth and have learned from it where evil is—that is learned the origin of the corruption by which Your substance cannot be violated. For there is no way in which corruption can affect our God, whether by His will or by necessity or by accident: for He is God, and what He wills is good, and Himself is Goodness; whereas to be corrupted is not good. Nor are You against Your will constrained to anything, for Your will is not greater than Your power. It would be greater, only if You were greater than Yourself: for God's will and God's power are alike God Himself. And what unlooked-for accident can befall You, since You know all things? No nature exists save because You know it. Why indeed should I multiply reasons to show that the substance which is God is not corruptible, since if it were, it would not be God?

v

I sought for the origin of evil, but I sought in an evil manner, and failed to see the evil that there was in my manner of enquiry. I ranged before the eyes of my mind the whole creation, both what we are able to see—earth and sea and air and stars and trees and mortal creatures; and what we cannot see—like the firmament of the Heaven above, and all its angels and spiritual powers: though even these I imagined as if they were bodies disposed each in its own place. And I made one great mass of God's Creation, distinguished according to the kinds of bodies in it, whether they really were bodies, or only such bodies as I imagined spirits to be. I made it huge, not as huge as it is, which I had no means of knowing, but as huge as might be necessary, though in every direction finite. And I saw You, Lord, in every part containing and penetrating it, Yourself altogether infinite: as if Your Being were a sea, infinite and immeasurable everywhere, though still only a sea: and within it there were some mighty but not infinite sponge, and that sponge filled in every part with the immeasurable sea. Thus I conceived Your Creation as finite, and filled utterly by Yourself, and You were Infinite. And I said: "Here is God, and here is what God has created; and God is good, mightily and incomparably better than all these; but of His goodness He created them good: and see how He contains and fills them.

"Where then is evil, and what is its source, and how has it crept into the Creation? What is its root, what is its seed? Can it be that it is wholly without being? But why should we fear and be on guard against what is not? Or if our fear of it is groundless, then our very fear is itself an evil thing. For by it the heart is driven and tormented for no cause; and that evil is all the worse, if there is nothing to fear yet we do fear. Thus either there is evil which we fear, or the fact that we fear is evil.

"Whence then is evil, since God who is good made all things good? It was the greater and supreme Good who made these lesser goods, but Creator and Creation are alike good. Whence then comes evil? Was there perhaps some evil matter of which He made this creation, matter which He formed and ordered, while yet leaving in it some element which He did not convert into good? But why? Could He who was omnipotent be unable to change matter wholly so that no evil might remain in it? Indeed why did He choose to make anything of it and not rather by the same omnipotence cause it wholly not to be? Could it possibly have existed against His will? And if it had so existed from eternity, why did He allow it so long to continue through the infinite spaces of time past, and then after so long a while choose to make something of it? If He did suddenly decide to act, surely the Omnipotent should rather have caused it to cease to be, that He Himself, the true and supreme and infinite Good, alone should be. Or, since it was not good that He who was good should frame and create something not good, could He not have taken away and reduced to nothing that matter which was evil, and provided good matter of which to create all things? For He would not be omnipotent if He could not create something good without the aid of matter which He had not created."

Such thoughts I revolved in my unhappy heart, which was further burdened and gnawed at by the fear that I should die without having found the truth. But at least the faith of Your Christ, Our Lord and Saviour, taught by the Catholic Church, stood firm in my heart, though on many points I was still uncertain and swerving from the norm of doctrine. Yet my mind did not forsake it, but drank of it more deeply with every day that passed.

VI

By now I had rejected the ridiculous prophesyings and blasphemous follies of the astrologers. Let Your own mercies, O my God, confess to You from the very depths of my soul. For who else recalls us from the death that all error is, except the Life which cannot die, and the Wisdom which illumines the minds that need it and needs no illumination from any other, by which the world is governed even to the wind-blown leaves of the trees? It was You then who provided the cure for the obstinacy with which I argued with Vindicianus, an old man of great mental acuteness, and with Nebridius a young man of very fine soul. Vindicianus maintained with great vehemence, Nebridius not quite so vehemently but repeatedly, that there was no art for foreseeing the future, but that human guesses sometimes chanced to fall out right: those who said a great deal would often say things that did in fact come to pass, although those who said them did not really know, but merely happened to say them in the course of saying so many things. Then by Your provision came a man to help me in this matter, one who was a fairly frequent consulter of the astrologers. He was not himself skilled in the art, but as I have said he followed it up with some curiosity. One thing he did know, which he said that he had heard from his father: but he did not realize how utterly destructive it was to any belief in their art. This man, Firminus by name, an educated man and trained in Rhetoric, consulted me as one very dear to him concerning certain affairs of his own in which he placed very considerable worldly hopes, wishing to know how I thought his constellations, as the astrologers call them, stood in the matter. I had now begun to turn towards Nebridius' opinion, yet for all my own uncertainty I did not absolutely refuse to read the stars and tell him what I saw; but I added that I was practically persuaded that the whole business was an empty folly. Thereupon he told me that his father had been deeply interested in the books of the astrologers and had had a friend as keen as himself in studying them. They studied and conferred together upon these follies each with the same burning zeal: they observed the moments at which the dumb animals about their houses brought forth their young, and noted the position of the sky at those moments, by way of getting experience in the art. And he said that he had heard from his father that when his mother was pregnant with him [Firminus], a female slave belonging to his father's friend happened to be pregnant at the same time. This her master could not be unaware of since he took such minute care to know about the whelping of his very dogs. The friends had numbered the days and hours and even the smallest parts of the hours, the one for his wife and the other for his servant, with the most careful observation. And it chanced that both women brought forth their child at the same instant. Thus they were compelled to cast the very same horoscope even to the exact minute for both children, the one for his son, the other for his slave. For when the women began to be in labor, each man let the other know what was happening in his own house, and they had messengers ready to send to each other as soon as either should know that the child had been born —and each of course would know instantly, since it was happening in his own household; and the messengers sent by each, so my friend said, met at a point equidistant from both houses, so that neither could observe any position of the stars or any moment of time different from the other. Yet Firminus, born to wealth in his parents' house, trod the pleasanter ways of life, grew in riches and was raised to positions of honour; whereas the slave did not find the yoke of his condition relaxed, but served his masters. So Firminus who knew him told me.

I heard all this, and I believed it, because of the man who told it. All my doubt was resolved and fell away. First I tried to win Firminus from his interest, by telling him that if I had had to consult his stars and truly foretell his future, I should surely have had to see in his horoscope that his parents had been people of standing in their neighborhood, that his family was noble in his own city, that he was born free, that he was to have a sound education in the liberal arts. Whereas if the slave had consulted me upon the same constellations, for they were the very same, and asked me to foretell him the truth, then I ought to have seen in them that his family was low-born, his condition servile, and

all sorts of other particulars very different and very far removed from the first child's. Thus looking at the same constellations I must utter different things if I were to tell the
truth, and if I said the same things I should be foretelling
falsely. Thus I saw it as obvious that such things as happened to be said truly from the casting of horoscopes were
true not by skill but by chance; and such things as were
false were not due to want of skill in the art but merely that
luck had fallen the other way.

Having started upon this line of reasoning I began to consider what I should answer if any one of those fools who got
their living by astrology and whom I was already longing to
assail and overwhelm with ridicule, should simply reply
that either Firminus had told me, or his father had told him,
falsely: so I set myself to considering the case of those who
are born twins, who usually emerge from the womb so close
to each other that the small interval of time involved—
however much influence they claim that it has in nature—
cannot be estimated by any human observation so as to be
set down in the tables which the astrologer has to inspect
in order to pronounce the truth. It will not be the truth.
For instance anyone inspecting those tables would have had
to foretell the same future for Esau and Jacob, but the
same things did not happen to them. Therefore he would
either have had to foretell falsely, or else if he foretold
truly then he would have had to see different things in the
same horoscope. So again we see that any truth he spoke
would have been by chance not skill. For You, O Lord, the
most just ruler of the universe can so act by Your secret
influence upon both those who consult and those who are
consulted—neither of them knowing what they do—that
when a man consults he hears what it behooves him to hear,
given the hidden merits of souls, from the abyss of Your
just judgment. Let no man say to You: What is this or why
is this? He must not say it, he must not say it. For he is a
man.

## VII

Thus, O God my aid, from those chains You had freed me. But I was still seeking what might be the source of evil and I could see no answer. Yet with all the ebb and flow of my thought You did not let me be carried away from the faith by which I believed that You were, and that Your substance was unchangeable, and that You cared for men and would judge them; and that in Christ Your Son Our Lord, and in the Holy Scriptures which the authority of Your Catholic Church acknowledges, You had established the way of man's salvation unto that life which is to be after death. But with these truths held safe and inviolably rooted in my mind, I was still on fire with the question whence comes evil. What were the agonies, what the anguish of my heart in labour, O my God!

But though I knew it not, You were listening. And when in silence I sought so vehemently, the voiceless contritions of my soul were strong cries to Your mercy. You knew what I was suffering and no man knew it. For how little it was that my tongue uttered of it in the ears even of my closest friends! Could they hear the tumult of my soul, for whose utterance no time or voice of mine would have been sufficient? Yet into Your hearing came all that I cried forth in the anguish of my heart, and my desire was in Your sight, and the light of my eyes shone not for me. For that light was within, I looking outward. Nor was that light in space: but I was intent upon things that are contained in space, and in them I found no place to rest. The things of space neither so received me that I could say "It is enough, it is well," nor yet allowed me to return where I might find sufficiency and well-being. They were not good enough for me, I was not good enough for You: You are my true joy, and I am subject to You, and You have made subject to me the things below me that You have created. This was the right order and the middle way of salvation for me, that I should remain in Your image, and so in You should dominate my body. But when I rose against You in my pride and *ran upon my Lord with the thick neck of my shield*, those lower things became greater than I and pressed me under so that I could neither loosen their grip nor so much as breathe. Wherever I looked they bore in upon me, massed thick; and when I tried to think, the images of corporeal things barred me from turning back towards the truth, as though they said: "Where are you going, base and unclean?" All these things had grown out of my wound, for You humble the proud like one wounded; and I was separated from You by my own swollenness, as though my cheeks had swelled out and closed up my eyes.

## VIII

But You, O Lord, abide forever, nor are You angry with us forever, for You have pity upon our dust and ashes. It was pleasing in Your sight to reshape what was deformed in me. And You kept stirring me with Your secret goad so that I should remain unquiet until You should become clear to the gaze of my soul. And from the secret hand of Your healing my swollenness abated, and the troubled and darkened sight of my mind was daily made better by the stinging ointment of sorrow.

## IX

And first You willed to show me how You resist the proud and give grace to the humble, and with how great mercy You have shown men the way of humility in that the Word was made flesh and dwelt among men. Therefore You brought in my way by means of a certain man—an incredibly conceited man—some books of the Platonists translated from Greek into Latin. In them I found, though not in the very words, yet the thing itself and proved by all sorts of reasons: that *in the beginning was the Word and the Word was with God and the Word was God: the same was in the beginning with God; all things were made by Him and without him was made nothing that was made; in Him was*

*life and the life was the light of men, and the light shines
in darkness and the darkness did not comprehend* it. And
I found in those same writings that the soul of man, though
*it gives testimony of the light, yet is not itself the light;* but
the Word, God Himself, is *the true light which enlightens
every man that comes into this world; and that He was in
the world and the world was made by Him, and the world
knew Him not.* But I did not read in those books that *He
came unto His own, and His own received Him not, but to as
many as received Him He gave power to be made the sons
of God, to them that believed in His name.*

Again I found in them that the Word, God, was *born
not of flesh nor of blood, nor of the will of man nor of the
will of the flesh, but of God;* but I did not find that *the
Word became flesh.*

I found it stated, differently and in a variety of ways, that
the Son *being in the form of the Father thought it not
robbery to be equal with God,* because by nature He was
God. But these books did not tell me that *He emptied Himself, taking the form of a servant, being made in the likeness
of men, and in habit found as a man;* or that *He humbled
Himself becoming obedient unto death, even to the death of
the cross; for which cause God also hath exalted Him from
the dead and given Him a name which is above all names,
that in the name of Jesus every knee should bow of those
that are in heaven, on earth, and under the earth; and that
every tonguge should confess that the Lord Jesus is in the
glory of God the Father.*

Further I read there that Your only-begotten Son was before all times and beyond all times and abides unchangeably,
co-eternal with You, and that *of His fullness souls receive,*
that they may be blessed, and that by participation in that
wisdom which abides in them they are renewed that they
may be wise. But I did not read that *in due time He died
for the ungodly,* and that *Thou didst not spare Thy only-
begotten Son but delivered Him up for us all.* For *Thou
hast hid these things from the wise and hast revealed them*

*to little ones,* that *those who labor and are burdened should come to Him and He should refresh them, because He is meek and humble of heart;* and *the meek He directs in judgement, and the gentle He teaches His ways, beholding our lowness and our trouble and forgiving all our sins.* But those who wear the high boots of their sublimer doctrine do not hear Him saying: *Learn of me for I am meek and humble of heart and you shall find rest for your souls;* and *if they know God, they have not glorified him as God or given thanks: but become vain in their thoughts; and their foolish heart is darkened. Professing themselves to be wise they become fools.*

Again I read in these books that they had *changed the glory of Thy incorruption* into idols and divers images, *into the likeness of the image of a corruptible man and of birds, and of four-footed beasts, and of creeping things*—in fact into that Egyptian food for which Esau had lost his birthright, since the people which was Your firstborn worshipped the head of a four-footed beast instead of You, turning in their heart back towards Egypt and bowing down their soul, Your image, before the image of a calf that eats hay. I found these things there and I did not feed upon them. For it pleased You, O Lord, to take away the reproach of inferiority from Jacob, so that the elder brother served the younger: and You have called the Gentiles into Your inheritance. From the Gentiles indeed I had come to You; and I fixed my mind upon the gold which You willed that Your people should bring with them from Egypt: for it was Yours, wherever it was. And You had said to the Athenians by Your apostle that in You we live and move and are; as certain of their own writers had said; and obviously it was from Athens that these books came. But I did not fix my mind upon the idols of the Egyptians which they served with the gold that was Yours, *changing the truth of God into a lie and worshipping and serving a creature rather than the Creator.*

## x

Being admonished by all this to return to myself, I entered into my own depths, with You as guide; and I was able to do it because You were my helper. I entered, and with the eye of my soul, such as it was, I saw Your unchangeable Light shining over that same eye of my soul, over my mind. It was not the light of everyday that the eye of flesh can see, nor some greater light of the same order, such as might be if the brightness of our daily light should be seen shining with a more intense brightness and filling all things with its greatness. Your Light was not that, but other, altogether other, than all such lights. Nor was it above my mind as oil above the water it floats on, nor as the sky is above the earth; it was above because it made me, and I was below because made by it. He who knows the truth knows that Light, and he that knows the Light knows eternity. Charity knows it. O eternal truth and true love and beloved eternity! Thou art my God, I sigh to Thee by day and by night. When first I knew Thee, Thou didst lift me up so that I might see that there was something to see, but that I was not yet the man to see it. And Thou didst beat back the weakness of my gaze, blazing upon me too strongly, and I was shaken with love and with dread. And I knew that I was far from Thee in the region of unlikeness, as if I heard Thy voice from on high: "I am the food of grown men: grow and you shall eat Me. And you shall not change Me into yourself as bodily food, but into Me you shall be changed." And I learned that *Thou hast corrected man for iniquity and Thou didst make my soul shrivel up like a moth.* And I said "Is truth then nothing at all, since it is not extended either through finite spaces or infinite?" And Thou didst cry to me from afar: "I am who am." And I heard Thee, as one hears in the heart; and there was from that moment no ground of doubt in me: I would more easily have doubted my own life than have doubted that truth is: which is *clearly seen, being understood by the things that are made.*

## XI

Then I thought upon those other things that are less than You, and I saw that they neither absolutely are nor yet totally are not: they are, in as much as they are from You: they are not, in as much as they are not what You are. For that truly is, which abides unchangeably. But *it is good for me to adhere to my God,* for if I abide not in Him, I cannot abide in myself. But He, abiding in Himself, renews all things; and *Thou art my God for Thou hast no need of my goods.*

## XII

And it became clear to me that corruptible things are good: if they were supremely good they could not be corrupted, but also if they were not good at all they could not be corrupted: if they were supremely good they would be incorruptible, if they were in no way good there would be nothing in them that might corrupt. For corruption damages; and unless it diminished goodness, it would not damage. Thus either corruption does no damage, which is impossible or—and this is the certain proof of it—all things that are corrupted are deprived of some goodness. But if they were deprived of all goodness, they would be totally without being. For if they might still be and yet could no longer be corrupted, they would be better than in their first state, because they would abide henceforth incorruptibly. What could be more monstrous than to say that things could be made better by losing all their goodness? If they were deprived of all goodness, they would be altogether nothing: therefore as long as they are, they are good. Thus whatsoever things are, are good; and that evil whose origin I sought is not a substance, because if it were a substance it would be good. For either it would be an incorruptible substance, that is to say, the highest goodness; or it would be a corruptible substance, which would not be corruptible unless it were good. Thus I saw and clearly realized that You have made all things good, and that there are no substances not made by You. And because all the things You have made are not equal, they have a goodness [over and above] as a totality: because they are good individually, and they are very good altogether, for our God has made all things very good.

XIII

To You, then, evil utterly is not—and not only to You, but to Your whole creation likewise, evil is not: because there is nothing over and above Your creation that could break in or derange the order that You imposed upon it. But in certain of its parts there are some things which we call evil because they do not harmonize with other things; yet these same things do harmonize with still others and thus are good; and in themselves they are good. All these things which do not harmonize with one another, do suit well with that lower part of creation which we call the earth, which has its cloudy and windy sky in some way apt to it. God forbid that I should say: "I wish that these things were not"; because even if I saw only them, though I should want better things, yet even for them alone I should praise You: for that You are to be praised, things of earth show —*dragons, and all deeps, fire, hail, snow, ice, and stormy winds, which fulfill Thy word; mountains and all hills, fruitful trees and all cedars; beasts and all cattle, serpents and feathered fowl; kings of the earth and all people, princes and all judges of the earth; young men and maidens, old men and young, praise Thy name.* And since from the heavens, O our God, *all Thy angels praise Thee in the high places, and all Thy hosts, sun and moon, all the stars and lights, the heavens of heavens, and the waters that are above the heavens, praise thy name*—I no longer desired better, because I had thought upon them all and with clearer judgement I realized that while certain higher things are better than lower things, yet all things together are better than the higher alone.

## XIV

There is no sanity in those whom anything in creation displeases, any more than there was in me when I was dis-pleased with many things that You had made. Because my soul did not dare to be displeased with my God, it would not allow that what displeased it was Yours. Thus it strayed off into the error of holding two substances, and it found no rest but talked wildly. Turning from that error it had made for itself a god occupying the infinite measures of all space, and had thought this god to be You, and had placed it in its heart, and thus had once again become the temple of its own idol, a temple abominable to You. But You caressed my head, though I knew it not, and closed my eyes that they should not see vanity; and I ceased from myself a little and found sleep from my madness. And from that sleep I awakened in You, and I saw You infinite in a different way; but that sight was not with the eyes of flesh.

## XV

And I looked upon other things, and I saw that they owed their being to You, and that all finite things are in You: but in a different manner, being in You not as in a place, but because You are and hold all things in the hand of Your truth, and all things are true inasmuch as they are: nor is falsehood anything, save that something is thought to be which is not. And I observed that all things harmonized not only with their places but also with their times; and that You, who alone are eternal, did not begin to work after innumer-able spaces of time had gone by: since all the spaces of time, spaces past, spaces to come, could neither go nor come if You did not operate and abide.

## XVI

My own experience had shown me that there was nothing extraordinary in the same bread being loathsome to a sick palate and agreeable to a healthy, and in light being painful to sore eyes which is a joy to clear. Your justice displeases the wicked: but so do the viper and the smaller worms: yet these You have created good, and suited to the lower parts of Your creation—to which lower parts indeed the wicked themselves are well suited, insofar as they are unlike You, though they become suited to the higher parts as they grow more like You. So that when I now asked what is iniquity, I realized that it was not a substance but a swerving of the will which is turned towards lower things and away from You, O God, who are the supreme substance: so that it casts away what is most inward to it and swells greedily for outward things.

## XVII

And I marvelled to find that at last I loved You and not some phantom instead of You; yet I did not stably enjoy my God, but was ravished to You by Your beauty, yet soon was torn away from You again by my own weight, and fell again with torment to lower things. Carnal habit was that weight. Yet the memory of You remained with me and I knew without doubt that it was You to whom I should cleave, though I was not yet such as could cleave to You: *for the corruptible body is a load upon the soul, and the earthly habitation presses down the mind that muses upon many things.* I was altogether certain that Your *invisible things are clearly seen from the creation of the world, being understood by the things that are made:* so too are Your everlasting power and Your Godhead. I was now studying the ground of my admiration for the beauty of bodies, whether celestial or of earth, and on what authority I might rightly judge of things mutable and say: "This ought to be so, that not so." Enquiring then what was the source of my judgement, when I did so judge I had discovered the immutable and true eternity of truth above my changing mind. Thus by stages I passed from bodies to the soul which uses the body for its perceiving, and from this to the soul's inner power, to which the body's senses present external things, as indeed the beasts are able; and from there I passed on to the reasoning power, to which is referred for judgement what is received from the body's senses. This too realised that it was mutable in me, and rose to its own understanding. It withdrew my thought from its habitual way, abstracting from the confused crowds of fantasms that it might find what light suffused it, when with utter certainty it cried aloud that the immutable was to be preferred to the mutable, and how it had come to know the immutable itself: for if it had not come to some knowledge of the immutable, it could not have known it as certainly preferable to the mutable. Thus in the thrust of a trembling glance my mind arrived at That Which Is. Then indeed I saw clearly Your *invisible things which are understood by the things that are made;* but I lacked the strength to hold my gaze fixed, and my weakness was beaten back again so that I returned to my old habits, bearing nothing with me but a memory of delight and a desire as for something of which I had caught the fragrance but which I had not yet the strength to eat.

## XVIII

So I set about finding a way to gain the strength that was necessary for enjoying You. And I could not find it until I embraced the *Mediator between God and man, the man Christ Jesus, who is over all things, God blessed forever,* who was calling unto me and saying: *I am the Way, the Truth, and the Life;* and who brought into union with our nature that Food which I lacked the strength to take: for *the Word was made flesh* that Your Wisdom, by which You created all things, might give suck to our souls' infancy. For I was not yet lowly enough to hold the lowly Jesus as my God, nor did I know what lesson His embracing of our weakness was to teach. For Your Word, the eternal Truth, towering above the highest parts of Your creation, lifts up to Himself those that were cast down. He built for Himself here below a lowly house of our clay, that by it He might bring down from themselves and bring up to Himself those who were to be made subject, healing the swollenness of their pride and

fostering their love: so that their self-confidence might grow
no further but rather diminish, seeing the deity at their
feet, humbled by the assumption of our coat of human
nature: to the end that weary at last they might cast themselves down upon His humanity and rise again in its rising.

## XIX

But I realised none of this at that time. I thought of Christ
my Lord as of a man of marvellous wisdom, whom no other
could possibly equal; and I saw His miraculous birth from
a virgin—with the example it gave that temporal things are
to be despised for the sake of immortality—as a mark of divine care for us, which surely merited for Him complete
authority as our master. But the mystery contained in the
truth that the Word was made flesh, I could not even faintly
glimpse. From what had come down in writing about
him—that he ate and drank, slept, walked, was glad, was
sad, preached—I had gathered that his body did not cleave
to Your Word save through a human mind and soul. This
anyone knows who grasps the immutability of Your Word,
as I now grasped it in my own fashion and indeed held it
unwaveringly. For at one moment to be moving the limbs by
the will, at another keeping them still; now feeling some
particular emotion, now not feeling it; now uttering wisdom
in human speech, now silent—all these are properties of
a mutable soul and a mutable mind. If Scripture told falsely
of Christ on this matter, all of it would be involved in
the peril of falsehood, and there would be no sure faith for
mankind left in it. Taking then what was written there as
truth, I saw Christ as complete man: not the body of a man
only, or an animating soul without a rational mind, but altogether man; and I thought he was to be preferred to all
others not as the very Person of Truth but because of the
great excellence of his human nature and his more perfect
participation in wisdom.

Alypius, on the other hand, imagined that Catholics believed that in Christ God was clothed in flesh—meaning that
there was the godhead and a body in Him, but no soul.

He thought they held that He had not a human mind. And since it seemed quite clear to him that what had been handed down to us concerning Christ could not have been done save by a creature both vital and rational, he was slower in his movement towards the Christian faith itself. But once he realized that this was the error of the Apollinarian heretics, he liked the Catholic faith better and accepted it. But I admit that it was only some time later that I learned how, in the truth that the Word was made flesh, Catholic doctrine is distinguished from the error of Photinus. In fact the refutation of heretics serves to bring into clearer light what Your church holds and what sound doctrine is. *For there must be also heresies: that they who are approved may be made manifest among the weak.*

## xx

Now that I had read the books of the Platonists and had been set by them towards the search for a truth that is incorporeal, I came to see Your *invisible things which are understood by the things that are made.* I was at a standstill, yet I *felt* what through the darkness of my mind I was not able actually to see; I was certain that You are and that You are infinite, but not as being diffused through space whether finite or infinite: that You truly are and are ever the same, not in any part or by any motion different or otherwise; and I knew that all other things are from You from the simple fact that they are at all. Of these things I was utterly certain, yet I had not the strength to enjoy You. I talked away as if I knew a great deal; but if I had not sought the way to You in Christ our Saviour, I would have come not to instruction but to destruction. For I had begun to wish to appear wise, and this indeed was the fulness of my punishment; and I did not weep for my state, but was badly puffed up with my knowledge. Where was that charity which builds us up upon the foundation of humility, which is Christ Jesus? Or when would those books have taught me that? Yet I think it was Your will that I should come upon these books before I had made study of the Scriptures, that it might be impressed on my memory how they had affected me: so that, when later I should have become responsive to You through Your Books with my wounds healed by the care of Your fingers, I might be able to discern the difference that there is between presumption and confession, between those who see what the goal is but do not see the way, and [those who see] the Way which leads to that country of blessedness, which we are meant not only to know but to dwell in. If I had been first formed by Your Holy Scriptures so that You had grown sweet to me through their familiar use, and had come later upon these books of the Platonists, they might have swept me away from the solid ground of piety; and even if I had remained firm in that disposition which for my health Scripture had taught me, I might perhaps have thought that the same disposition could have been acquired from those books if a man studied them alone.

### XXI

So now I seized greedily upon the adorable writing of Your Spirit, and especially upon the apostle Paul. And I found that those difficulties, in which it had once seemed to me that he contradicted himself and that the text of his discourse did not agree with the testimonies of the law and the prophets, vanished away. In that pure eloquence I saw One Face, and I learned to rejoice with trembling. I found that whatever truth I had read in the Platonists was said here with praise of Your grace: that he who sees should *not so glory as if he had not received*—and received, indeed, not only what he sees but even the power to see, *for what has he that he has not received?* And further, that he [who sees] is not only taught to *see* You who are always the same, but is also strengthened to take hold of You; and that he who cannot see You from afar off, may yet walk on that way by which he may come and see and take hold. For though a man be *delighted with the law of God according to the inward man*, what shall he do about that *other law in his members, fighting against the law of his mind and capti-*

*vating him in the law of sin that is in his members?* For *Thou art just, O Lord,* but *we have sinned, we have committed iniquity, we have done wickedly* and Thy hand has grown heavy upon us and we are justly delivered over to that first sinner, the ruler of death, because he has turned our will to the likeness of his will, whereby he stood not in Thy truth. But what shall unhappy man do? *Who shall deliver him from the body of this death,* save *the grace of God by Jesus Christ our Lord* whom Thou hast begotten coeternally with Thee and *possessed in the beginning of Thy ways; in whom the prince of this world found nothing worthy of death yet killed Him; and the handwriting was blotted out of the decree which was contrary to us.*

The writings of the Platonists contain nothing of all this. Their pages show nothing of the face of that love, the tears of confession, Your sacrifice, an afflicted spirit, a contrite and humbled heart, the salvation of Your people, the espoused city, the promise of the Holy Spirit, the chalice of our redemption. In them no one sings: *Shall not my soul be submitted unto God? From Him is my salvation: for He is my God, my salvation, and my defense: I shall be no more moved.* And we hear no voice calling: *Come unto me, all you that labour.* They scorned to learn from Him, *because He is meek and humble of heart. For Thou hast hidden these things from the wise and prudent and hast revealed them to the little ones.* It is one thing to see the land of peace from a wooded mountaintop, yet not find the way to it and struggle hopelessly far from the way, with hosts of those fugitive deserters from God, under their leader the Lion and the Dragon, besetting us about and ever lying in wait; and quite another to hold to the way that leads there, a way guarded by the care of our heavenly General, where there are no deserters from the army of heaven to practice their robberies—for indeed they avoid that way as a torment. Marvellously these truths graved themselves in my heart when I read that latest of Your apostles and looked upon Your works and trembled.

# BOOK EIGHT

## AGED THIRTY-ONE

# I

L ET me, O my God, remember with thanks to Thee and confess Thy mercies upon me. Let my bones be pierced through with Thy love, and let them say: *Who is like unto Thee, O Lord? Thou hast broken my bonds, I will sacrifice to Thee the sacrifice of praise.* How Thou hast broken them I shall tell and all who adore Thee will say as they listen: Blessed be the Lord in heaven and on earth, great and wonderful is His name.

Your words had rooted deep in my heart and I was fenced about on all sides by You. Of Your eternal life I was now certain, though I saw it *in a dark manner and as through a glass.* All my former doubt about an incorruptible substance from which every substance has its being was taken from me. My desire now was not to be more sure of You but more steadfast in You.

But in my temporal life all was uncertain; my heart had to be purged of the old leaven. The way, our Saviour himself, delighted me; but I still shrank from actually walking a way so strait. Then by You it came into my mind, and the idea appealed strongly to me, to go to Simplicianus whom I knew to be Your good servant, for Your grace shone in him. I had heard that from his youth he had lived in great love of You. He was now grown old; and it seemed to me that from a long lifetime spent in so firm a following of Your way he must have experienced much and learned much. And truly so it was. I hoped that if I conferred with him about my problems he might from that experience and learning show me the best way for one affected as I was to walk in Your path.

For I saw the Church full; and one went this way, and one that. But I was unhappy at the life I led in the world, and it was indeed a heavy burden, for the hope of honour and

profit no longer inflamed my desire, as formerly, to help me
bear so exacting a servitude. These things delighted me no
longer in comparison with Your sweetness and the beauty of
Your house which I loved. But what still held me tight bound
was my need of woman: nor indeed did the apostle forbid
me to marry, though he exhorted to a better state, wishing
all men to be as he was himself. But I in my weakness was for
choosing the softer place, and this one thing kept me from
taking a sure line upon others. I was weary and wasted with
the cares that were eating into me, all because there were
many things which I was unwilling to suffer but had to put up
with for the sake of living with a wife, a way of life to which I
was utterly bound. I had heard from the mouth of Truth
itself that *there are eunuchs who have made themselves
eunuchs for the kingdom of heaven;* but Christ had said,
*He that can take it, let him take it.* Certainly *all men are
vain in whom there is not the knowledge of God and who
cannot, by these good things that are seen, find Him that is.*
Now I was no longer in that sort of vanity; I had gone beyond
it and in the testimony of the whole creation I had found
You, our Creator, and Your Word who is with You and one
God with You, by whom You created all things. But there is
another sort of godlessness, that of the men who *knowing
God have not glorified Him as God or given thanks.* Into
this also I had fallen, but Your right hand upheld me and
taking me out of it, placed me where I might find health. For
You have said to man: *Behold, the fear of the Lord is wisdom;* and again: *Be not desirous to seem wise, for those
who affirm themselves to be wise become fools.* I had
now found the pearl of great price, and I ought to have sold
all I had and bought it. But I hesitated still.

II

So I went to Simplicianus, who had begotten Ambrose,
now bishop, into Your grace, and whom indeed Ambrose
loved as a father. I told him all the wanderings of my error.
But when I told him that I had read certain books of the

Platonists which had been translated into Latin by Victorinus, one time professor of Rhetoric in Rome—who had, so
I heard, died a Christian—he congratulated me for not having fallen upon the writings of other philosophers which are
full of vain deceits, according to the elements of this world,
whereas in the Platonists God and his Word are everywhere
implied. Then to draw me on to the humility of Christ,
hidden from the wise and revealed to little ones, he began
to speak of Victorinus himself whom he had known inti-
mately when he was in Rome. Of Victorinus he told me
what I shall now set down, for the story glorifies Your grace
and it should be told to Your glory. For here was an old man
deeply learned, trained in all the liberal sciences, a man who
had read and weighed so many of the philosophers' writings,
the teacher of so many distinguished senators, a man who on
account of the brilliance of His teaching had earned and
been granted a statue in the Roman forum—an honour the
citizens of this world think so great. He had grown old in
the worship of idols, had taken part in their sacrilegious
rites, for almost all the Roman nobility at that time was
enthusiastic for them and was ever talking of "prodigies and
the monster gods of every kind, and of the jackal-headed
Anubis—who all had once fought against the Roman deities
Neptune and Venus and Minerva" and had been beaten:
yet Rome was on its knees before these gods it had conquered.
All this Victorinus with his thunder of eloquence had
gone on championing for so many years even into old age:
yet he thought it no shame to be the child of Your Christ, an
infant at Your font, bending his neck under the yoke of
humility and his forehead to the ignominy of the Cross.

O Lord, Lord, who dost *bow down Thy heavens and
descend, dost touch the mountains and they smoke,* by what
means didst Thou find thy way into that breast? He read, so
Simplicianus said, Holy Scripture; he investigated all the
Christian writings most carefully and minutely. And he
said not publicly but to Simplicianus privately and as one
friend to another: "I would have you know that I am now

a Christian." Simplicianus answered: "I shall not believe it nor count you among Christians unless I see you in the Church of Christ." Victorinus asked with some faint mockery: "Then is it the walls that make Christians?" He went on saying that he was a Christian, and Simplicianus went on with the same denial, and Victorinus always repeated his retort about the walls. The fact was that he feared to offend his friends, important people and worshippers of these demons; he feared that their enmity might fall heavily upon him from the height of their Babylon-dignity as from the cedars of Lebanon which the Lord had not yet brought down. But when by reading in all earnestness he had drawn strength, he grew afraid that Christ might deny him before His angels if he were ashamed to confess Christ before men. He felt that he was guilty of a great crime in being ashamed of the sacraments of the lowliness of Your Word, when he had not been ashamed of the sacrilegious rites of those demons of pride whom in his pride he had worshipped. So he grew proud towards vanity and humble towards truth. Quite suddenly and without warning he said to Simplicianus, as Simplicianus told me: "Let us go to the Church. I wish to be made a Christian." Simplicianus, unable to control his joy, went with him. He was instructed in the first mysteries of the faith, and not long after gave in his name that he might be regenerated by baptism, to the astonishment of Rome and the joy of the Church. The proud saw it and were enraged, ground their teeth and were livid with envy: but the Lord God was the hope of his servant, so that he had no regard for vanities and lying follies.

Finally when the hour had come for his profession of faith —which at Rome was usually made by those who were about to enter into Your grace in a set form of words learned and memorized and spoken from a platform in the sight of the faithful—Simplicianus told me that the priests offered Victorinus to let him make the profession in private, as the custom was with such as seemed likely to find the ordeal embarrassing. But he preferred to make profession of salvation

in the sight of the congregation in church. For there had been
no salvation in the Rhetoric he had taught, yet he had
professed it publicly. Obviously therefore he should be in
less fear of Your meek flock when he was uttering Your word,
since he had had no fear of the throng of the deluded when
uttering his own. When therefore he had gone up to make his
profession all those who knew him began whispering his
name to one another with congratulatory murmurs. And
indeed who there did not know him? And from the lips of
the rejoicing congregation sounded the whisper, "Victorinus,
Victorinus." They were quick to utter their exultation at
seeing him and as quickly fell silent to hear him. He uttered the true faith with glorious confidence, and they would
gladly have snatched him to their very heart. Indeed, they
did take him to their heart in their love and their joy: with
those hands they took him.

### III

O loving God, what is it in men that makes them rejoice
more for the salvation of a soul that was despaired of or one
delivered from a major peril, than if there had always been
hope or the peril had been less? Even You, O Merciful
Father, rejoice more *upon one sinner doing penance than
upon ninety and nine just who need not penance.* It is with
special joy that we hear how the lost sheep is brought home
upon the exultant shoulders of the shepherd and how the
coin is put back into Your treasury while the neighbors
rejoice with the woman who found it. And the joy we feel
at mass in Your church brings tears as we hear of that
younger son who was dead and made alive again, who
had been lost and was found. You rejoice in us and in
Your angels who stand fast in holy charity. For You are
ever the same because You ever know, and in the one way
of knowing, all those things which are not always existent
nor always the same.

What is it in the soul, I ask again, that makes it delight
more to have found or regained the things it loves than if

it had always had them? Creatures other than man bear the same witness, and all things are filled with testimonies acclaiming that it is so. The victorious general has his triumph; but he would not have been victorious if he had not fought; and the greater danger there was in the battle, the greater rejoicing in the triumph. The storm tosses the sailors and threatens to wreck the ship; all are pale with the threat of death. But the sky grows clear, the sea calm, and now they are as wild with exultation as before with fear. A friend is sick and his pulse threatens danger; all who want him well feel as if they shared his sickness. He begins to recover, though he cannot yet walk as strongly as of old: and there is more joy than there was before, when he was still well and could walk properly. Note too that men procure the actual pleasures of human life by way of pain—I mean not only the pain that comes upon us unlooked for and beyond our will, but unpleasantness planned and willingly accepted. There is no pleasure in eating or drinking, unless the discomfort of hunger and thirst come before. Drunkards eat salty things to develop a thirst so great as to be painful, and pleasure arises when the liquor quenches the pain of the thirst. And it is the custom that promised brides do not give themselves at once lest the husband should hold the gift cheap unless delay had set him craving.

We see this in base and dishonourable pleasure, but also in the pleasure that is licit and permitted, and again in the purest and most honourable friendship. We have seen it in the case of him who had been dead and was brought back to life, who had been lost and was found. Universally the greater joy is heralded by greater pain. What does this mean, O Lord my God, when Thou art an eternal joy to Thyself, Thou Thyself art joy itself, and things about Thee ever rejoice in Thee? What does it mean that this part of creation thus alternates between need felt and need met, between discord and harmony? Is this their mode of being, this what Thou didst give them, when from the heights of heaven to the lowest earth, from the beginning of time to

the end, from the angel to the worm, from the first movement to the last, Thou didst set all kinds of good things
and all Thy just works each in its place, each in its season?
Alas for me, how high art Thou in the highest, how deep in
the deepest! And Thou dost never depart from us, yet with
difficulty do we return to Thee.

### IV

Come, Lord, work upon us, call us back, set us on fire
and clasp us close, be fragrant to us, draw us to Thy loveliness: let us love, let us run to Thee. Do not many from
a deeper pit of blindness than Victorinus come back to
Thee, enlightened by that light in which they receive from
Thee the power to be made Thy sons? But because they
are not so well-known, there is less rejoicing over them even
by those who do know them. For when many rejoice together, the joy of each one is richer: they warm themselves at each other's flame. Further in so far as they are
known widely, they guide many to salvation and are bound
to be followed by many. So that even those who have
gone before rejoice much on their account, because the rejoicing is not only on their account. It would be shameful
if in Your tabernacle the persons of the rich should be welcome before the poor, or the nobly born before the rest:
since *Thou has rather chosen the weak things of the world
to confound the strong, and hast chosen the base things of
the world and the things that are contemptible, and things
that are not, in order to bring to nought things that are*. It
was by Paul's tongue that You uttered these words. Yet when
Paulus the proconsul came under the light yoke of Christ
and became a simple subject of the great King, his pride
brought low by the apostle's spiritual might, even that least
of Your apostles now desired to be called Paul, in place of
his former name of Saul, for the glory of so great a victory.
Victory over the enemy is greater when we win from him
a man whom he holds more strongly and through whom he
holds more people. He has a firmer hold on the eminent by

reason of their noble rank, and through them he holds very
many people by reason of their authority. Therefore the heart
of Victorinus was all the more welcome because the devil had
held it as an impregnable fortress; and the tongue of Victorinus because it was a strong sharp weapon with which the
devil had slain many. It was right for Your sons to rejoice with
more abounding joy because our King had bound the strong
man, and they saw his vessels taken from him and cleansed
and made available unto Your honour and *profitable to the
Lord unto every good work.*

v

Now when this man of Yours, Simplicianus, had told me
the story of Victorinus, I was on fire to imitate him: which
indeed was why he had told me. He added that in the
time of the emperor Julian, when a law was made prohibit-
ing Christians from teaching Literature and Rhetoric, Victorinus had obeyed the law, preferring to give up his own
school of words rather than Your word, by which You make
eloquent the tongues of babes. In this he seemed to me not
only courageous but actually fortunate, because it gave him
the chance to devote himself wholly to You. I longed for the
same chance, but I was bound not with the iron of another's
chains, but by my own iron will. The enemy held my will;
and of it he made a chain and bound me. Because my will was
perverse it changed to lust, and lust yielded to became habit.
and habit not resisted became necessity. These were like
links hanging one on another—which is why I have called
it a chain—and their hard bondage held me bound hand
and foot. The new will which I now began to have, by
which I willed to worship You freely and to enjoy You, O
God, the only certain Joy, was not yet strong enough to
overcome that earlier will rooted deep through the years.
My two wills, one old, one new, one carnal, one spiritual, were in conflict and in their conflict wasted my soul.

Thus, with myself as object of the experiment, I came to
understand what I had read, how the *flesh lusts against the*

*spirit and the spirit against the flesh*. I indeed was in both camps, but more in that which I approved in myself than in that which I disapproved. For in a sense it was now no longer I that was in this second camp, because in large part I rather suffered it unwillingly than did it with my will. Yet habit had grown stronger against me by my own act, since I had come willingly where I did not now will to be. Who can justly complain when just punishment overtakes the sinner? I no longer had the excuse which I used to think I had for not yet forsaking the world and serving You, the excuse namely that I had no certain knowledge of the truth. By now I was quite certain; but I was still bound to earth and refused to take service in Your army; I feared to be freed of all the things that impeded me, as strongly as I ought to have feared the being impeded by them. I was held down as agreeably by this world's baggage as one often is by sleep; and indeed the thoughts with which I meditated upon You were like the efforts of a man who wants to get up but is so heavy with sleep that he simply sinks back into it again. There is no one who wants to be asleep always—for every sound judgment holds that it is best to be awake—yet a man often postpones the effort of shaking himself awake when he feels a sluggish heaviness in the limbs, and settles pleasurably into another doze though he knows he should not, because it is time to get up. Similarly I regarded it as settled that it would be better to give myself to Your love rather than go on yielding to my own lust; but the first course delighted and convinced my mind, the second delighted my body and held it in bondage. For there was nothing I could reply when You called me: *Rise, thou that sleepest and arise from the dead: and Christ shall enlighten thee;* and whereas You showed me by every evidence that Your words were true, there was simply nothing I could answer save only laggard lazy words: "Soon," "Quite soon," "Give me just a little while." But "soon" and "quite soon" did not mean any particular time; and "just a little while" went on for a long while. It was in vain that *I delighted in Thy law according to the inner man, when that other law in my members rebelled against the law of my mind and led me captive in the law of sin that was in my members.* For the law of sin is the fierce force of habit, by which the mind is drawn and held even against its will, and yet deservedly because it had fallen wilfully into the habit. *Who then should deliver me from the body of this death, but Thy grace only, through Jesus Christ Our Lord?*

## VI

Now, O Lord, my Helper and my Redeemer, I shall tell and confess to Your name how You delivered me from the chain of that desire of the flesh which held me so bound, and the servitude of worldly things. I went my usual way with a mind ever more anxious, and day after day I sighed for You. I would be off to Your church as often as my business, under the weight of which I groaned, left me free. Alypius was with me, at liberty from his legal office after a third term as Assessor and waiting for private clients, to whom he might sell his legal advice—just as I sold skill in speaking, if indeed this can be bought. Nebridius had yielded to our friendship so far as to teach under Verecundus, a great friend of all of us, a citizen and elementary school teacher of Milan, who had earnestly asked and indeed by right of friendship demanded from our company the help he badly needed. Nebridius was not influenced in the matter by any desire for profit, for he could have done better had he chosen, in a more advanced school; but he was a good and gracious friend and too kindly a man to refuse our requests. But he did it all very quietly, for he did not want to draw the attention of those persons whom the world holds great; he thus avoided distraction of mind, for he wanted to have his mind free and at leisure for as many hours as possible to seek or read or hear truths concerning wisdom. On a certain day—Nebridius was away for some reason I cannot recall—there came to Alypius and me at our house

one Ponticianus, a fellow countryman of ours, being from
Africa, holder of an important post in the emperor's court.
There was something or other he wanted of us and we
sat down to discuss the matter. As it happened he noticed
a book on a gaming table by which we were sitting. He
picked it up, opened it, and found that it was the apostle
Paul, which surprised him because he had expected that it
would be one of the books I wore myself out teaching. Then
he smiled a little and looked at me, and expressed pleasure
but surprise too at having come suddenly upon that book,
and only that book, lying before me. For he was a Christian
and a devout Christian; he knelt before You in church, O
our God, in daily prayer and many times daily. I told him
that I had given much care to these writings. Whereupon
he began to tell the story of the Egyptian monk Antony,
whose name was held in high honour among Your servants,
although Alypius and I had never heard it before that time.
When he learned this, he was the more intent upon telling
the story, anxious to introduce so great a man to men ignorant of him, and very much marvelling at our ignorance.
But Alypius and I stood amazed to hear of Your wonderful
works, done in the true faith and in the Catholic Church so
recently, practically in our own times, and with such numbers of witnesses. All three of us were filled with wonder,
we because the deeds we were now hearing were so great,
and he because we had never heard them before.

From this story he went on to the great groups in the
monasteries, and their ways all redolent of You, and the
fertile deserts of the wilderness, of all of which we knew nothing. There was actually a monastery at Milan, outside the
city walls. It was full of worthy brethren and under the
care of Ambrose. And we had not heard of it. He continued
with his discourse and we listened in absolute silence. It
chanced that he told how on one occasion he and three of
his companions—it was at Treves, when the emperor was
at the chariot races in the Circus—had gone one afternoon
to walk in the gardens close by the city walls. As it happened

they fell into two groups, one of the others staying with him, and the other two likewise walking their own way. But as those other two strolled on they came into a certain house, the dwelling of some servants of Yours, poor in spirit, of whom is the kingdom of God. There they found a small book in which was written the life of Antony. One of them began to read it, marvelled at it, was inflamed by it. While he was actually reading he had begun to think how he might embrace such a life, and give up his worldly employment to serve You alone. For the two men were both state officials. Suddenly the man who was doing the reading was filled with a love of holiness and angry at himself with righteous shame. He looked at his friend and said to him: "Tell me, please, what is the goal of our ambition in all these labours of ours? What are we aiming at? What is our motive in being in the public service? Have we any higher hope at court than to be friends of the emperor? And at that level, is not everything uncertain and full of perils? And how many perils must we meet on the way to this greater peril? And how long before we are there? But if I should choose to be a friend of God, I can become one now." He said this, and all troubled with the pain of the new life coming to birth in him, he turned back his eyes to the book. He read on and was changed inwardly, where You alone could see; and the world dropped away from his mind, as soon appeared outwardly. For while he was reading and his heart thus tossing on its own flood, at length he broke out in heavy weeping, saw the better way and chose it for his own. Being now Your servant he said to his friend, "Now I have broken from that hope we had and have decided to serve God; and I enter upon that service from this hour, in this place. If you have no will to imitate me, at least do not try to dissuade me."

The other replied that he would remain his companion in so great a service for so great a prize. So the two of them, now Your servants, built a spiritual tower at the only cost that is adequate, the cost of leaving all things and following

You. Then Ponticianus and the man who had gone walking with him in another part of the garden came looking for them in the same place, and when they found them suggested that they should return home as the day was now declining. But they told their decision and their purpose, and how that will had arisen in them and was now settled in them; and asked them not to try to argue them out of their decision, even if they would not also join them. Ponticianus and his friend, though not changed from their former state, yet wept for themselves, as he told us, and congratulated them in God and commended themselves to their prayers. Then with their own heart trailing in the dust they went off to the palace, while the other two, with their heart fixed upon heaven, remained in the hut. Both these men, as it happened, were betrothed, and when the two women heard of it they likewise dedicated their virginity to You.

### VII

This was the story Ponticianus told. But You, Lord, while he was speaking, turned me back towards myself, taking me from behind my own back where I had put myself all the time that I preferred not to see myself. And You set me there before my own face that I might see how vile I was, how twisted and unclean and spotted and ulcerous. I saw myself and was horrified; but there was no way to flee from myself. If I tried to turn my gaze from myself, there was Ponticianus telling what he was telling; and again You were setting me face to face with myself, forcing me upon my own sight, that I might see my iniquity and loathe it. I had known it, but I had pretended not to see it, had deliberately looked the other way and let it go from my mind.

But this time, the more ardently I approved those two as I heard of their determination to win health for their souls by giving themselves up wholly to Your healing, the more detestable did I find myself in comparison with them. For many years had flowed by—a dozen or more—from the time when I was nineteen and was stirred by the reading of

Cicero's Hortensius to the study of wisdom; and here was I still postponing the giving up of this world's happiness to devote myself to the search for that of which not the finding only but the mere seeking is better than to find all the treasures and kingdoms of men, better than all the body's pleasures though they were to be had merely for a nod. But I in my great worthlessness—for it was greater thus early— had begged You for chastity, saying: "Grant me chastity and continence, but not yet." For I was afraid that You would hear my prayer too soon, and too soon would heal me from the disease of lust which I wanted satisfied rather than extinguished. So I had gone wandering in my sacrilegious superstition through the base ways of the Manicheans: not indeed that I was sure they were right but that I preferred them to the Christians, whom I did not inquire about in the spirit of religion but simply opposed through malice.

I had thought that my reason for putting off from day to day the following of You alone to the contempt of earthly hopes was that I did not see any certain goal towards which to direct my course. But now the day was come when I stood naked in my own sight and my conscience accused me: "Why is my voice not heard? Surely you are the man who used to say that you could not cast off vanity's baggage for an uncertain truth. Very well: now the truth is certain, yet you are still carrying the load. Here are men who have been given wings to free their shoulders from the load, though they did not wear themselves out in searching nor spend ten years or more thinking about it."

Thus was I inwardly gnawed at. And I was in the grip of the most horrible and confounding shame, while Ponticianus was telling his story. He finished the tale and the business for which he had come; and he went his way, and I to myself. What did I not say against myself, with what lashes of condemnation did I not scourge my soul to make it follow me now that I wanted to follow You! My soul hung back. It would not follow, yet found no excuse for not following. All its arguments had already been used and refuted. There

remained only trembling silence: for it feared as very death
the cessation of that habit of which in truth it was dying.

VIII

In the midst of that great tumult of my inner dwelling
place, the tumult I had stirred up against my own soul in
the chamber of my heart, I turned upon Alypius, wild in
look and troubled in mind, crying out: "What is wrong with
us? What is this that you heard? The unlearned arise and take
heaven by force, and here are we with all our learning,
stuck fast in flesh and blood! Is there any shame in following because they have gone before us, would it not be a
worse shame not to follow at once?" These words and more
of the same sort I uttered, then the violence of my feeling
tore me from him while he stood staring at me thunder-
struck. For I did not sound like myself. My brow, cheeks,
eyes, flush, the pitch of my voice, spoke my mind more
powerfully than the words I uttered. There was a garden
attached to our lodging, of which we had the use, as indeed
we had of the whole house: for our host, the master of the
house, did not live there. To this garden the storm in my
breast somehow brought me, for there no one could inter-
vene in the fierce suit I had brought against myself, until
it should reach its issue: though what the issue was to be,
You knew, not I: but there I was, going mad on my way to
sanity, dying on my way to life, aware how evil I was, unaware that I was to grow better in a little while. So I went
off to the garden, and Alypius close on my heels: for it was
still privacy for me to have him near, and how could he
leave me to myself in that state? We found a seat as far as
possible from the house. I was frantic in mind, in a frenzy
of indignation at myself for not going over to Your law and
Your covenant, O my God, where all my bones cried out
that I should be, extolling it to the skies. The way was not by
ship or chariot or on foot: it was not as far as I had
gone when I went from the house to the place where we sat.
For I had but to will to go, in order not merely to go but

to arrive: I had only to will to go—but to will powerfully and wholly, not to turn and twist a will half-wounded this way and that, with the part that would rise struggling against the part that would keep to the earth.

In the torment of my irresolution, I did many bodily acts. Now men sometimes will to do bodily acts but cannot, whether because they have not the limbs, or because their limbs are bound or weakened with illness or in some other way unable to act. If I tore my hair, if I beat my forehead, if I locked my fingers and clasped my knees, I did it because I willed to. But I might have willed and yet not done it, if my limbs had not had the pliability to do what I willed. Thus I did so many things where the will to do them was not at all the same thing as the power to do them: and I did not do what would have pleased me incomparably more to do—a thing too which I could have done as soon as I willed to, given that willing means willing *wholly*. For in that matter, the power was the same thing as the will, and the willing *was* the doing. Yet it was not done, and the body more readily obeyed the slightest wish of the mind, more readily moved its limbs at the mind's mere nod, than the mind obeyed itself in carrying out its own great will which could be achieved simply by willing.

IX

Why this monstrousness? And what is the root of it? Let Your mercy enlighten me, that I may put the question: whether perhaps the answer lies in the mysterious punishment that has come upon men and some deeply hidden damage in the sons of Adam. Why this monstrousness? And what is the root of it? The mind gives the body an order, and is obeyed at once: the mind gives itself an order and is resisted. The mind commands the hand to move and there is such readiness that you can hardly distinguish the command from its execution. Yet the mind is mind, whereas the hand is body. The mind commands the mind to will, the mind is itself, but it does not do it. Why this monstrousness? And

what is the root of it? The mind I say commands itself to
will: it would not give the command unless it willed: yet
it does not do what it commands. The trouble is that it does
not totally will: therefore it does not totally command. It
commands in so far as it wills; and it disobeys the command in so far as it does not will. The will is commanding
itself to be a will—commanding itself, not some other. But
it does not in its fullness give the command, so that what
it commands is not done. For if the will were so in its
fullness, it would not command itself to will, for it would
already will. It is therefore no monstrousness, partly to
will, partly not to will, but a sickness of the soul to be
so weighted down by custom that it cannot wholly rise even
with the support of truth. Thus there are two wills in us,
because neither of them is entire: and what is lacking to
the one is present in the other.

x

Let them perish from thy presence, O God, as perish vain
talkers and seducers of the soul, who observing that there
are two wills at issue in our coming to a decision proceed
to assert [as the Manichees do] that there are two minds in
us of different natures, one good, one evil. For they are evil
themselves in holding such evil opinions; and they will become good only if they perceive truth and come to it as
your Apostle says to them: *You were heretofore darkness
but now light in the Lord.* But these men though they want
to be light, want to be light in themselves and not in the
Lord, imagining the nature of the soul to be the same as
God. Thus they become not light but deeper darkness, since
in their abominable arrogance they have gone further from
You, *the true Light that enlightens every man that comes
into this world.* Take heed what you say and blush for
shame: *draw near unto Him and be enlightened, and your
faces shall not be ashamed.* When I was deliberating about
serving the Lord my God, as I had long meant to do, it was
I who willed to do it, I who was unwilling. It was I. I did

not wholly will, I was not wholly unwilling. Therefore I strove with myself and was distracted by myself. This distraction happened to me though I did not want it, and it showed me not the presence of some second mind, but the punishment of my own mind. Thus it was not I who caused it but *the sin that dwells in me*, the punishment of a sin freely committed by Adam, whose son I am.

For if there be as many contrary natures in man as there are wills in conflict with one another, then there are not two natures in us but several. Take the case of a man trying to make up his mind whether he would go to the Manichees' meeting-house or to the theatre. The Manichees would say: "Here you have two natures, one good, bringing him to the meeting-house, the other evil, taking him away. How else could you have this wavering between two wills pulling against each other?" Now I say that both are bad, the will that would take him to the Manichees and the will that would take him to the theatre. But they hold that the will by which one comes to them is good. Very well! Supposing one of us is trying to decide and wavering between two wills in conflict, whether to go to the theatre or to *our* church, will not the Manichees be in some trouble about an answer? For either they must admit, which they do not want to, that a good will would take a man to our church as they think it is a good will that brings those who are receivers of their sacrament and belong to them to their church; or they must hold that there are two evil natures and two evil wills at conflict in one man, and what they are always saying will not be true—namely that there is one good will and one evil will. Otherwise, they must be converted to the truth and not deny that when a man is taking a decision there is one soul drawn this way and that by diverse wills.

Therefore, when they perceive that there are two wills in conflict in man, they must not say that there are two opposing minds in conflict, one good, one bad, from two opposing substances and two opposing principles. For you, O God of truth, refute them and disprove them and convict them of error: as in the case where both wills are bad, when, for instance, a man is deliberating whether he shall kill another man by poison or by dagger; whether he should seize this or that part of another man's property, when he cannot seize both; whether he should spend his money on lust or hoard his money through avarice; whether he should go to the games or the theatre if they happen both to come on the same day. Let us add a third possibility to this last man, whether he should go and commit a theft from someone else's house, if the occasion should arise: and indeed a fourth, whether he should go and commit adultery, if the chance occurs at the same time. If all four things come together at the same point of time, and all are equally desired, yet all cannot be done, then they tear the mind by the conflicting pull of four wills—or even more, given the great mass of things which can be desired. Yet the Manichees do not hold such a multitude of different substances.

The same reasoning applies to wills that are good. For I ask them whether it is good to find delight in the reading of the Apostle, and good to find delight in the serenity of a Psalm, and good to discuss the Gospel. To each of these they answer that it is good: but, if all these things attract us at the same moment, are not different wills tugging at the heart of man while we deliberate which we should choose? Thus they are all good, yet they are all in conflict until one is chosen, and then the whole will is at rest and at one, whereas it had been divided into many. Or again, when eternity attracts the higher faculties and the pleasure of some temporal good holds the lower, it is one same soul that wills both, but not either with its whole will; and it is therefore torn both ways and deeply troubled while truth shows the one way as better but habit keeps it to the other.

## XI

Thus I was sick at heart and in torment, accusing myself with a new intensity of bitterness, twisting and turning in my chain in the hope that it might be utterly broken, for

what held me was so small a thing! But it still held me.
And You stood in the secret places of my soul, O Lord, in
the harshness of Your mercy redoubling the scourges of fear
and shame lest I should give way again and that small slight
tie which remained should not be broken but should grow
again to full strength and bind me closer even than before.
For I kept saying within myself: "Let it be now, let it be
now," and by the mere words I had begun to move towards
the resolution. I almost made it, yet I did not quite make
it. But I did not fall back into my original state, but as
it were stood near to get my breath. And I tried again and
I was almost there, and now I could all but touch it and
hold it: yet I was not quite there, I did not touch it or hold it.
I still shrank from dying unto death and living unto life. The
lower condition which had grown habitual was more powerful than the better condition which I had not tried. The
nearer the point of time came in which I was to become
different, the more it struck me with horror; but it did not
force me utterly back nor turn me utterly away, but held
me there between the two.

Those trifles of all trifles, and vanities of vanities, my one-
time mistresses, held me back, plucking at my garment of
flesh and murmuring softly: "Are you sending us away?"
And "From this moment shall we not be with you, now or
forever?" And "From this moment shall this or that not
be allowed you, now or forever?" What were they suggesting
to me in the phrase I have written "this or that," what were
they suggesting to me, O my God? Do you in your mercy
keep from the soul of Your servant the vileness and uncleanness they were suggesting. And now I began to hear
them not half so loud; they no longer stood against me face
to face, but were softly muttering behind my back and, as
I tried to depart, plucking stealthily at me to make me look
behind. Yet even that was enough, so hesitating was I, to keep
me from snatching myself free, from shaking them off and
leaping upwards on the way I was called: for the strong force

of habit said to me: "Do you think you can live without them?"

But by this time its voice was growing fainter. In the direction towards which I had turned my face and was quivering in fear of going, I could see the austere beauty of Continence, serene and indeed joyous but not evilly, honourably soliciting me to come to her and not linger, stretching forth loving hands to receive and embrace me, hands full of multitudes of good examples. With her I saw such hosts of young men and maidens, a multitude of youth and of every age, gray widows and women grown old in virginity, and in them all Continence herself, not barren but the fruitful mother of children, her joys, by You, Lord, her Spouse. And she smiled upon me and her smile gave courage as if she were saying: "Can you not do what these men have done, what these women have done? Or could men or women have done such in themselves, and not in the Lord their God? The Lord their God gave me to them. Why do you stand upon yourself and so not stand at all? Cast yourself upon Him and be not afraid; He will not draw away and let you fall. Cast yourself without fear, He will receive you and heal you."

Yet I was still ashamed, for I could still hear the murmuring of those vanities, and I still hung hesitant. And again it was as if she said: "Stop your ears against your unclean members, that they may be mortified. They tell you of delights, but not of such delights as the law of the Lord your God tells." This was the controversy raging in my heart, a controversy about myself against myself. And Alypius stayed by my side and awaited in silence the issue of such agitation as he had never seen in me.

### XII

When my most searching scrutiny had drawn up all my vileness from the secret depths of my soul and heaped it in my heart's sight, a mighty storm arose in me, bringing a mighty rain of tears. That I might give way to my tears and lamentations, I rose from Alypius: for it struck me that solitude was more suited to the business of weeping. I went far enough from him to prevent his presence from being an embarrassment to me. So I felt, and he realized it. I suppose I had said something and the sound of my voice was heavy with tears. I arose, but he remained where we had been sitting, still in utter amazement. I flung myself down somehow under a certain fig tree and no longer tried to check my tears, which poured forth from my eyes in a flood, *an acceptable sacrifice to Thee.* And much I said not in these words but to this effect: *"And Thou, O, Lord, how long? How long, Lord; wilt Thou be angry forever? Remember not our former iniquities."* For I felt that I was still bound by them. And I continued my miserable complaining: "How long, how long shall I go on saying tomorrow and again tomorrow? Why not now, why not have an end to my uncleanness this very hour?"

Such things I said, weeping in the most bitter sorrow of my heart. And suddenly I heard a voice from some nearby house, a boy's voice or a girl's voice, I do not know: but it was a sort of sing-song, repeated again and again, "Take and read, take and read." I ceased weeping and immediately began to search my mind most carefully as to whether children were accustomed to chant these words in any kind of game, and I could not remember that I had ever heard any such thing. Damming back the flood of my tears I arose, interpreting the incident as quite certainly a divine command to open my book of Scripture and read the passage at which I should open. For it was part of what I had been told about Anthony, that from the Gospel which he happened to be reading he had felt that he was being admonished as though what he read was spoken directly to himself: *Go, sell what thou hast and give to the poor and thou shalt have treasure in heaven; and come follow Me.* By this experience he had been in that instant converted to You. So I was moved to return to the place where Alypius was sitting, for I had put down the Apostle's book there when I arose. I snatched it up, opened it and in silence read the passage upon which my eyes first fell: *Not in rioting and drunkenness, not in chambering and impurities, not in contention and envy, but put ye on the Lord Jesus Christ and make not provision for the flesh in its concupiscences.* [*Romans* xiii, 13.] I had no wish to read further, and no need. For in that instant, with the very ending of the sentence, it was as though a light of utter confidence shone in all my heart, and all the darkness of uncertainty vanished away. Then leaving my finger in the place or marking it by some other sign, I closed the book and in complete calm told the whole thing to Alypius and he similarly told me what had been going on in himself, of which I knew nothing. He asked to see what I had read. I showed him, and he looked further than I had read. I had not known what followed. And this is what followed: *"Now him that is weak in faith, take unto you."* He applied this to himself and told me so. And he was confirmed by this message, and with no troubled wavering gave himself to God's good-will and purpose—a purpose indeed most suited to his character, for in these matters he had been immeasurably better than I.

Then we went in to my mother and told her, to her great joy. We related how it had come about: she was filled with triumphant exultation, and praised You who are mighty beyond what we ask or conceive: for she saw that You had given her more than with all her pitiful weeping she had ever asked. For You converted me to Yourself so that I no longer sought a wife nor any of this world's promises, but stood upon that same rule of faith in which You had shown me to her so many years before. Thus You changed her mourning into joy, a joy far richer than she had thought to wish, a joy much dearer and purer than she had thought to find in grandchildren of my flesh.

# BOOK NINE

## AGED THIRTY-TWO

O LORD, *I am Thy servant: I am Thy servant and the son of Thy handmaid. Thou hast broken my bonds. I will sacrifice to Thee the sacrifice of praise.* Let my heart and my tongue praise Thee, and *let all my bones say, O Lord, who is like to Thee?* Let them say and do Thou answer me and say to my soul: *I am Thy salvation.* Who am I and what kind of man am I? What evil has there not been in my deeds, or if not in my deeds, in my words, or if not in my words, then in my will? But You, Lord, are good and merciful, and Your right hand had regard to the profundity of my death and drew out the abyss of corruption that was in the bottom of my heart. By Your gift I had come totally not to will what I willed but to will what You willed. But where in all that long time was my free will, and from what deep sunken hiding-place was it suddenly summoned forth in the moment in which I bowed my neck to Your easy yoke and my shoulders to Your light burden, Christ Jesus, my Helper and my Redeemer? How lovely I suddenly found it to be free from the loveliness of those vanities, so that now it was a joy to renounce what I had been so afraid to lose. For You cast them out of me, O true and supreme Loveliness, You cast them out of me and took their place in me, You who are sweeter than all pleasure, yet not to flesh and blood; brighter than all light, yet deeper within than any secret; loftier than all honour, but not to those who are lofty to themselves. Now my mind was free from the cares that had gnawed it, from aspiring and getting and weltering in filth and rubbing the scab of lust. And I talked with You as friends talk, my glory and my riches and my salvation, my Lord God.

II

And I thought it would be good in Your sight if I did not dramatically snatch my tongue's service from the speech

market but quietly withdrew; but that in any event with-
draw I must, so that youths—not students of Your law or
Your peace but of lying follies and the conflicts of the law—
should no longer buy at my mouth the tools of their madness. Fortunately it happened that there were only a few
days left before the Vintage Vacation; and I decided to
endure them so that I might leave with due deliberation,
seeing that I had been redeemed by You and was not going
to put myself up for sale again. Our purpose therefore was
known to You, but not to men other than our own friends.
We had agreed among ourselves not to spread the news
abroad at all, although, in our ascent from *the valley of
tears* and our singing of the *song of degrees*, You had given
us *sharp arrows* and *burning coals* against *cunning tongues*
that might argue against us with pretended care for our
interest, might destroy us saying that they loved us: as men
consume food saying that they love it.

You had pierced our hearts with the arrow of Your love,
and our minds were pierced with the arrows of Your words.
To burn away and utterly consume our slothfulness so that
we might no more be sunk in its depths, we had the depths
of our thought filled with the examples of Your servants
whom You had changed from darkness to light and from
death to life; and these inflamed us so powerfully that any
false tongue of contradiction did not extinguish our flame
but set us blazing more fiercely. But because for Your
name, which You have sanctified throughout the earth, our
decision would find many to praise it, I was afraid that it
would look like ostentation if I did not wait for the approaching vacation but immediately resigned from a profession which everyone knew I practiced: for the faces of all
about would be turned on my act, in that I had not chosen
to wait for the vacation when it was so close, and it would
be widely said that I had done it to make myself seem important. And what would it have profited me to have people
discussing and arguing about my purpose and to have our
good ill-spoken of?

Furthermore that very summer, under the too heavy labor of teaching, my lungs had begun to give way and I breathed with difficulty; the pain in my breast showed that they were affected and they no longer let me talk with any strength for too long at a time. At first this had disturbed me, because it made it practically a matter of necessity that I should lay down the burden of teaching, or at least give it up for the time if I was to be cured and grow well again. But when the full purpose of giving myself leisure to meditate on how You are the Lord arose in me and became a settled resolve—as you know, O my God—I actually found myself glad to have this perfectly truthful excuse to offer parents who might be offended and for their children's sake would never willingly have let me give up teaching. So I was full of joy, and I put up with the space of time that still had to run—I fancy it was about twenty days. But to bear the time took considerable fortitude. Desire for money, which formerly had helped me to bear the heavy labor of teaching, was quite gone; so that I should have [had nothing to help me bear it and so] found it altogether crushing if patience had not taken the place of covetousness. Some of Your servants, my brethren, may think that I sinned in this, since having enrolled with all my heart in Your service, I allowed myself to sit for so much as an hour in the chair of untruthfulness. It may be so. But, most merciful Lord, have You not pardoned and remitted this sin, along with others most horrible and deadly, in the holy water of baptism?

III

Meanwhile Verecundus was worrying himself ill over the good that had come to us. He saw himself losing our company by reason of his own chains, which bound him very tight. He was not yet a Christian, though his wife was, and indeed she was the strongest obstacle of all in the way of his setting out upon that journey on which we had started. For he said that he would not be a Christian in any

other way, than the way that was beyond his power. But
he very generously offered that as long as we were in the
country, we might stay in his house. You will reward him, O
Lord, with the reward of the just, for You have already
given him the lot of the just. At a time when we were
away in Rome he was seized with some bodily illness, and
in the course of it became a Christian and was baptized, and
so departed this life. Thus you had mercy not only upon
him, but upon us too: otherwise, thinking of the wonderful kindness our friend had shown us, we should have
been tormented with unbearable sorrow if we had not been
able to number him in Your flock. Thanks be to our God!
We are Yours, as Your exhortations and consolations prove.
You are faithful to Your promises, and you will repay Verecundus for his country house at Cassiciacum, where we
rested in You from the world's troubles, with the loveliness
and eternal freshness of Your paradise: for You forgave him
his sins upon earth in the mountain of abundance, Your
mountain, the mountain of richness.

At the time, however, Verecundus was very much perturbed; but Nebridius altogether joyful. For although before
he was a Christian he had fallen into that same pit of deadly
error and believed the true body of Your Son to be a phan-
tasm, he had emerged from that error; and though he had not
yet received any sacraments of Your church, he was a most
zealous seeker of the truth. Not long after our conversion
and regeneration by Your baptism, You took him from this
life, by then a baptized Catholic and serving You in Africa
in perfect chastity among his own people, for he had made
his whole family Christian. And now he lives in Abraham's
bosom. Whatever is meant by that bosom, there my Nebridius lives, my most beloved friend, Your son by adoption and no longer a freed-man only. There he lives. For
what other place is there for such a soul? There he lives,
in the place of which he asked me, an ignorant poor creature, so many questions. He no longer puts his bodily ear
to my lips, but the lips of his spirit to Your fountain,

drinking his fill of wisdom, all that his thirst requires, happy without end. Nor do I think he is so intoxicated with the draught of that wisdom as to forget me, since You, O Lord, of whom he drinks are mindful of us.

There then we were, consoling the unhappy Verecundus, for our friendship was not impaired by conversion, and exhorting him to fidelity in his state, namely the married life. As for Nebridius, we were merely waiting for him to follow us. He was so close that he might well follow, and he was indeed on the point of doing so when at last those days of waiting for the vacation came to an end. For they seemed long and many to me, because of the longing I had for that freedom and leisure in which I might sing to You from the depths of my heart: *My heart hath said to Thee: I have sought Thy face. Thy face, O Lord, will I still seek.*

IV

And now the day was come on which I was to be set free from the teaching of Rhetoric in fact, as I was already free in mind. And so it came about. You delivered my tongue as You had already delivered my heart, and I rejoiced and praised You, and so went off with my friends to the country-house. The amount of writing I did there—the writing was now in your service but during this breathing-space still smacked of the school of pride—my books exist to witness, with the record they give of discussions either with my friends there present or with Yourself when I was alone with You; and there are my letters to show what correspondence I had with Nebridius while he was away. But when shall I have the time to relate all Your great acts of goodness towards me, especially at that time, since I must hasten to tell of matters greater still?

For my memory reminds me, and pleasant it is, O Lord, to confess to You, what inner goads you used to tame me, and how you brought me low, *making low the mountains and hills of my thoughts, making straight what was crooked, and plain what was rough.* And I remember too how You

subdued my heart's brother Alypius to the name of Jesus
Christ Your only-begotten Son, Our Lord and Saviour, which
at first he thought it would be in some sense lowering to put
into my writings. For he would have had them redolent
of the high cedars of the schools, which the Lord had now
broken down, rather than of the health-giving herbs of
the Church which are of such avail against the bites of serpents.

When I read the Psalms of David, songs of faithfulness and
devotion in which the spirit of pride has no entry, what
cries did I utter to You, O my God, I but a novice in your
true love, a catechumen keeping holiday in a country house
with that other catechumen Alypius: though my mother also
was with us, a woman in sex, with the faith of a man, with
the serenity of great age, the love of a mother, the piety of a
Christian. What cries did I utter to You in those Psalms and
how was I inflamed towards You by them, and on fire to set
them sounding through all the world, if I could, against the
pride of man! But in truth they are already sung throughout the world and *there is none who can hide himself from
Thy heat.* I thought of the Manichees with indignation and
a burning anguish of sorrow. I pitied them because they
did not know our sacraments and our healing, but were
insanely set against the medicine that would have cured their
insanity. I wished that they might be somewhere close
at hand—without my knowing that they were there—and
could see my face and hear my words, when in that time
of leisure I read the Fourth Psalm; and that they could see
what that Psalm did in me: *When I called upon Thee, Thou,
God of my justice, didst hear me; when I was in distress,
Thou hast enlarged me: have mercy on me, O Lord, and
hear my prayer.* Would that they could have heard me—
without my knowing that they heard me, lest they might
think it was on their account I was speaking as I spoke when
I recited these words: and indeed I would not have said those
things or said them in the same way, if I had realized that I
was being heard and seen by them: nor, if I *had* said them,

would they have understood how I was speaking with myself and to myself in Your presence from the natural movement of my spirit.

I was in fear and horror, and again I was on fire with hope and exultation in your mercy, O Father. And all these emotions found expression in my eyes and in my voice when Your Holy Spirit turned to us and said: *O ye sons of men, how long will ye be dull of heart? Why do you love vanity so much and seek after lying?* For I myself had loved vanity and sought after lying. *And Thou, Lord,* hadst already *made Thy holy one wonderful,* raising Him from the dead and setting Him at Thy right hand, whence He should send from on high His promise, the Paraclete, the Spirit of Truth. And He had already sent Him, though I knew it not. He had sent Him because already He was magnified and risen from the dead and ascended into heaven. For till then the Spirit was not yet given, because Jesus was not yet glorified. And the prophet cried aloud: *How long will you be dull of heart? Why do you love vanity and seek after lying? Know ye also that the Lord hath made His holy one wonderful?* He cries out "How long," he cries out "Know ye." And I so long was ignorant and loved vanity and sought after lying.

I heard these things and trembled to hear them, for they were spoken to such as I remembered myself to have been. For in those phantasms which I had taken for truth were vanity and lying. And I cried out many things strongly and earnestly in the grief I felt at what I remembered. If only those could have heard me who still loved vanity and sought after lying. Perchance they would have been troubled, and have vomited up their error; and You would have heard them when they cried to You: for He who intercedes with You for us died for us with a true death of the body.

I read, *Be angry and sin not.* And by this I was much moved, O my God, for I had by then learned to be angry with myself for the past, that I might not sin in what re-

mained of life: and to be angry with good reason, because
it was not some other nature of the race of darkness that
had sinned in me, as the Manichees say: and they are not
angry at themselves, but treasure up to themselves wrath
against the day of wrath and of the revelation of the just
judgement of God.

The good I now sought was not in things outside me,
to be seen by the eye of flesh under the sun. For those
that find their joy outside them easily fall into emptiness
and are spilled out upon the things that are seen and the
things of time, and in their starved minds lick shadows. If
only they could grow weary of their own hunger and say:
*Who shall show us good things?* And we should say and
they should hear: *The light of Thy countenance is sealed
upon us,* O Lord. For we are not *the Light that enlightens
every man* but we are enlightened by Thee that *as we
were heretofore darkness we are now light in Thee.* If they
could but see the Light interior and eternal: for now that
I had known it, I was frantic that I could not make them
see it even were they to ask: *Who shall show us good things?*
For the heart they would bring me would be in their eyes,
eyes that looked everywhere but at You. But there, where
I had been angry with myself, in my own room where I
had been pierced, where I had offered my sacrifice, slaying
the self that I had been, and, in the newly-taken purpose of
newness of life, hoping in You—there You began to make me
feel Your love and to give *gladness in my heart.* I cried
out as I read this aloud and realized it within: and I no
longer wished any increase of earthly goods, in which a man
wastes time and is wasted by time, since in the simplicity
of the Eternal I had other corn and wine and oil.

It was with a deep cry of my heart that I uttered the
next verse: *O in peace! O in the selfsame!* O how he has
said: *I will sleep and I will rest.* For who shall stand against
us *when the saying that is written will come to pass: Death
is swallowed up in victory?* You supremely are that selfsame,
for You are not changed and in You is that rest in which all

cares are forgotten, since there is no other besides You, and we have not to seek other things which are not what You are: but You, Lord, alone have *made me dwell in hope*. All these things I read and was on fire; nor could I find what could be done with those deaf dead, of whom indeed I had myself been one for I had been a scourge, a blind raging snarler against the Scriptures, which are all honeyed with the honey of heaven and all luminous with Your light: and now I was fretting my heart out over the enemies of these same Scriptures.

When shall I recall and set down all that belongs to those days in the country? I have not forgotten, nor shall I pass in silence, the bite of Your scourge and the wonderful swiftness of Your mercy. During those days You sent me the torture of toothache, and when it had grown so agonizing that I could not speak, it came into my heart to ask all my friends there present to pray for me to You, the God of every kind of health. I wrote this down on my tablet and gave it to them to read. As soon as we had gone on our knees in all simplicity, the pain went. But what was the pain or how did it go? I admit that I was terrified, O my Lord, my God, for as far back as my earliest infancy I had never experienced any such thing. Thus in that depth I recognized the act of Your will, and I gave praise to Your name, rejoicing in faith. But this faith would not let me feel safe about my past sins, since Your baptism had not yet come to remit them.

### v

When the Vintage Vacation was over I gave the people of Milan notice that they must find someone else to sell the art of words to their students, because I had chosen to serve You, and because owing to my difficulty in breathing and the pain in my lungs I could not continue my teaching. And in a letter I told Your bishop, the holy Ambrose, of my past errors and my present purpose, that he might advise me which of Your Scriptures I should especially read to prepare me and make me more fit to receive so great a grace. He told me to read Isaias the prophet, I imagine because he more clearly foretells the gospel and the calling of the gentiles than the other Old Testament writers; but I did not understand the first part of his book, and thinking that it would be all of the same kind, put it aside meaning to return to it when I should be more practised in the Lord's way of speech.

VI

When the time had come to give in my name for baptism, we left the country and returned to Milan. Alypius had decided to be born again in You at the same time, for he was already endowed with the humility that Your sacraments require, and had brought his body so powerfully under control that he could tread the icy soil of Italy with bare feet, which required unusual fortitude. We also took with us the boy Adeodatus, carnally begotten by me in my sin. You had made him well. He was barely fifteen, yet he was more intelligent than many a grave and learned man. In this I am but acknowledging to You Your own gifts, O Lord my God, Creator of all and powerful to reshape our shapelessness: for I had no part in that boy but the sin. That he had been brought up by us in Your way was because You had inspired us, no other. I do but acknowledge to You Your own gifts. There is a book of mine called *De Magistro:* it is a dialogue between him and me. You know, O God, that all the ideas which are put into the mouth of the other party to the dialogue were truly his, though he was but sixteen. I had experience of many other remarkable qualities in him. His great intelligence filled me with a kind of awe: and who but You could be the maker of things so wonderful? But You took him early from this earth, and I think of him utterly without anxiety, for there is nothing in his boyhood or youth or anywhere in him to cause me to fear. We took him along with us, the same age as ourselves in Your grace, to be brought up in Your discipline: and we were baptised, and all anxiety as to our past life fled away. The days were not long enough as I meditated, and found wonderful delight in meditating, upon the depth of Your design for the salvation of the human race. I wept at the beauty of Your hymns and canticles, and was powerfully moved at the sweet sound of Your Church's singing. Those sounds flowed into my ears, and the truth streamed into my heart: so that my feeling of devotion overflowed, and the tears ran from my eyes, and I was happy in them.

## VII

It was only a little while before that the church of Milan had begun to practise this kind of consolation and exultation, to the great joy of the brethren singing together with heart and voice. For it was only about a year, or not much more, since Justina, the mother of the boy emperor Valentinian, was persecuting Your servant Ambrose in the interests of her own heresy: for she had been seduced by the Arians. The devoted people had stayed day and night in the church, ready to die with their bishop, Your servant. And my mother, Your handmaid, bearing a great part of the trouble and vigil, had lived in prayer. I also, though still not warmed by the fire of Your Spirit, was stirred to excitement by the disturbed and wrought-up state of the city. It was at this time that the practice was instituted of singing hymns and psalms after the manner of the Eastern churches, to keep the people from being altogether worn out with anxiety and want of sleep. The custom has been retained from that day to this, and has been imitated by many, indeed in almost all congregations throughout the world.

At this time You revealed to Your bishop Ambrose in a vision the place where the bodies of the martyrs Protasius and Gervasius lay hid, which You had for so many years kept incorrupt in the treasury of Your secret knowledge that You might bring them forth at the proper moment to check a woman's fury—the woman being the ruler of the Empire! For when they were discovered and dug up and with due honour brought to Ambrose's basilica, not only were people cured who had been tormented by evil spirits—and the devils themselves forced to confess it—but also there was a man, a citizen well known to the city, who had been blind for many years: he asked what was the cause of the tumultuous joy of the people, and when he heard, he sprang up and asked his guide to lead him into the place. When he arrived there he asked to be allowed to touch with his handkerchief the place on which lay the saints, whose death is precious in Your sight. He did so, put the handkerchief to his eyes, and immediately they were opened. The news spread abroad, Your praises glowed and shone, and if the mind of that angry woman was not brought to the sanity of belief, it was at least brought back from the madness of persecution. Thanks be to my God! From what and towards what have You led my memory, that it should confess to You these great things which I had altogether forgotten? Yet even then, *when the odor of Thy ointments was so sweet smelling,* I did not *run after Thee:* and for this I wept all the more now when I heard Your hymns and canticles, as one who had then sighed for You and now breathed in You, breathed so far as the air allows in this our house of grass.

### VIII

You, Lord, who make men of one mind to dwell in one house brought to our company a young man of our own town, Evodius. He had held office in the civil service, had been converted and baptised before us, had resigned from the state's service, and given himself to Yours. We kept together, meaning to live together in our devout purpose. We thought deeply as to the place in which we might serve You most usefully. As a result we started back for Africa. And when we had come as far as Ostia on the Tiber, my mother died. I pass over many things, for I must make haste. Do You, O my God, accept my confessions and my gratitude for countless things of which I say nothing. But I will not

omit anything my mind brings forth concerning her, Your
servant, who brought me forth—brought me forth in the
flesh to this temporal light, and in her heart to light eternal.
Not of her gifts do I speak but of Your gifts in her. For she
did not bring herself into the world or educate herself in
the world: it was You who created her, nor did her father
or mother know what kind of being was to come forth from
them. It was the scepter of Your Christ, the discipline of your
Only-Begotten, that brought her up in holy fear, in a
Catholic family which was a worthy member of Your church.
Yet it was not the devotion of her mother in her upbring-
ing that she talked most of, but of a certain aged servant,
who had indeed carried my mother's father on her back
when he was a baby, as little ones are accustomed to be
carried on the backs of older girls. Because of this, because also of her age and her admirable character, she was
very much respected by her master and mistress in their
Christian household. As a result she was given charge of
her master's daughters. This charge she fulfilled most con-
scientiously, checking them sharply when necessary with
holy severity and teaching them soberly and prudently.
Thus, except at the times when they ate—and that most
temperately—at their parents' table, she would not let them
even drink water, no matter how tormenting their thirst.
By this she prevented the forming of a bad habit, and she
used to remark very sensibly: "Now you drink water because
you are not allowed to have wine; but when you are married, and thus mistresses of food-stores and wine-cellars,
you will despise water, but the habit of drinking will still
remain." By this kind of teaching and the authority of her
commands she moderated the greediness that goes with
childhood and brought the little girls' thirst to such a control that they no longer wanted what they ought not to
have.

Yet, as Your servant told me, her son, there did steal
upon my mother an inclination to wine. For when, in the
usual way, she was sent by her parents, as a well-behaved

child, to draw wine from the barrel, she would dip the cup in, but before pouring the wine from the cup into the flagon, she would sip a little with the very tip of her lips, only a little because she did not yet like the taste sufficiently to take more. Indeed she did it not out of any craving for wine, but rather from the excess of childhood's high spirits, which tend to boil over in absurdities, and are usually kept in check by the authority of elders. And so, adding to that daily drop a little more from day to day—for he that despises small things, falls little by little—she fell into the habit, so that she would drink off greedily cups almost full of wine. Where then was that wise old woman with her forceful prohibitions? Could anything avail against the evil in us, unless Your healing, O Lord, watched over us? When our father and mother and nurses are absent, You are present, who created us, who call us, who can use those placed over us for some good unto the salvation of our souls. What did You do then, O my God? How did You cure her, and bring her to health? From another soul you drew a harsh and cutting sarcasm, as though bringing forth a surgeon's knife from Your secret store, and with one blow amputated that sore place. A maidservant with whom she was accustomed to go to the cellar, one day fell into a quarrel with her small mistress when no one else chanced to be about, and hurled at her the most biting insult possible, calling her a drunkard. My mother was pierced to the quick, saw her fault in its true wickedness, and instantly condemned it and gave it up. Just as the flattery of a friend can pervert, so the insult of an enemy can sometimes correct. Nor do You, O God, reward men according to what You do by means of them, but according to what they themselves intended. For the girl being in a temper wanted to enrage her young mistress, not to amend her, for she did it when no one else was there, either because the time and place happened to be thus when the quarrel arose, or because she was afraid that elders would be angry because she had not told it sooner. But You, O Lord, Ruler of heavenly things and earthly, who turn to Your own purposes the very depths of rivers as they run and order the turbulence of the flow of time, did by the folly of one mind bring sanity to another; thus reminding us not to attribute it to our own power if another is amended by our word, even if we meant to amend him.

## IX

My mother, then, was modestly and soberly brought up, being rather made obedient to her parents by You than to You by her parents. When she reached the age for marriage, and was bestowed upon a husband, she served him as her lord. She used all her effort to win him to You, preaching You to him by her character, by which You made her beautiful to her husband, respected and loved by him and admirable in his sight. For she bore his acts of unfaithfulness quietly, and never had any jealous scene with her husband about them. She awaited Your mercy upon him, that he might grow chaste through faith in You. And as a matter of fact, though generous beyond measure, he had a very hot temper. But she knew that a woman must not resist a husband in anger, by deed or even by word. Only, when she saw him calm again and quiet, she would take the opportunity to give him an explanation of her actions, if it happened that he had been roused to anger unreasonably. The result was that whereas many matrons with much milder husbands carried the marks of blows to disfigure their faces, and would all get together to complain of the way their husbands behaved, my mother—talking lightly but meaning it seriously—advised them against their tongues: saying that from the day they heard the matrimonial contract read to them they should regard it as an instrument by which they became servants; and from that time they should be mindful of their condition and not set themselves up against their masters. And they often expressed amazement —for they knew how violent a husband she had to live with— that it had never been heard, and there was no mark to show, that Patricius had beaten his wife or that there had been any family quarrel between them for so much as a single day. And when her friends asked her the reason, she taught them her rule, which was as I have just said. Those who followed it, found it good and thanked her; those who did not, went on being bullied and beaten.

Her mother-in-law began by being angry with her because of the whispers of malicious servants. But my mother won her completely by the respect she showed, and her unfailing patience and mildness. She ended by going to her son, telling him of the tales the servants had bandied about to the destruction of peace in the family between herself and her daughter-in-law, and asking him to punish them for it. So he, out of obedience to his mother and in the interests of order in the household and peace among his womenfolk, had the servants beaten whose names he had been given, as she had asked when giving them. To which she added the promise that anyone must expect a similar reward from her own hands who should think to please her by speaking ill of her daughter-in-law. And as no one had the courage to do so, they lived together with the most notable degree of kindness and harmony.

This great gift also, O my God, my Mercy, You gave to Your good servant, in whose womb You created me, that she showed herself, wherever possible, a peacemaker between people quarreling and minds at discord. For swelling and undigested discord often belches forth bitter words when in the venom of intimate conversation with a present friend hatred at its rawest is breathed out upon an absent enemy. But when my mother heard bitter things said by each of the other, she never said anything to either about the other save what would help to reconcile them. This might seem a small virtue, if I had not had the sorrow of seeing for myself so many people who—as if by some horrible widespreading infection of sin—not only tell angry people the things their enemies said in anger, but even add things that were never said at all. Whereas, on the contrary, ordinary humanity would seem to require not merely that we refrain from ex-

citing or increasing wrath among men by evil speaking, but
that we study to extinguish wrath by kind speaking. Such
a one was she: and You were the master who taught her
most secretly in the school of her heart.

The upshot was that towards the very end of his life she
won her husband to You; and once he was a Christian she
no longer had to complain of the things she had had to
bear with before he was a Christian. Further, she was a servant of Your servants. Such of them as knew her praised
and honoured and loved You, O God, in her; for they felt
Your presence in her heart, showing itself in the fruit of her
holy conversation. She had been *the wife of one husband,
had requited her parents, had governed her house* piously,
*was well reported of for good works*. She had *brought up her
children*, being in labour of them as often as she saw them
swerving away from You. Finally of all of us Your servants,
O Lord—since by Your gift You suffer us to speak—who before her death were living together after receiving the grace
of baptism, she took as much care as if she had been the
mother of us all, and served us as if she had been the daughter
of us all.

x

When the day was approaching on which she was to depart this life—a day that You knew though we did not—it
came about, as I believe by Your secret arrangement, that
she and I stood alone leaning in a window, which looked
inwards to the garden within the house where we were
staying, at Ostia on the Tiber; for there we were away from
everybody, resting for the sea-voyage from the weariness of
our long journey by land. There we talked together, she
and I alone, in deep joy; and *forgetting the things that were
behind and looking forward to those that were before*, we
were discussing in the presence of Truth, which You are,
what the eternal life of the saints could be like, *which eye has
not seen nor ear heard, nor has it entered into the heart of
man*. But with the mouth of our heart we panted for the high

waters of Your fountain, the fountain of the life which is
with You: that being sprinkled from that fountain according
to our capacity, we might in some sense meditate upon so
great a matter.

And our conversation had brought us to this point, that
any pleasure whatsoever of the bodily senses, in any brightness whatsoever of corporeal light, seemed to us not worthy
of comparison with the pleasure of that eternal Light, not
worthy even of mention. Rising as our love flamed upward
towards that Selfsame, we passed in review the various levels
of bodily things, up to the heavens themselves, whence sun
and moon and stars shine upon this earth. And higher still
we soared, thinking in our minds and speaking and marvelling at Your works: and so we came to our own souls, and
went beyond them to come at last to that region of richness
unending, where You feed Israel forever with the food
of truth: and there life is that Wisdom by which all things
are made, both the things that have been and the things that
are yet to be. But this Wisdom itself is not made: it is
as it has ever been, and so it shall be forever: indeed "has
ever been" and "shall be forever" have no place in it, but it
simply is, for it is eternal: whereas "to have been" and "to
be going to be" are not eternal. And while we were thus
talking of His Wisdom and panting for it, with all the
effort of our heart we did for one instant attain to touch
it; then sighing, and leaving the first fruits of our spirit
bound to it, we returned to the sound of our own tongue,
in which a word has both beginning and ending. For what
is like to your Word, Our Lord, who abides in Himself forever, yet grows not old and makes all things new!

So we said: If to any man the tumult of the flesh grew
silent, silent the images of earth and sea and air: and if the
heavens grew silent, and the very soul grew silent to herself
and by not thinking of self mounted beyond self: if all
dreams and imagined visions grew silent, and every tongue
and every sign and whatsoever is transient—for indeed
if any man could hear them, he should hear them saying

with one voice: We did not make ourselves, but He made us who abides forever: but if, having uttered this and so set us to listening to Him who made them, they all grew silent, and in their silence He alone spoke to us, not by them but by Himself: so that we should hear His word, not by any tongue of flesh nor the voice of an angel nor the sound of thunder nor in the darkness of a parable, but that we should hear Himself whom in all these things we love, should hear Himself and not them: just as we two had but now reached forth and in a flash of the mind attained to touch the eternal Wisdom which abides over all: and if this could continue, and all other visions so different be quite taken away, and this one should so ravish and absorb and wrap the beholder in inward joys that his life should eternally be such as that one moment of understanding for which we had been sighing—would not this be: *Enter Thou into the joy of Thy Lord?* But when shall it be? Shall it be when *we shall all rise again* and *shall not all be changed?*

Such thoughts I uttered, though not in that order or in those actual words; but You know, O Lord, that on that day when we talked of these things the world with all its delights seemed cheap to us in comparison with what we talked of. And my mother said: "Son, for my own part I no longer find joy in anything in this world. What I am still to do here and why I am here I know not, now that I no longer hope for anything from this world. One thing there was, for which I desired to remain still a little longer in this life, that I should see you a Catholic Christian before I died. This God has granted me in superabundance, in that I now see you His servant to the contempt of all worldly happiness. What then am I doing here?"

## XI

What answer I made, I do not clearly remember; within five days or not much longer she fell into a fever. And in her sickness, she one day fainted away and for the moment lost consciousness. We ran to her but she quickly returned to consciousness, and seeing my brother and me standing by her she said as one wondering: "Where was I?" Then looking closely upon us as we stood wordless in our grief, she said: "Here you will bury your mother." I stayed silent and checked my weeping. But my brother said something to the effect that he would be happier if she were to die in her own land and not in a strange country. But as she heard this she looked at him anxiously, restraining him with her eye because he savored of earthly things, and then she looked at me and said: "See the way he talks." And then she said to us both: "Lay this body wherever it may be. Let no care of it disturb you: this only I ask of you that you should remember me at the altar of the Lord wherever you may be." And when she had uttered this wish in such words as she could manage, she fell silent as her sickness took hold of her more strongly.

But as I considered Your gifts, O unseen God, which You send into the hearts of Your faithful to the springing up of such wonderful fruits, I was glad and gave thanks to You, remembering what I had previously known of the care as to her burial which had always troubled her: for she had arranged to be buried by the body of her husband. Because they had lived together in such harmony, she had wished—so little is the human mind capable of rising to the divine—that it should be granted her, as an addition to her happiness and as something to be spoken of among men, that after her pilgrimage beyond the sea the earthly part of man and wife should lie together under the same earth. Just when this vain desire had begun to vanish from her heart through the fullness of Your goodness, I did not know; but I was pleased and surprised that it had now so clearly vanished: though indeed in the conversation we had had together at the window, when she said: "What am I still doing here?" there had appeared no desire to die in her own land. Further I heard afterwards that in the time we were at Ostia, she had talked one day to some of my friends, as a mother talking to her children, of the contempt of this life and of the attraction of death. I was not there at the time. They marvelled at such courage in a woman—but it was You who had given it to her—and asked if she was not afraid to leave her body so far from her own city. But she said: "Nothing is far from God, and I have no fear that He will not know at the end of the world from what place He is to raise me up." And so on the ninth day of her illness, in the fifty-sixth year of her life and the thirty-third of mine, that devout and holy soul was released from the body.

## XII

I closed her eyes; and an immeasurable sorrow flowed into my heart and would have overflowed in tears. But my eyes under the mind's strong constraint held back their flow and I stood dry-eyed. In that struggle it went very ill with me. As she breathed her last, the child Adeodatus broke out into lamentation and we all checked him and brought him to silence. But in this very fact the childish element in me, which was breaking out into tears, was checked and brought to silence by the manlier voice of my mind. For we felt that it was not fitting that her funeral should be solemnized with moaning and weeping and lamentation, for so it is normal to weep when death is seen as sheer misery or as complete extinction. But she had not died miserably, nor did she wholly die. Of the one thing we were sure by reason of her character, of the other by the reality of our faith.

What then was it that grieved my heart so deeply? Only the newness of the wound, in finding the custom I had so loved of living with her suddenly snapped short. It was a joy to me to have this one testimony from her: when her illness was close to its end, meeting with expressions of endearment such services as I rendered, she called me a dutiful loving son, and said in the great affection of her love that she had never heard from my mouth any harsh or reproachful word addressed to herself. But what possible comparison was there, O my God who made us, between the honour I showed her and the service she had rendered me?

Because I had now lost the great comfort of her, my soul was wounded and my very life torn asunder, for it had been one life made of hers and mine together. When the boy had been quieted and ceased weeping, Evodius took up the psalter and began to chant—with the whole house making the responses—the psalm *Mercy and judgment I will sing to Thee, O Lord.* And when they heard what was being done, many of the brethren and religious women came to us; those whose office it was were making arrangement for the burial, while, in another part of the house where it could properly be done I discoursed, with friends who did not wish to leave me by myself, upon matters suitable for that time. Thus I used truth as a kind of fomentation to bring relief to my torment, a torment known to You, but not known to those others: so that listening closely to me they thought that I lacked all feeling of grief. But in Your ears, where none of them could hear, I accused the emotion in me as weakness; and I held in the flood of my grief. It was for the moment a little diminished, but returned with fresh violence, not with any pouring of tears or change of countenance: but I knew what I was crushing down in my heart. I was very much ashamed that these human emotions could have such power over me—though it belongs to the due order and the lot of our earthly condition that they should come to us—and I felt a new grief at my grief and so was afflicted with a twofold sorrow.

When the body was taken to burial, I went and returned without tears. During the prayers which we poured forth to you when the sacrifice of our redemption was offered for her—while the body, as the custom there is, lay by the grave before it was actually buried—during those prayers I did not weep. Yet all that day I was heavy with grief within and in the trouble of my mind I begged of You in my own fashion to heal my pain; but You would not—I imagine because You meant to impress upon my memory by this proof how strongly the bond of habit holds the mind even when it no longer feeds upon deception. The idea

came to me to go and bathe, for I had heard that the bath
—which the Greeks call αλανείον —is so called because it
drives anxiety from the mind. And this also I acknowledge to Your mercy, O Father of orphans, that I bathed and
was the same man after as before. The bitterness of grief had
not sweated out of my heart. Then I fell asleep, and woke
again to find my grief not a little relieved. And as I was in bed
and no one about, I said over those true verses that Your
servant Ambrose wrote of You:

> Deus creator omnium
> polique rector vestiens
> diem decoro lumine,
> noctem sopora gratia,
>
> artus solutos ut quies
> reddat laboris usui
> mentesque fessas allevet
> luctusque solvat anxios.

And then little by little I began to recover my former feeling about Your handmaid, remembering how loving and
devout was her conversation with You, how pleasant and
considerate her conversation with me, of which I was thus
suddenly deprived. And I found solace in weeping in Your
sight both about her and for her, about myself and for myself. I no longer tried to check my tears, but let them flow
as they would, making them a pillow for my heart: and
it rested upon them, for it was Your ears that heard my
weeping, and not the ears of a man, who would have mis-
understood my tears and despised them. But now, O Lord,
I confess it to You in writing, let him read it who will and
interpret it as he will: and if he sees it as sin that for so small
a portion of an hour I wept for my mother, now dead and
departed from my sight, who had wept so many years for
me that I should live ever in Your sight—let him not scorn
me but rather, if he is a man of great charity, let him weep
for my sins to You, the Father of all the brethren of Your
Christ.

### XIII

Now that my heart is healed of that wound, in which there was perhaps too much of earthly affection, I pour forth to You, O our God, tears of a very different sort for Your handmaid—tears that flow from a spirit shaken by the thought of the perils there are for every soul that dies in Adam. For though she had been made alive in Christ, and while still in the body had so lived that Your name was glorified in her faith and her character, yet I dare not say that from the moment of her regeneration in baptism no word issued from her mouth contrary to Your Command. Your Son, who is Truth, has said: *Whosoever shall say to his brother, Thou fool, shall be in danger of hell fire;* and it would go ill with the most praiseworthy life lived by men, if You were to examine it with Your mercy laid aside! But because You do not enquire too fiercely into our sins, we have hope and confidence of a place with You. Yet if a man reckons up before You the merits he truly has, what is he reckoning except Your own gifts? If only men would know themselves to be but men, so that he that glories would glory in the Lord!

Thus, my Glory and my Life, God of my heart, leaving aside for this time her good deeds, for which I give thanks to Thee in joy, I now pray to Thee for my mother's sins. Grant my prayer through the true Medicine of our wounds, who hung upon the cross and who now sitting at Thy right hand makes intercession for us. I know that she dealt mercifully, and from her heart forgave those who trespassed against her: do Thou also forgive such trespasses as she may have been guilty of in all the years since her baptism, forgive them, Lord, forgive them, I beseech Thee: enter not into judgment with her. Let Thy mercy be exalted above Thy justice for Thy words are true and Thou hast promised that the merciful shall obtain mercy. That they should be merciful is Thy gift who *hast mercy on whom Thou wilt, and wilt have compassion on whom Thou wilt.*

And I believe that Thou hast already done what I am now asking; but be not offended, Lord, at the things my mouth would utter. For on that day when her death was so close, she was not concerned that her body should be sumptuously wrapped or embalmed with spices, nor with any thought of choosing a monument or even for burial in her own country. Of such things she gave us no command, but only desired to be remembered at Thy altar, which she had served without ever missing so much as a day, on which she knew that the holy Victim was offered, *by whom the handwriting is blotted out of the decree that was contrary to us,* by which offering too the enemy was overcome who, reckoning our sins and seeking what may be laid to our charge, found nothing in Him, in whom we are conquerors. Who shall restore to Him his innocent blood? Who shall give Him back the price by which He purchased us and so take us from Him? To this sacrament of our redemption Thy handmaid had bound her soul by the bond of faith. Let none wrest her from Thy protection; let neither the lion nor the dragon bar her way by force or craft. For she will not answer that she owes nothing, lest she should be contradicted and confuted by that cunning accuser: but she will answer that her debts have been remitted by Him, to whom no one can hand back the price which He paid for us, though He owed it not.

So let her rest in peace, together with her husband, for she had no other before nor after him, but served him, in patience bringing forth fruit for Thee, and winning him likewise for Thee. And inspire, O my Lord my God, inspire Thy servants my brethren, Thy sons my masters, whom I serve with heart and voice and pen, that as many of them as read this may remember at Thy altar Thy servant Monica, with Patricius, her husband, by whose bodies Thou didst bring me into this life, though how I know not. May they with loving mind remember these who were my parents in this transitory light, my brethren who serve Thee as our Father in our Catholic mother, and those who are to be fellow-

citizens with me in the eternal Jerusalem, which Thy people
sigh for in their pilgrimage from birth until they come there:
so that what my mother at her end asked of me may be fulfilled more richly in the prayers of so many gained for her
by my Confessions than by my prayers alone.

# BOOK TEN

## CONCLUDES AUGUSTINE'S CONFESSION

Lᴇᴛ me know Thee who knowest me, *let me know Thee even as I am known.* O Thou, the Power of my soul, enter into it and fit it for Thyself, that Thou mayest have it and possess it without spot or wrinkle. This is my hope, this is my prayer, and in this hope do I rejoice when I rightly rejoice. But as for the other things of this life, the more we weep for them the less they deserve our tears, and the less we weep for them, the more we should weep. For behold Thou lovest the truth, and *he that does the truth comes to the light.* I wish to do it in confession, in my heart before Thee, in my writing before many witnesses.

II

And even if I would not confess to You, what could be hidden in me, O Lord, from You to whose eyes the deepest depth of man's conscience lies bare? I should only be hiding You from myself, not myself from You. But now that my groaning is witness that I am displeasing to myself, You shine unto me and I delight in You and love You and yearn for You, so that I am ashamed of what I am and renounce myself and choose You and please neither You nor myself save in You. To You then, O Lord, I am laid bare for what I am. And I have said with what profit I confess to You. For my confession is not by bodily words, or bodily cries, but with the words of the soul and the upward cry of my thought, which Your ear knows. For when I am wicked, confession to You simply means being displeased at myself; when I am good, confession to You means simply not attributing my goodness to myself: for You, O Lord, bless the just man, but first You turn him from ungodliness to justice. And so my confession, O my God, in Your sight is made silently: and yet not silently, for if it makes no sound, yet it cries aloud in my heart. For whatever good I utter to men, You have heard from me before I utter it; and whatever good You hear from me, You have first spoken to me.

### III

What therefore have I to do with men that they should hear my confessions, as if it were they who would cure all that is evil in me? Men are a race curious to know of other men's lives, but slothful to correct their own. Why should they wish to hear from me what I am, when they do not wish to hear from You what they are themselves? And when they hear me confessing of myself, how do they know whether I speak the truth, since *no man knows the things of a man but the spirit of a man that is in him?* Whereas if they hear from You something about themselves, they cannot say: "The Lord is lying." For to hear from You about themselves is simply to know themselves. And who, knowing himself, can say: "It is false," unless himself is lying? But because charity believes all things—that is, all things spoken by those whom it binds to itself and makes one—I, O Lord, confess to You that men may hear, for though I cannot prove to them that my confession is true, yet those will believe me whose ears charity has opened to me.

But do You, O my inmost Physician, make clear to me what profit I gain by it. When the confessions of my past sins—which You have forgiven and covered up, giving me joy in You, changing my life by faith and Your sacrament—are read and heard, they stir up the heart. It no longer lies in the lethargy of despair and says "I cannot," but keeps wakeful in the love of Your mercy and the loveliness of Your grace, by which every weak man is made strong, since by it he is made conscious of his weakness. As for the good, it rejoices them to hear of sins committed in the past by men now free from them: not because these things are sins, but because they were and no longer are.

But again, O Lord my God, to whom daily my conscience makes confession, relying more in the hope of Your mercy than in its own innocence, with what profit, I beseech You, do I confess unto men in Your sight by this book, not what I once was, but what I now am? I have seen and spoken of that other profit. But as to what I now am while I am writing my Confessions, there are many who desire to know —both people who know me personally, and people who do not, but have heard something from me or about me. Yet they have not their ear at my heart, where I am what I am. They wish, therefore, to hear from my own confession what I am inwardly, where they cannot pierce with eye or ear or mind. They desire to know and are prepared to believe, but will they know? The charity by which they are good, tells them that in my confession I do not lie about myself; and this charity in them believes me.

## IV

But for what profit do they wish to hear it? Do they desire to rejoice with me when they hear how close by Your grace I have come to You, and to pray for me when they hear how far I am held from You by my own weight? To such shall I show myself. For it is no small fruit, O Lord my God, that many should give thanks to You for me and many should pray to You for me. Let the mind of my brethren love that in me which You teach to be worthy of love, and grieve for that in me which You teach to be worthy of grief. So let the mind of my brethren act—not the mind of strangers nor the children of strangers, *whose mouth has spoken vanity, and whose right hand is the right hand of iniquity*—but the mind of my brethren who rejoice for what they see good in me and are grieved for what they see ill, but whether they see good or ill still love me. To such shall I show myself: let their breath come faster for my good deeds: let them sigh for my ill. For my good deeds are Your act and Your gift, my ill deeds are my own faults and Your punishments. Let their breath come faster for the one, let them sigh for the other, and let the hymn of praise and the weeping rise up together in Your sight from Your censers which are the hearts of my brethren. And do Thou, Lord, delighted with the odour of Thy holy temple, *have mercy upon me according to Thy great mercy,* and for Thy Name's sake; and in no point deserting what Thou hast begun, supply what is imperfect in me.

This then is the fruit of my confession—the confession not of what I have been, but of what I am—in that I confess not only before You, with inward exultation yet trembling, with inward sorrow yet with hope as well: but also in the ears of the believing sons of men, companions of my joy and sharers of my mortality, my fellow citizens, fellow pilgrims: those who have gone before, and those who are to come after, and those who walk the way of life with me. These are Your servants, my brethren, whom You have chosen that they should be Your sons, my masters whom You have commanded me to serve if I am to live with You and in You. And this Your word to me would be a lesser thing, if it merely commanded me by word and did not go before me in the doing. Thus I do it, in deed and in word, I do it under Your wings, for the peril would be too great were not my soul under Your wings and subject to You, and my infirmity known to You. I am but a little one, yet my Father lives forever and my Protector is sufficient for me. For He is the same who begot me and who watches over me: and You are all my good, You the almighty who are with me even before I am with You. To such then as You command me to serve will I show, not what I was, but what I now am, what I continue to be. But I do not judge myself. Thus therefore let me be heard.

v

For You, O Lord, are my judge, because though *no man knows the things of a man, save the spirit of a man that is in him,* yet there is something of man that the very spirit of man that is in him does not know. But You, Lord, know all of him, for You made him. As for me, although I despise myself in Your sight, and hold myself but dust and ashes, yet

I know something of You which I do not know of myself.
It is true that *now we see through a glass in a dark manner
and not yet face to face*; so that as long as I am on pilgrimage
and not with You, I am more present to myself than to You;
yet I know that You cannot in any way suffer violence,
whereas I do not know which temptations I myself can resist
and which I cannot. But there is hope, because You are *faithful and will not suffer us to be tempted above that which we
are able: but will also make issue with temptation, that we
may be able to bear it.* I will confess therefore what I know of
myself and what I do not know; for what I know of myself
I know through the shining of Your light; and what I do
not know of myself, I continue not to know until my
darkness shall be made as noonday in Your countenance.

VI

It is with no doubtful knowledge, Lord, but with utter
certainty that I love You. You have stricken my heart with
Your word and I have loved You. And indeed heaven and
earth and all that is in them tell me wherever I look that I
should love You, and they cease not to tell it to all men, so
that there is no excuse for them. For *You will have mercy on
whom You will have mercy, and You will show mercy to
whom You will show mercy*: otherwise heaven and earth cry
their praise of You to deaf ears.

But what is it that I love when I love You? Not the beauty
of any bodily thing, nor the order of seasons, not the brightness of light that rejoices the eye, nor the sweet melodies of
all songs, nor the sweet fragrance of flowers and ointments
and spices: not manna nor honey, not the limbs that carnal
love embraces. None of these things do I love in loving my
God. Yet in a sense I do love light and melody and fragrance
and food and embrace when I love my God—the light and
the voice and the fragrance and the food and embrace in
the soul, when that light shines upon my soul which no place
can contain, that voice sounds which no time can take from
me, I breathe that fragrance which no wind scatters, I **eat**

the food which is not lessened by eating, and I lie in the embrace which satiety never comes to sunder. This it is that I love, when I love my God.

And what is this God? I asked the earth and it answered: "I am not He"; and all things that are in the earth made the same confession. I asked the sea and the deeps and the creeping things, and they answered: "We are not your God; seek higher." I asked the winds that blow, and the whole air with all that is in it answered: "Anaximenes was wrong; I am not God." I asked the heavens, the sun, the moon, the stars, and they answered: "Neither are we God whom you seek." And I said to all the things that throng about the gateways of the senses: "Tell me of my God, since you are not He. Tell me something of Him." And they cried out in a great voice: "He made us." My question was my gazing upon them, and their answer was their beauty. And I turned to myself and said: "And you, who are you?" And I answered: "A man." Now clearly there is a body and a soul in me, one exterior, one interior. From which of these two should I have enquired of my God? I had already sought Him by my body, from earth to heaven, as far as my eye could send its beams on the quest. But the interior part is the better, seeing that all my body's messengers delivered to it, as ruler and judge, the answers that heaven and earth and all things in them made when they said: "We are not God," and, "He made us." The inner man knows these things through the ministry of the outer man: I the inner man knew them, I, I the soul, through the senses of the body. I asked the whole frame of the universe about my God and it answered me: "I am not He, but He made me."

Is not the face of the earth clearly seen by all whose senses function properly? Then why does it not give the same answer to all? Animals great and small see it, but cannot interrogate it. For reason does not preside in them to judge upon the evidence their senses bring. But man can interrogate it, and so should be able clearly to see *the invisible things of God understood by things which are made*; but they love these last too much and become subject to them, and subjects cannot judge. All these things refuse to answer those who ask, unless they ask with power to judge. If one man merely sees the world, while another not only sees but interrogates it, the world does not change its speech—that is, its outward appearance which speaks—in such a way as to appear differently to the two men; but presenting exactly the same face to each, it says nothing to the one, but gives answer to the other: or rather it gives its answer to all, but only those understand who compare its voice as it comes through their senses, with the truth that is within them. For truth says to me: "Your God is not heaven or earth or any corporeal thing." So their very nature tells us. For clearly there is less bulk in the part than in the whole. And I tell you, my soul, you are better, since you vivify the whole bulk of the body: you give the body life, which no body can give to a body. But your God is the Life of your life.

VII

I ask again what it is that I love when I love my God? Who is He that is above the topmost point of my soul? By that same soul I shall ascend to Him. I shall mount beyond the power by which I am united to my body, and by which I fill its whole structure with life. Not by that can I find my God: for by that *the horse and the mule which have no understanding* could equally find Him, for there is in them the same power giving life to their bodies. There is another faculty, by which not only do I give life to my body but sense perception likewise, a faculty which the Lord created for me when He commanded the eye not to hear and the ear not to see, but gave me the eye to see by and the ear to hear by, and gave to all the other senses their respective places and functions: which, in their diversity, I the one soul act by. But this faculty also I must mount beyond: for this also the horse and the mule have. They perceive by means of the body.

### VIII

I shall mount beyond this power of my nature, still rising by degrees towards Him who made me. And so I come to the fields and vast palaces of memory, where are stored the innumerable images of material things brought to it by the senses. Further there is stored in the memory the thoughts we think, by adding to or taking from or otherwise modifying the things that sense has made contact with, and all other things that have been entrusted to and laid up in memory, save such as forgetfulness has swallowed in its grave. When I turn to memory, I ask it to bring forth what I want: and some things are produced immediately, some take longer as if they had to be brought out from some more secret place of storage; some pour out in a heap, and while we are actually wanting and looking for something quite different, they hurl themselves upon us in masses as though to say: "May it not be we that you want?" I brush them from the face of my memory with the hand of my heart, until at last the thing I want is brought to light as from some hidden place. Some things are produced just as they are required, easily and in right order; and things that come first give place to those that follow, and giving place are stored up again to be produced when I want them. This is what happens, when I say anything by heart.

In the memory all the various things are kept distinct and in their right categories, though each came into the memory by its own gate. For example, light and all the colors and shapes of bodies come in by the eyes, all the kinds of sound by the ears, all scents by the nostrils, all tastes by the mouth; and by a sense that belongs to the whole body comes in what is hard and what is soft, what is hot or cold, rough or smooth, heavy or light, whether outside the body or inside. All these things the vast recesses, the hidden and unsearchable caverns, of memory receive and store up, to be available and brought to light when need arises: yet all enter by their own various gates to be stored up in memory. Nor indeed do the things themselves enter: only the images of the things perceived by the senses are there for thought to remember them.

And even though we know by which senses they were brought in and laid up in the memory, who can tell how these images were formed? Even when I am in darkness and in silence, I can if I will produce colors in my memory, and distinguish black from white and any other colors if I choose; and sounds do not break in and disturb the image I am considering that came in through the eye, since the sounds themselves were already there and lie stored up apart. For I can summon them too, if I like, and they are immediately present; and though my tongue is at rest and my throat silent I can sing as I will; nor do the images of the colors, although they are as truly present, interfere or interrupt when I call from the storehouse some other thing which came in by the ear. Similarly all other things that were brought in by the other senses and stored up in the memory can be called up at my pleasure: I distinguish the scent of lilies from the scent of violets, though at that instant I smell nothing; and I like honey better than wine, some smooth thing better than rough, though I am not tasting or handling but only remembering.

All this I do inside me, in the huge court of my memory. In my memory are sky and earth and sea, ready at hand along with all the things that I have ever been able to perceive in them and have not forgotten. And in my memory too I meet myself—I recall myself, what I have done, when and where and in what state of mind I was when I did it. In my memory are all the things I remember to have experienced myself or to have been told by others. From the same store I can weave into the past endless new likenesses of things either experienced by me or believed on the strength of things experienced; and from these again I can picture actions and events and hopes for the future; and upon them all I can meditate as if they were present. "I shall do this or that," I say to myself in the vast recess of my mind with its immeasurable store of images of things so great: and this or that follows. "O, if only this or that could be!" or again, "May God prevent this or that!" Such things I say within myself, and when I speak of them the images of all the things I mention are to hand from the same storehouse of memory, and if the images were not there I could not so much as speak of the things.

Great is this power of memory, exceedingly great, O my God, a spreading limitless room within me. Who can reach its uttermost depth? Yet it is a faculty of my soul and belongs to my nature. In fact I cannot totally grasp all that I am. Thus the mind is not large enough to contain itself: but where can that part of it be which it does not contain? Is it outside itself and not within? How can it not contain itself? [How can there be any of itself that is not *in* itself?] As this question struck me, I was overcome with wonder and almost stupor. Here are men going afar to marvel at the heights of mountains, the mighty waves of the sea, the long courses of great rivers, the vastness of the ocean, the movements of the stars, yet leaving themselves unnoticed and not seeing it as marvellous that when I spoke of all these things, I did not see them with my eyes, yet I could not have spoken of them unless these mountains and waves and rivers and stars which I have seen, and the ocean of which I have heard, had been inwardly present to my sight: in my memory, yet with the same vast spaces between them as if I saw them outside me. When I saw them with my eyes, I did not by seeing them swallow them into me; nor are they themselves present in me, but only their images; and I know by what sense of my body each one of them was impressed upon my mind.

IX

These are not the only thoughts to which the immense capaciousness of memory gives rise. In memory also are all such things as we have learned of the liberal sciences and have not forgotten, lying there as if in a more inward place, which yet is no place; and of these I have not the images but the things themselves. For what grammar is or the art of disputation, how many kinds of questions there are—whatever I know of such matters is in my memory not as though I retained the image and left the thing outside, or as though it had sounded in my mind then passed away, like a voice heard by the ear which leaves something by which it can be recalled as though it were sounding, though it sounds no more; or like an odor which, though it passes and is borne away on the wind, affects the sense of smell and so impresses on the memory some image of itself which we can recall and recreate; or like food which certainly has no taste as far as the belly is concerned, yet has a kind of taste in the memory; or like something that has touched the body and been felt and can still be imagined in memory although no longer in contact with us. In these cases the things themselves are not brought into the memory; it is only their images which are seized with such marvellous speed, and stored away marvellously as if in cabinets, and as marvellously brought forth again when we remember.

X

Now when I hear that there are three kinds of questions: whether a thing is, what it is, of what sort it is: I do indeed retain the images of the sounds of which those words are composed, and I know that they passed through the air with a certain noise and now no longer are. But the things themselves which the sounds signified I could not come at by any bodily sense nor see them at all save by my mind; and what I stored in my memory was not their images but the truths themselves. But how they got into me, it is for them to tell if they can. For I run my mind over all the doorways of my body, but I cannot find any door by which they could have come in. For my eyes say: "If they were coloured, we reported them to you"; my ears say: "If they sounded, we gave you notice of them"; the nostrils say: "If they had any smell, they went in through us"; the sense of taste says: "Unless there was any taste in them, there is no use in my being asked"; the sense of touch says: "If the thing is not a body,

I did not handle it, and if I did not handle it, I did not report it to you." Very well then, whence and how did they get into my memory? I do not know. For when I first learned them I was not trusting some other man's mind, but recognized them in my own; and I saw them as true and committed them to my mind as if placing them where I could get at them again whenever I desired. Thus they must have been in my mind even before I learned them, though they were not in my memory. Then where were they, or how did it come that when I heard them spoken I recognized them and said: "It is so, it is true," unless they *were* in my memory already, but so far back, thrust away as it were in such remote recesses, that unless they had been drawn forth by some other man's teaching, I might perhaps never have managed to think of them at all?

## XI

Thus we find that to learn those things which do not come into us as images by the senses, but which we know within ourselves without images and as they actually are, is in reality only to take things that the memory already contained, but scattered and unarranged, and by thinking bring them together, and by close attention have them placed within reach in that same memory: so that things which had formerly lain there scattered and not considered, now come easily and familiarly to us. And my memory carries an immense number of things of this sort, which have already been discovered and, as I have said, placed within reach—the things we are said to have learned and to know. Yet if I ceased to give thought to them for quite a short space of time, they would sink again and fall away into the more remote recesses of the memory, and I should have to think them out afresh and put them together again from the same place—for there is nowhere else for them to have gone—if I am to know them: in other words they must be collected out of dispersion, and indeed the verb *to cogitate* is named from this drawing together. For *cogito* (I think) has the same relation to *cogo* (I put together) as *agito* to *ago* and *factito* to *facio*. But the mind of man has claimed the word *cogitate* completely for its own: not what is put together anywhere else but only what is put together in the mind is called cogitation.

### XII

The memory also contains the innumerable principles and laws of numbers and dimensions; and none of these have been impressed upon it by any bodily sense, seeing that they have neither colour nor sound nor scent nor taste nor feel. I have heard the sounds of the words by which they are expressed when we discuss them, but the sounds are not the same as the truths themselves. For the sounds are of one kind in Greek, quite different in Latin, but the things themselves are neither Greek nor Latin nor of any other language. I have seen the lines drawn by architects, some of them as fine as a spider's web; but the truths are different, they are not the images of such things as the eye of my body has shown me. To know them is to recognize them interiorly without any concept of any kind of body whatsoever. With all my bodily senses I have perceived the numbers we use in counting; but the basic numbers *by* which we count are not the same as these, nor images of these; but really are. Let whoever does not see these truths laugh at me for talking thus: while he laughs at me I shall be sorry for him.

### XIII

All these things I have in my memory, and how I learned them I have in my memory. And I have also heard and have in my memory notions that have been falsely urged against them; and though the notions are false yet it is not false that I remember them. I recall distinguishing between the truths and the fallacious objections: and to see myself now making the distinction is different from remembering the times I made it in the past. Thus I remember that I formerly saw them so, and I lay up in my memory how I see and understand them now, so that I may remember later that I understood them at the present time. And I remember that I remembered just as, if later I recall that I was now able to remember these things, it will be by the power of memory that I shall recall it.

### XIV

My memory also contains the feelings of my mind, not in the mode in which the mind itself has them when it is experiencing them, but in a different mode, proper to the power of memory. For I remember that in the past I was cheerful, but I am not cheerful now; and I remember past sadness yet am not sad. I remember past fears without fear, and past desire without desire. Sometimes the thing is exactly contrary —when I am joyful I remember past sorrow, and in present sorrow remember past joy. Now this would not be remarkable if my memories were only of the body: for the mind is one thing and the body another, and it would not be strange if my mind's joy were not affected by remembering the body's past pain. But the mind and the memory are not two separate things—for when we tell another to remember something we say: "See that you have it in mind"; and when we forget something, we say: "It was not in my mind" or "It escaped my mind." Thus we call the memory mind. Since this is so, how comes it that when I am joyful yet remember past sorrow, so that the mind has joy and the memory sorrow, my mind is joyful because there is joy in it, but my memory is not sorrowful because there is sorrow in it? Surely no one would say that the memory does not belong to the mind. Perhaps one might say that the memory is like the mind's stomach, and joy and sorrow like nice or nasty food; when joy and sorrow are committed to the memory it is as though they had passed into the stomach, where they can lie but not be tasted. It is of course ridiculous to see it like this, yet some sort of resemblance there is.

But note again: when I name these four movements of the mind—desire, joy, fear, sadness—I draw them from my memory; and any discussion I can make of them by defining, or by dividing each according to its own genus and species, I find in my memory what to say and it is from my memory that I bring it forth: yet I am not perturbed by their emotional quality when in memory I call them back; and before I recalled them and meditated upon them, they were there, otherwise it would not have been possible for me to fetch them forth. Perhaps therefore just as food is brought up from the stomach by chewing the cud, so things are brought up from the memory by remembering. But if that is so, why is not the pleasure of the joy or the pain of the sorrow felt in the mouth of his thinking by the man who thus remembers them? Or is this the point of dissimilarity which makes the resemblance incomplete? Indeed would any one be willing to speak of sorrow or fear, if as often as we named them we had to feel sorrow or fear? Yet we could not speak of them unless we found in our memory not only the sound of their names according to images impressed upon it by the senses of the body, but also the notions of the things themselves, which notions we did not receive by any gate of the body; it was the mind, aware of them through the experience of its own passions, which committed them to the memory; or, as often happens, the memory of itself retained them, although the mind did not commit them to it.

## XV

But whether all this is by images or not, it is not easy to say. For I mention a stone or the sun, when the things themselves are not present to my senses, yet images of the things are present in my memory. When I name some pain of the body, it is not present, since I am not in pain; yet unless there were some image of it in my memory, I should not know what to say of it or how to differentiate it in thought from pleasure. I name bodily health, when I am in bodily health, and the thing itself is present in me; all the same, unless there were some image of it in my memory, I could not possibly recall what the sound of the name signified; nor would sick people know what was meant by the word health, in the absence of the thing itself from the body, unless some image were preserved by the power of memory. I name the numbers we use in counting: and it is not their images that are in my memory but themselves. I mention the sun's image, and this too is in my memory: yet it is not the image of its image that I recall but the image itself: that is what is present when I remember it. I name memory and I recognize what I am naming, but where do I recognize it except in my memory? Can the memory possibly be present to itself by its image and not rather by its own being?

XVI

I can also name forgetfulness and know what I mean by the word; but how should I recognize the thing itself unless I remembered it? I am not speaking of the sound of the word, but of the thing the sound signifies; for if I had forgotten the thing, I should be unable to remember what the sound stood for. When I remember memory my memory itself is present to itself by itself; but when I remember forgetfulness, then memory and forgetfulness are present together—forgetfulness which I remember, memory by which I remember. But what is forgetfulness except absence of memory? How then can that be present for me to remember, which when it is present means that I cannot remember? If what we remember we hold in our memory, and if, unless we remembered forgetfulness, we should not on hearing the word recognize what is meant by it, then forgetfulness is contained in the memory. Therefore that is present, to keep us from forgetting it, which when it is present we do forget. Are we to understand from this that when we remember forgetfulness, it is not present to the memory in itself but by its image: because if it were present in itself it would cause us not to remember but to forget? Who can analyze this, or understand how it can be?

Assuredly, Lord, I toil with this, toil within myself: I have become to myself a soil laborious and of heavy sweat. For I am not now considering the parts of the heavens, or measur-

ing the distances of the stars, or seeking how the earth is
held in space; it is I who remember, I, my mind. It is not
remarkable if things that I am not are far from my knowledge: but what could be closer to me than myself? Yet the
power of memory in me I do not understand, though without memory I could not even name myself. What am I to
say, when I see so clearly that I remember forgetfulness? Am
I to say that something I remember is not in my memory?
Or am I to say that forgetfulness is in my memory to keep
me from forgetting? Either would be absurd. Is there a third
possibility? Could I say that the image of forgetfulness is
retained in my memory, not forgetfulness itself, when I
remember it? But how could I say this since if the image of
a thing is imprinted on the memory, the thing itself must
first have been present, for the image to be able to be imprinted? Thus I remember Carthage and such other places
as I have been in; I remember the faces of men I have
seen and things reported by the other senses; I remember
the health or sickness of the body. For when these were
present, the memory received their images from them, and
these remained present to be gazed on and thought about by
the mind when in their absence I might choose to remember
them. It follows that if forgetfulness is retained in the memory by means of an image and not in itself, then itself must
at some time have been present for its image to be received.
But when it was present, how did it write its image in my
memory since by its presence it destroys what it finds noted
there? At any rate whatever the manner of it, however incomprehensible and inexplicable, I am certain that I do remember forgetfulness, although by forgetfulness what we remember is effaced.

## XVII

Great is the power of memory, a thing, O my God, to be
in awe of, a profound and immeasurable multiplicity; and
this thing is my mind, this thing am I. What then am I, O my
God? What nature am I? A life powerfully various and mani-

fold and immeasurable. In the innumerable fields and dens and caverns of my memory, innumerably full of innumerable kinds of things, present either by their images as are all bodies, or in themselves as are our mental capacities, or by certain notions or awarenesses, like the affections of the mind —for even when the mind is not experiencing these, the memory retains them, although whatever is in the memory is in the mind too—in and through all these does my mind range, and I move swiftly from one to another and I penetrate them as deeply as I can, but find no end. So great is the force of memory, so great the force of life even while man lives under sentence of death here.

What am I to do now, O my true Life, my God? I shall mount beyond this my power of memory, I shall mount beyond it, to come to You, O lovely Light. What have You to say to me? In my ascent by the mind to You who abide above me, I shall mount up beyond that power of mine called memory, longing to attain to touch You at the point where that contact is possible and to cleave to You at the point where it is possible to cleave. For the beasts and the birds have memory, or else they could never find their dens or their nests or all the other things their way of life needs; indeed without memory they would be unable to have a way of life. So I must pass beyond memory to come to Him who separated me from the four footed beasts and made me wiser than the birds of the air. I shall pass beyond memory to find You, O truly good and certain Loveliness, and where shall I find You? If I find You beyond my memory, then shall I be without memory of You. And how shall I find You if I am without memory of You?

### XVIII

The woman who had lost a groat sought it with a light. But she would not have found it if she had not remembered it. For when it was found, how should she have known whether it was what she sought, if she had not remembered it? I remember that I have often lost things and looked for them and found them again and I know this, that when I was looking for any such and someone asked me: "Is this it? Is that it?" I kept on saying "No," until the thing I was looking for was produced. But unless I had remembered it, whatever it was, even if it had been offered to me I should not have found it because I should not have recognized it. It is always thus when we seek and find anything we have lost. For if a thing is absent from the eye but not from the memory—as any visible body may be—its image is held within us and is sought for until the thing itself is restored to our sight. And when it has been found, it is recognized by the image within us. We do not say that we have found what was lost unless we recognize it, nor can we recognize it unless we remember it. It was only lost to the eyes; it was preserved in the memory.

## XIX

When then the memory itself loses anything, as happens when we forget something and try to recall it, where are we to look for it save in the memory? And if the memory chances to offer us something else instead, we reject it until we come upon the thing we are looking for. And when we come upon it we say: "This is it"; but we could not say this unless we recognized it, and we could not recognize it unless we remembered it. Yet certainly we had forgotten it. May it be that the whole of it had not escaped and that by the part which we still held we looked for the other part, because the memory—feeling that it did not have all that was accustomed to go together, and moving haltingly because of the loss of what it was used to—was demanding to have the missing part restored? Thus if we see or think about some man known to us, but have forgotten his name and are trying to remember it, if some other name occurs to us we do not accept it because it was not our habit to think of that name with that man; thus we go on rejecting until the name occurs with which the mind is satisfied, because it had been used to associating it with the man. But where does that name come back from except from the memory? For even when it is through being reminded by something else that we recognize someone's name, it is still by memory that we do it, for we do not hold it as some new thing learned, but by memory we are sure that this is what the name was. But were the name utterly blotted out of the mind, we should not remember it even if we were reminded. For even the thing we remember that we forgot, we had not utterly forgotten. For if we had utterly forgotten it, we should not even be able to think of looking for it.

XX

How then do I seek You, O Lord? For in seeking You, my God, it is happiness that I am seeking. I shall seek You, that my soul may live. For my body lives by my soul and my soul lives by You. What *is* the way to seek for happiness, then? Because I have no happiness till I can say, and say rightly: "Enough, it is there." How am I to seek it? Should it be by way of remembrance, as though I had forgotten it but am still aware that I have forgotten it, or is it by a kind of appetite to learn it as something unknown to me—whether as something I never have known, or something I have known and forgotten and do not even remember that I have forgotten? Is not happiness precisely what all seek, so that there is not one who does not desire it? But where did they know it, that they should desire it so? Where have they seen it, that they should love it? Obviously we have it in some way, but I do not know how. There is indeed a way by which one may have it and be blessed in having it, and there are some who have the hope of it and are blessed in that hope. These have it in a lesser way than those who are happy in its actual possession, yet they are better than those who are not happy either in the thing itself or in the hope of it. Even these last, unless they had it in some manner, could not even desire to be happy: yet it is quite certain that they do desire it. Somehow or other they have come to know it, that is they have some sort of knowledge of it. I strive to know whether or not this knowledge is in the memory, for if it is then we have at some past time been happy—whether individually, or in that man who committed the first sin, in whom we all died and of whom we are all in misery descended. Which of these two I do not ask now: my concern is whether happiness is in the memory. For I repeat we should not love it unless we had some knowledge of it. We have of course heard the name and we all admit that we want the thing, for we do not get any joy from the mere sound of the word. For when a Greek hears the word pronounced in Latin, he gets no pleasure because he does not know what has been said; but we who speak Latin get the same pleasure from it as he when he hears the word in Greek; for the thing itself is neither Greek nor Latin, but Greeks and Latins and men of all tongues are ever hot upon its pursuit. Thus happiness is known to all, for if they could be asked with one voice whether they wish for happiness, there is no doubt whatever that they would all answer yes. And this could not be unless the thing itself, signified by the word, lay somehow in their memory.

<h3 style="text-align:center">XXI</h3>

But does it lie in the memory in the way that I remember Carthage which I have seen? No. Happiness is not to be seen by the eye because it is not a body. Is it in the memory as we remember numbers? No. For he who has knowledge of numbers does not go on trying to gain it; but we do have knowledge of happiness, and so we love it, and yet wish to gain it in order to be happy. Is it in our memory then as eloquence is? No. For although when the word eloquence is heard, people recognize the thing signified, though they are not eloquent themselves: and again many would like to be eloquent, so that it appears that it must be in their knowledge: the position is different, because by their bodily senses they have observed eloquence in others, have enjoyed it, and so have wished to possess it. (Though obviously they would not enjoy it unless there were also an interior notion [as well as sense perception], and would not desire it unless they had enjoyed it.) But there is no bodily sense by which we experience happiness in others.

Is it in the memory as we remember joy? It may be so. For even when I am sad I remember my joy, just as when I am unhappy I remember happiness; nor did I ever by any bodily sense see my joy or hear it or smell it or taste it or touch it. But I experienced it in my mind, at such times as I happened to rejoice, and the knowledge of it remained in my memory, so that I am able to recall it—sometimes with loathing, sometimes with desire, according to the diversity of the things I remember having enjoyed. For I have in the past been all joyful at vile actions which I now detest and execrate when I recall them; at other times I rejoice in good and honourable things which I remember with longing, though I may no longer have them, so that it is with sadness that I recall former joy.

But where and when had I any experience of happiness, that I should remember it and love it and long for it? And not I alone, or a handful of men besides, but surely all men whatsoever want to be happy. And unless we knew the thing with certain knowledge, we could not will it with so certain a will. Yet notice this: If two men were asked whether they want to go with the army, it might happen that one of them would say Yes, and the other No: but if they were asked whether they wanted to be happy, each would instantly and without hesitation say Yes—and the one would have no reason for wanting to go with the army nor the other for not wanting to go, save to be happy. May it be that one gets joy from this, one from that? All agree that they desire happiness, just as they would agree, if they were asked, that they desire joy: and indeed they think joy and happiness are the same thing. One man may get it one way, another another, yet all alike are striving to attain this one thing, namely that they may be joyful. It is something that no one can say that he has had no experience of, which is why he finds it in his memory and recognizes it when he hears the word *happiness*.

## XXII

Far be it, O Lord, far be it from the heart of Thy servant who makes this confession to Thee, far be it from me to think that I am happy for any or every joy that I may have. For there is a joy which is not given to the ungodly but only to those who love Thee for Thy own sake, whose joy is Thyself. And this is happiness, to be joyful in Thee and for Thee and because of Thee, this and no other. Those who think happiness is any other, pursue a joy that is apart from Thee and is no true joy. Yet their will is not wholly without some image of joy.

## XXIII

Thus it is not certain that all men do desire to be happy, since there are those who do not desire to rejoice in You, O God: and as this rejoicing is the only happiness, they do not really desire happiness. Or it may be that all men do desire true happiness but because *the flesh lusts against the spirit and the spirit against the flesh, so that they cannot do what they would*, they fall to what they can, and thus are content: because what they cannot do they do not want to do with sufficient intensity to make them able to do it. I ask all men whether they would rather have their joy in the truth or in a falsehood: they reply as unhesitatingly that they would rather have their joy in the truth as that they wish for happiness. Now joy in truth is happiness: for it is joy in You, God, who are Truth, my Light, the Salvation of my countenance and my God. This happiness all desire, this which alone is happiness all desire, for all desire to have joy in truth. I have met many who wished to deceive, but not one who wished to be deceived. But where have they come to know happiness, save where they came to know truth likewise? For they love truth, since they do not wish to be deceived; and when they love happiness, which as we have seen is simply joy in truth, they must love truth also: and they could not love it unless there were some knowledge of it in their memory.

That being so, why do they not rejoice in it? Why are they not happy? Because they are much more concerned over things which are more powerful to make them unhappy than truth is to make them happy, for they remember truth so slightly. There is but a dim light in men; let them walk, let them walk, lest darkness overtake them.

Why does truth call forth hatred? Why is Your servant treated as an enemy by those to whom he preaches the truth, if happiness is loved, which is simply joy in truth? Simply because truth is loved in such a way that those who love some other thing want it to be the truth, and, precisely because they do not wish to be deceived, are unwilling to be convinced that they are deceived. Thus they hate the truth for the sake of that other thing which they love because they take it for truth. They love truth when it enlightens them, they hate truth when it accuses them. Because they do not wish to be deceived and do wish to deceive, they love truth when it reveals itself, and hate it when it reveals them. Thus it shall reward them as they deserve: those who do not wish to be revealed by truth, truth will unmask against their will, but it will not reveal itself to them. Thus, thus, even thus, does the human mind, blind and inert, vile and ill-behaved, desire to keep itself concealed, yet desire that nothing should be concealed from itself. But the contrary happens to it—it cannot lie hidden from truth, but only truth from it. Even so, for all its worthlessness, the human mind would rather find its joy in truth than falsehood. So that it shall be happy if, with no other thing to distract, it shall one day come to rejoice in that sole Truth by which all things are true.

## XXIV

See now how great a space I have covered in my memory, in search of Thee, O Lord; and I have not found Thee outside it. For I find nothing concerning Thee but what I have remembered from the time I first learned of Thee. From that time, I have never forgotten Thee. For where I found

truth, there I found my God, who is Truth Itself, and this I
have not forgotten from the time I first learned it. Thus
from the time I learned of Thee, Thou hast remained in my
memory, and there do I find Thee, when I turn my mind
to Thee and find delight in Thee. These are my holy delights, which in Thy mercy Thou hast given me, looking
upon my poverty.

### XXV

But where in my memory do You abide, Lord, where in
my memory do You abide? What resting-place have You
claimed as Your own, what sanctuary built for Yourself? You
have paid this honour to my memory, that You deign to
abide in it; but I now come to consider in what part of it
You abide. In recalling You to mind I have mounted
beyond those parts of memory which I have in common with
the beasts, in that I did not find You among the images of
corporeal things; and I came to those parts in which are kept
the affections of my mind, and I could not find You there.
And I came in to the innermost seat of my mind—which
the mind has in my memory, since the mind remembers itself—and You were not there: because, just as You are not
a corporeal image, or any affection of any living man such as
we have when we are glad or sad, when we desire, fear, remember, forget and all such things: so You are not the mind
itself, because You are the Lord God of the mind, and all
these things suffer change, but You remain unchangeable
over all: and yet You deign to dwell in my memory, ever since
the time I first learned of You. And indeed why do I seek
in what place of my memory You dwell as though there
were places in my memory? Certain I am that You dwell in
it, because I remember You since the time I first learned
of You, and because I find You in it when I remember You.

### XXVI

In what place then did I find You to learn of You? For
You were not in my memory, before I learned of You. Where

then did I find You to learn of You, save in Yourself, above myself? Place there is none, we go this way and that, and place there is none. You, who are Truth, reside everywhere to answer all who ask counsel of You, and in one act reply to all though all seek counsel upon different matters. And You answer clearly, but all do not hear clearly. All ask what they wish, but do not always hear the answer that they wish. That man is Your best servant who is not so much concerned to hear from You what he wills as to will what he hears from You.

### XXVII

Late have I loved Thee, O Beauty so ancient and so new; late have I loved Thee! For behold Thou wert within me, and I outside; and I sought Thee outside and in my unloveliness fell upon those lovely things that Thou hast made. Thou wert with me and I was not with Thee. I was kept from Thee by those things, yet had they not been in Thee, they would not have been at all. Thou didst call and cry to me and break open my deafness: and Thou didst send forth Thy beams and shine upon me and chase away my blindness: Thou didst breathe fragrance upon me, and I drew in my breath and do now pant for Thee: I tasted Thee, and now hunger and thirst for Thee: Thou didst touch me, and I have burned for Thy peace.

### XXVIII

When once I shall be united to Thee with all my being, there shall be no more grief and toil, and my life will be alive, filled wholly with Thee. Thou dost raise up him whom Thou dost fill; whereas being not yet filled with Thee I am a burden to myself. The pleasures of this life for which I should weep are in conflict with the sorrows of this life in which I should rejoice, and I know not on which side stands the victory. Woe is me, Lord, have pity on me! For I have likewise sorrows which are evil and these are in conflict with joys that are good, and I know not on which side stands the victory. Woe is me, Lord have mercy upon me! Woe is me! See, I do not hide my wounds: Thou art the physician, I the sick man; Thou art merciful, I need mercy. Is not the life of man on earth a trial? Who would choose trouble and difficulty? Thou dost command us to endure them, not to love them. No one loves what he endures, though he may love to endure. For though he rejoices at his endurance, yet he would rather that there were nothing to endure. In adversity I desire prosperity, in prosperity I fear adversity. Yet what middle place is there between the two, where man's life may be other than trial? There is woe and woe again in the prosperity of this world, woe from the fear of adversity, woe from the corruption of joy! There is woe in the adversity of this world, and a second woe and a third, from the longing for prosperity, and because adversity itself is hard, and for fear that endurance may break! Is not man's life upon earth trial without intermission?

### XXIX

All my hope is naught save in Thy great mercy. Grant what Thou dost command, and command what Thou wilt. Thou dost command continence. And *when I knew*, as it is said, *that no one could be continent unless God gave it, even this was a point of wisdom, to know whose gift it was.* For by continence we are collected and bound up into unity within ourself, whereas we had been scattered abroad in multiplicity. Too little does any man love Thee, who loves some other thing together with Thee, loving it not on account of Thee, O Thou Love, who art ever burning and never extinguished! O Charity, my God, enkindle me! Thou dost command continence: grant what Thou dost command and command what Thou wilt.

### XXX

Assuredly You command that I contain myself from *the lust of the flesh, the lust of the eyes, and the pride of life.* You commanded me also to abstain from fornication, and in the matter of marriage You advised me a better course though You allowed me a less good. And since You gave me the power, it was so done, even before I became a dispenser of Your Sacrament. Yet there still live in my memory the images of those things, of which I have already spoken much, which my long habit had fixed there. When I am awake they beset me though with no great power, but in sleep not only seeming pleasant, but even to the point of consent and the likeness of the act itself. The illusion of that image is of such avail in my soul and in my flesh, that mere visions persuade me in sleep as the realities could not persuade me when I am awake. Surely I am myself in sleep, O Lord my God? Yet there is such a difference between myself and myself, divided by that moment in which from waking I fall asleep, from sleeping I wake! Where is my reason, which when I am awake resists such suggestions, and would remain unshaken were the realities themselves presented? Is my reason closed when my eyes close? Does it fall asleep with the bodily senses? And if so how does it happen that even in dreams I often resist, mindful of my purpose, and remain most chastely fixed in it, giving no consent to such temptations? Yet there is this much difference that even when it falls out otherwise, upon waking I return to peace of conscience; and in the difference between the two states discover that I did not commit the act, though I grieve that in some way or other it was done in me.

Is not Thy hand powerful, O God almighty, to heal all the diseases of my soul, and with more abundant grace quench the lascivious motions even of my sleep? Thou, O Lord, wilt more and more increase Thy gifts in me, that my soul may follow me to Thee, utterly freed from the hold of concupiscence: so that it may not be in revolt against itself, and even in dreams may not commit, much less consent to, such baseness of corruption, by means of sense images, unto pollution of the body. For it is no great matter for the Almighty, who is able to do all things more abundantly than we can ask or understand, to pre-

vent any such thing—or even the smallest vestige of it,
so small that a mere nod would restrain it—winning the
chaste mind even in sleep, even while I am in the prime of
life. But now I confess to my good Lord what I still am, in
this way of evil; rejoicing with trembling in what Thou hast
given me and grieving that I am not yet made perfect, hoping
that Thou wilt perfect Thy mercies in me unto the fullness
of peace: the peace which my inward being and my outward shall have with Thee when *death shall be swallowed
up in victory*.

### XXXI

Another evil is of the day, and would that it were
sufficient unto it. We repair the daily deteriorations of the
body by eating and drinking, until the day when You will
*destroy both the belly and the meats*, for You will kill our
emptiness with a marvellous fullness, and You will clothe
this corruptible with eternal incorruption. But for the
present time the necessity is sweet to me, and I fight against
that sweetness lest I be taken captive by it. I wage daily
war upon it by fasting, bringing my body again and
again into subjection; but the pain this gives me is driven
away by the pleasure [of eating and drinking]. For hunger
and thirst really are painful: they burn and kill, like
fever, unless food comes as medicine for their healing. And
since this medicine is ready to hand, from the comfort of
Your gifts, in which earth and sea and sky serve our infirmity, this very infirmity is called delight.

This You taught me, that I should learn to take my food
as a kind of medicine. But while I am passing from the pain
of hunger to the satisfaction of sufficiency, in that very
passage the snare of concupiscence lies in wait for me. For
the passage is itself a pleasure, yet there is no other way to
achieve sufficiency than that which necessity forces us to
travel. And while we eat and drink for the sake of health,
yet a perilous enjoyment runs at the heels of health and often
enough tries to run ahead of it: so that what I say I am

doing and really desire to do for my health's sake, I do in fact for the sake of the enjoyment. For there happens not to be the same measure for both: what suffices for health is too little for enjoyment; so that often it is not at all clear whether it is the necessary care of my body calling for more nourishment, or the deceiving indulgence of greed wanting to be served. Because of this uncertainty my wretched soul is glad, and uses it as a cover and an excuse, rejoicing that it does not clearly appear what is sufficient for the needs of health, so that under the cloak of health it may shelter the business of pleasure.

Day after day I fight against these temptations, and I call upon Thy right hand and to Thee refer my perplexities, for I have no clear guidance upon this matter. I hear the word of my God commanding me: *Let not your hearts be overcharged with surfeiting and drunkenness and the cares of this life*. Drunkenness is far from me, and Thou wilt have mercy that it may never come near me, but overeating has sometimes crept up on Thy servant: Thou wilt have mercy, that it may depart from me. *For no man can be continent unless Thou give it.*

Many things You give us in answer to prayer, and whatever good we received before we prayed, we received from You: even that we should come to know that we had received it from You, we received from You. Never was I a drunkard, but I have known drunkards made sober by You. Therefore I know that it is Your doing that those are not drunkards who never were, just as it is Your doing that those who were drunkards are drunkards no longer, and by Your doing also that both sorts know that it is Your doing. Another voice of Yours I also heard: *Go not after thy lusts: but turn away from thy own will*. And this saying also I heard and very much loved: *For neither if we eat shall we have the more: nor if we eat not, shall we have the less*: that is to say, that the one will not make me abundant nor the other destitute. And again I heard: *For I have learned in whatsoever state I am, to be content therewith. I know both how to abound and how to suffer need. I can do all things in Him who strengthens me.* There truly speaks a soldier of a heavenly army, not dust, as we are. But remember, Lord, that we are dust, and that You made man of dust, that he was lost and is found. Nor could he do this of his own power, for he was dust too—I mean this same Paul, whom I loved as I heard him say in the breath of Your inspiration: *I can do all things in Him who strengthens me.*

Strengthen me, that I may be able, grant what Thou dost command and command what Thou wilt. Paul confesses that he has received and when he glories, it is in the Lord that he glories. Another also I heard begging: *Take from me the greediness of the belly.* From this it is clear, O holy God, that when what You command is done, it is You who give the power. You have taught me, Good Father, that *to the clean all things are clean,* but *it is evil for that man who eats with offense,* that *every creature of thine is good and nothing should be rejected that is received with thanksgiving;* that *meat does not commend us to God* and that *no man may judge us in meat or in drink;* that *he who eats should not despise him that eats not,* and that *he who eats not should not judge him that eats.* These things have I learned, thanks and praise unto Thee, my God, my Master, who dost knock at the door of my ears and illumine my heart: deliver me from all temptation for it is not any uncleanness in the meat that I fear but the uncleanness of my own gluttony. I know that permission was given to Noe to eat of every kind of meat that was good for food: that Elias was fed with flesh: that John the Baptist, though his abstinence was marvellous, ate of animals—the locusts to wit which were granted him for food—and was not polluted. And again I know that Esau was defrauded owing to his greediness for the pottage of lentils; and that David blamed himself for longing for a drink of water: and that our King was tempted not by meat but by bread. Therefore the Israelites in the desert deserved to be rebuked, not because they desired meat but because in their desire for meat they murmured against the Lord.

Placed amidst these temptations, I strive daily against greediness in eating and drinking. For this is not the kind of thing I can resolve once and for all to cut off and touch no more, as I could with fornication. For the reins of the throat are to be held somewhere between too lightly and too tightly. Who is he, Lord, that is not carried somewhat beyond the limits of the necessary? If such a man there be, he is great. Let him magnify Your name. But I am not he, for I am a sinful man. Yet I too magnify Your name, and He intercedes with You for my sins who conquered the world, who numbers me among the weak members of His body, for *Thy eyes did see my imperfect being, and in Thy book all shall be written.*

### XXXII

As for the allurement of sweet scents, I am not much troubled: when they are absent I do not seek them; when they are present, I do not refuse them: yet at any time I do not mind being without them. At least so I seem to myself; perhaps I am deceived. For that darkness is lamentable in which the possibilities in me are hidden from myself: so that my mind, questioning itself upon its own powers, feels that it cannot lightly trust its own report: because what is already in it does for the most part lie hidden, unless experience brings it to light: and in this life, which is rightly called one continuing trial, no man ought to be oversure that though he is capable of becoming better instead of worse, he is not actually becoming worse instead of better. Our one hope, our one confidence, our one firm promise is Your mercy.

### XXXIII

The pleasures of the ear did indeed draw me and hold me more tenaciously, but You have set me free. Yet still when I hear those airs, in which Your words breathe life, sung with sweet and measured voice, I do, I admit, find a certain satisfaction in them, yet not such as to grip me too close, for I can depart when I will. Yet in that that they are received into me along with the truths which give them life, such airs seek in my heart a place of no small honour, and I find it hard to know what is their due place. At times indeed it seems to me that I am paying them greater honour than is their due —when, for example, I feel that by those holy words my mind is kindled more religiously and fervently to a flame of piety because I hear them sung than if they were not sung: and I observe that all the varying emotions of my spirit have modes proper to them in voice and song, whereby, by some secret affinity, they are made more alive. It is not good that the mind should be enervated by this bodily pleasure. But it often ensnares me, in that the bodily sense does not accompany the reason as following after it in proper order, but having been admitted to aid the reason, strives to run before and take the lead. In this matter I sin unawares, and then grow aware.

Yet there are times when through too great a fear of this temptation, I err in the direction of over-severity—even to the point sometimes of wishing that the melody of all the lovely airs with which David's Psalter is commonly sung should be banished not only from my own ears, but from the Church's as well: and that seems to me a safer course, which I remember often to have heard told of Athanasius, bishop of Alexandria, who had the reader of the psalm utter it with so little modulation of the voice that he seemed to be saying it rather than singing it. Yet when I remember the tears I shed, moved by the songs of the Church in the early days of my new faith: and again when I see that I am moved not by the singing but by the things that are sung—when they are sung with a clear voice and proper modulation—I recognize once more the usefulness of this practice. Thus I fluctuate between the peril of indulgence and the profit I have found: and on the whole I am inclined—though I am not propounding any irrevocable opinion—to approve the custom of singing in church, that by the pleasure of the ear the weaker minds may be roused to a feeling of devotion. Yet whenever it happens that I am more moved by the singing than by the thing that is sung, I admit that I have grievously sinned, and then I should wish rather not to have heard the singing. See in what a state I am! Weep with me and weep for me, all you who feel within yourselves that goodness from which good actions come. Those of you who have no such feeling will not be moved by what I am saying. But do Thou, O Lord my God, hear me and look upon me and see me and pity me and heal me, Thou in whose eyes I have become a question to myself: and that is my infirmity.

### XXXIV

There remains the pleasure of the eyes of my flesh, of which I now make confession. Let the ear of Your Church, the fraternal loving ear of Your Church, hearken: that I may finish what I have to say of the temptations of bodily pleasure which still solicit me, while *I groan, desiring to be clothed with our habitation that is from heaven.* My eyes love the diverse forms of beauty, brilliant and pleasing colors. Let these things not take possession of my soul; let God possess it, who made these things and made them exceedingly good: yet He is my good, not they. For they affect me in all the waking hours of every day, nor do I find any respite from them such as I do sometimes find in silence from all the voices of song. For light, the queen of colors, suffusing all the things I see whenever I am abroad in daylight, entices me as it flows before my sight in all its variousness, even though I am busy upon something else and not observing it. For it works its way into me with such power that if it is suddenly withdrawn, I desire it with great longing; and if it is absent too long, it saddens my mind.

O Light that Tobias beheld when though his eyes were closed in blindness he taught his son the way of life, and went before him with the feet of charity and did not err; Light that Isaac beheld when the eyes of his body were heavy and dim

with age and it was granted him to bless his sons though
he could not discern one from the other, yet by the act of
blessing he did discern between them; Light that Jacob
beheld when, though his eyes were dim in his old age, his
heart was luminous and he shed light upon the tribes of the
people to come, foreshown in the persons of his sons: and
he laid upon his grandchildren, the sons of Joseph, hands
mystically reversed [the right hand upon the younger, the
left hand upon the older] not as their father seeing them
from without directed, but as though he were within them
and discerned from within. This is the true Light; it is one:
and all who see it and love it are one. But that corporeal
light of which I have spoken seasons the life of this world
for its blind lovers with a dangerous enticingness. Yet those
who have the knowledge to praise You for that light take
up its praise in Your hymn, "O God, Creator of all," and
are not carried away by it in sleep [of soul]. Of such I desire
to be. I resist the enticements of the eye lest the feet with
which I walk Your road should be tangled in their snare,
and I raise the eyes of my soul to You that You may pluck
my feet from that snare. Repeatedly You pluck them out
for indeed they are ensnared. But You do not cease to pluck
them out, however often I fall into the snares that are spread
all about us. For *Thou shalt neither slumber nor sleep, that
keepest Israel.*

How innumerable are the things made by every kind of
art and workmanship in clothes, shoes, vessels and such like,
in pictures also and every kind of statue—far beyond necessary and moderate use and any meaning of devotion—that
men have added for the delight of their eyes, going abroad
from themselves after the things they have themselves
made, interiorly abandoning Him by whom they were
made and destroying what He made in them. But I, O my
God and my Glory, I too utter a hymn to Thee and offer
my praise as sacrifice to Him who sanctifies me: for all that
loveliness which passes through men's minds into their skill-
ful hands comes from that supreme Loveliness which is above

our souls, which my soul sighs for day and night. From the Supreme Beauty those who make and seek after exterior beauty derive the measure by which they judge of it, but not the measure by which it should be used. Yet this measure too is there, and they do not see it: for if they did they would not wander far from it, but would preserve their strength only for Thee and would not dissipate it upon delights that grow wearisome. But I, who speak thus and see thus, yet entangle my feet in these lower things of beauty; but Thou wilt pluck me forth, Lord, Thou wilt pluck me forth, because Thy mercy is before my eyes. For I in my wretchedness am caught and held captive, and Thou in Thy mercy wilt pluck me out—sometimes without my feeling it, because I had not wholly fallen within the trap: but sometimes I feel the pain of being drawn out, because I had fallen deep.

## XXXV

At this point I mention another form of temptation, more various and dangerous. For over and above that lust of the flesh which lies in the delight of all our senses and pleasures —whose slaves are wasted unto destruction as they go far from You—there can also be in the mind itself, through those same bodily senses, a certain vain desire and curiosity, not of taking delight in the body, but of making experiments with the body's aid, and cloaked under the name of learning and knowledge. Because this is in the appetite to know, and the eyes are the chief of the senses we use for attaining knowledge, it is called in Scripture the lust of the eyes. For "to see" belongs as a property to the eyes; yet we apply the word also to the other senses, when we use them for gaining knowledge. Thus we do not say: "Hear how it flashes," or "Smell how bright it is," or "Taste how it shines," or "Touch how it glows": because all these things are said to be seen. Yet we do say not only "See how it shines," something that only the eyes can perceive; but also "See how it sounds," "see how it smells," "see how it tastes," "see how hot it is." Thus the experience of the senses as a whole, as has been said, is called the lust of the eyes. Because though the function of seeing belongs properly to the eyes, yet we apply it to the other senses by analogy when they are in pursuit of the truth about anything.

In this it is easy to distinguish between the way in which the senses serve pleasure and the way in which they serve curiosity. Pleasure goes after objects that are beautiful to see, hear, smell, taste, touch; but curiosity for the sake of experiment can go after quite contrary things, not in order to experience their unpleasantness, but through a mere itch to experience and find out. What pleasure can there be in seeing a mangled corpse, which is only horrible? Yet if there happens to be one anywhere about, people flock to it to be saddened and sickened: indeed they are in terror that they may dream about it. So that you would think that when they are awake they would not go to see it unless either they were dragged there by force, or some false report that the sight was beautiful had drawn them. It is the same with the other senses which it would be long to follow up. Because of this disease of curiosity you have the various freaks shown in the theatres. Thus men proceed to investigate the phenomena of nature—the part of nature external to us—though the knowledge is of no value to them: for they wish to know simply for the sake of knowing. We have a similar thing when for the sake of the same perverted learning inquiry is made by way of magic. And the same happens even in religion: God is tempted when signs and wonders are demanded, not for any purpose of salvation, but solely for the experience of seeing them.

In this immense forest of snares and perils, I have cut off and thrust from my heart many sins, as You have given me to do, O God of my salvation; yet when would I dare to say —with so many things of the sort buzzing about our daily life on every side—when dare I say that no such thing can draw me to look at it or through vain curiosity to desire it? Certainly the theatres no longer attract me, nor do I care to know the course of the stars, nor has my mind ever sought answers from the dead: all sacrilegious rites I detest. But, O Lord my God, to whom I owe my humble undivided service, by what subtleties of suggestion has the enemy worked upon me to desire some sign from You! I beseech You, by our King and by Jerusalem our one pure homeland, that just as any consent to such a temptation has been far from me, so it may be ever further. When I ask You for the salvation of anyone, the end of my intention is quite different: for You do as You will, and You give me the grace, and ever will give me the grace, to accept and not question.

Yet in how many tiny and inconsiderable trifles is this curiosity of ours daily tempted: and how often we slip, who shall number? When people tell idle stories, it happens only too often that we first endure them, lest we give offense to the weak, and then little by little find ourselves listening willingly. I no longer go to the Games to see a dog chasing a hare, but if in going through a field I come upon the same thing, the chase may easily draw me off from some serious thought and concentrate me upon itself, forcing me from my path not by the body of my horse but by the inclination of my heart; and indeed unless You quickly showed me my infirmity and admonished me, either by some train of thought to rise from the actual sight to You, or at least to despise and pass by the thing itself, I would simply stand gaping at it. What is to be said of me when a lizard catching flies or a spider tangling them as they fall into her net often holds my attention so close, when I am sitting at home? These are small animals, but it is precisely the same thing. I do indeed go on to praise You, the marvellous Creator and Disposer of all things, but it is not in that state that I begin to gaze so attentively. It is one thing to get up quickly, but a better thing not to fall. And of such things my life is full, and my one hope is Your immeasurable mercy. For when our heart is made the stage for such things and is overladen with the throngs of this endless vanity, our prayers are often interrupted and distracted; and though we are in Your presence, and directing the voice of our heart to Your ears, the great business of prayer is broken off through the inrush of every sort of idle thought.

### XXXVI

Surely I must reckon this among things to be condemned: and is there anything to bring me back to hope save the knowledge of Your mercy, in that You have already begun to change me? And You know in what degree You have changed me, in that You have already healed me of the craving for revenge, so that You may be merciful also to my other iniquities, and heal all my diseases, redeem my life from destruction, crown me with mercy and compassion, and satisfy my desire with good things—You who have curbed my pride with Your fear and tamed my neck to Your yoke. I now bear Your yoke and it is light on me, for so You have promised, so You have done; and indeed it was always light, but I did not know it in the days when I feared to take it on me.

But tell me, Lord, You who alone reign without arrogance, because You alone are the true Lord who have no Lord: tell me whether a third kind of temptation has passed from me or can it ever pass wholly in this life—the desire to be feared and loved by men for no other reason than the joy I get from it, which is no true joy? It is a lamentable state, a base vaingloriousness. From this it comes that men neither love You utterly nor fear You with righteous fear: thus it is that You resist the proud but give grace to the humble: You thunder upon the ambition of this world and the foundations of the mountains tremble. But because certain offices in human society require the holder to be loved and feared by men, the enemy of our true beatitude presses hard upon me, spreading all about me his snares of Well done, Well done; and while I receive praises too eagerly, I lose caution and am caught by them, and so separate my joy from the truth and place it in the deceitfulness of men: I delight to be praised and feared, not for Your sake but in Your stead, and in this way the enemy has me like himself—not in any concord of charity, of course, but in the fellowship of like punishment—the devil who resolved *to establish his throne in the north,* that men darkened and frozen may serve him while he makes perverse and distorted imitation of You.

But we, O Lord, are Thy little flock: do Thou keep possession of us. Spread forth Thy wings, and let us shelter under them. Be Thou our glory; let us be loved because of Thee and let Thy word be feared in us.

A man who wishes to be praised by men when You do not praise him, will not be defended by men when You judge him, nor delivered by men when You condemn him. But it can happen, not that a sinner is praised in the desires of his soul, not that a man is blessed who does ungodlily, but that he is praised on account of some gift that You have given him: even so, if he rejoices more because he is praised than because he has the gift, then this man too is praised by men but blamed by You, and the man who praised him is better than himself who is praised: for the one took pleasure in God's gift in man, whereas the other took more pleasure in what man gave than in what God gave.

### XXXVII

Daily, O Lord, are we assailed by these temptations, unceasingly are we assailed. We are daily tried in the furnace of the human tongue. And in this matter also You command us to continence: grant what You command and command what You will. You know how my heart has groaned to You about this and the tears my eyes have shed. For I cannot easily know how far I am clean from this disease, and I am in great fear of my secret sins—sins that Your eyes see, though mine do not. For in those other kinds of temptation I have some power of examining myself, but in this almost none. For I can see how far I have advanced in power to control my mind in the matter of the pleasures of the flesh and curiosity for vain knowledge: I can see it when I am without these things, either because I choose to be or because they are not to be had. For then I can ask myself how much or how little it troubles me not to have them. Similarly in the matter of riches—which are sought to the end that they may serve a man for any one of those three concupiscences, or any two of them or all three of them—if the soul cannot discern while it possesses them whether or not it despises them, it can let them go and make trial of itself that way. But how are we to be without praise in order to discover our true attitude to praise? Are we to live evilly, to live a life so monstrous and abandoned, that everyone who knows us will detest us? What greater folly could be said or thought? On the contrary if praise both is and ought to be the normal accompaniment of a good life and good works, we ought no more to abandon that accompaniment than goodness of life itself. Yet unless I am deprived of something, I cannot know whether I can bear being without it well or ill?

What then am I to confess, Lord, in this field of temptation? What, save that I rejoice at praise?—but more for the truth than for the praise. For if I were given the choice whether on the one hand I would rather be a madman, or completely wrong in everything, and yet praised by all men: or on the contrary firm and sure in the truth and abused by all men, I see clearly which I would choose. Yet I wish that the praise of another's mouth did not increase the joy I feel in any good I may have: it does increase it, I admit: worse, dispraise diminishes it. And when I am troubled at this wretchedness in myself, an excuse comes into my head, how good an excuse You know, O God, for it leaves me uncertain! You have commanded us not only continence—that is, that we should restrain our affections from certain things —but also justice—by which we must bestow love on certain things: and it is not Your will that we should love You only, but our neighbor also. Now it often seems to me that what I rejoice in is the competence or promise I see in my neighbor. I am pleased with his praise as evidence of his understanding; and similarly I am sorry for the defect in him when I hear him blame what he does not understand or what is in fact good. For I am sometimes sorry to hear my own praise, either when qualities are praised in me which I see in myself with regret, or else good qualities of no great importance are praised more than they deserve. Yet I do not know: it may be that I feel thus, simply because I do not wish the man who praises me to differ from me about myself, and this not because I am concerned about what is good for him, but simply because those good qualities which please me in myself please me all the more when they please someone else as well. For in a sense I am not being praised, when my own opinion of myself is not praised—when, that is, things are praised in me which do not please me at all, or praised more though they please me less. So it seems that I am uncertain about myself in this matter.

Behold, O Truth, in You I see that I should be moved by praise of myself, not for my own sake but for the good of my neighbor. But whether this is so with me, I do not know. For in this matter I know more of You than of myself. I beseech You, O my God, show me to myself that I may confess to my brethren what I find defective in myself and they will pray for me. Again let me examine myself more closely. If in rejoicing to hear myself praised I am moved by the good of my neighbor, why am I less moved if someone else is blamed unjustly than when it happens to me? Why does that reproach bite me deeper which is cast upon me than when another is accused of the same sin in my presence? Am I ignorant of this too? Or does this remain as the real truth—that I deceive myself, and neither think nor speak the truth in Your sight? Put such madness far from me, O Lord, lest my mouth should be *the oil of the sinner to fatten my own head.*

## XXXVIII

I am poor and needy: yet I am better when with anguish of soul I see myself as hateful and seek your mercy, till what is damaged in me is repaired and made perfect, to the attaining of that peace which the eye of the proud knows not. The report of men's mouths, and deeds known to men, bring with them a most perilous temptation from the love of praise, which goes round almost begging for compliments and piles them up for our own personal glory. Love of praise tempts me even when I reprove it in myself, indeed in the very fact that I do reprove it: a man often glories the more vainly for his very contempt of vainglory: for which reason he does not really glory in his contempt of glory; in that he glories in it, he does not contemn it.

### XXXIX

Within us there is another evil in the same category of temptation, by which men are made vain though they do not please others or even displease others, and in any event have no desire to please others: but are interiorly pleased with themselves. They please themselves but they mightily displease You: not because they are pleased with things not good as though they were good, but because they are pleased with things good as though they were their own: or even if they rejoice in them as Yours, they think they have merited them: or even if they know that they are wholly of Your grace, yet they do not rejoice with their fellow-men, but as grudging Your grace to others. In all these and other similar perils and toils, You see the trembling of my heart: and truly I feel my wounds rather as things ever and again healed by You than as things never inflicted upon me.

### XL

Where have You not walked with me, O Truth, teaching me both what to shun and what to seek, when I set before You such things as I have been able to see here below and begged Your counsel? With my bodily senses I surveyed the external world as best I could, and considered the life my body has from me and the senses themselves. From that I turned inwards to the depths of my memory, like so many vast rooms filled so wonderfully with things beyond number: and I considered and stood awe-stricken: for no one of these could I discern without You, and I found that no one of these was You. Nor was I their finder. I did indeed go through them all and I tried to distinguish and evaluate each thing according to its worth, receiving some things with the feebleness of the senses and inquiring of them, perceiving other things in which there was some admixture of myself, observing and enumerating the messengers that had brought them to me, meditating upon things preserved in the vast stores of memory, putting some of them back, drawing others out. Yet it was not myself that did these things—that is, the power by which I did them was not myself: nor was it You, because you are that unfailing Light which I consulted upon all these things, as to whether they are, and what they are, and what they are worth. But I heard You teaching and commanding. And all this I do often; for it gives me pleasure and whenever I can relax from the duties necessity lays upon me, I have recourse to this same pleasure. Nor in all these things that my mind traverses in search of You, do I find any sure place for my mind save in You, in whom all that is scattered in me is brought into one, so that nothing of me may depart from You. And sometimes You admit me to a state of mind that I am not ordinarily in, a kind of delight which could it ever be made permanent in me would be hard to distinguish from the life to come. But by the weight of my imperfections I fall back again, and I am swallowed up by things customary: I am bound, and I weep bitterly, but I am bitterly bound. So much does the burden of custom count for. I can remain in my ordinary state though unwilling, I would remain in that other state but am not able, in both states I know my misery.

## XLI

Thus under the heads of that threefold concupiscence I have considered the damage wrought in me by my sins, and I have called Thy right hand to my aid. For in my wounded heart I have seen the shining of Thy splendor, and been beaten back, and have said: "Who can attain thither? *I am cast away from before Thy eyes.*" Thou art the Truth presiding over all things. But in my avarice I was unwilling to lose Thee, yet desired to possess a lie along with Thee: just as no man wishes to say what is false so that he himself shall not know what is true. So I lost Thee because Thou didst not deign to be possessed together with a lie.

XLII

Whom could I find to reconcile me to You? Was I to try to approach the Angels? But with what prayer? What sacraments? Many seeking to return to You and lacking the strength by themselves have, as I hear, made trial of that way, and have fallen into a seeking for curious visions, and been found worthy to be deluded. For they set out to find You in the conceit of their learning, swelling their breasts instead of beating them; and they drew to themselves through likeness in heart *the powers of this air* [fallen angels] as ministers and companions of their pride; and by these they were deceived with various effects of magic, seeking a mediator by whom they might be cleansed. But it was not a mediator they found. It was the devil, transforming himself into an angel of light. And it powerfully attracted proud flesh, that he was himself not a fleshly body. For they were mortal and sinners; You, Lord, to whom they wished to be reconciled, are immortal and sinless. Now clearly a mediator between God and men should have something in common with God, something in common with men; if he were in both points like men, he would be too far from God; if he were in both points like God, he would be too far from men: and in neither event could he be a mediator. But that sham mediator, by whom in Your secret judgments pride merits to be mocked, has one thing in common with men, namely sin, and pretends to have another thing in common with God— because he is not clothed with the mortality of flesh, he would pass for immortal. But because the wages of sin is

death, he has this in common with men, to be condemned
with them to the same death.

## XLIII

But the true Mediator, whom in the secret of Your mercy
You have shown to men and sent to men, that by His example
they might learn humility—the Mediator between God and
men, the man Christ Jesus, appeared between sinful mortals
and the immortal Just One: for like men He was mortal,
like God He was Just; so that, the wages of justice being life
and peace, He might, through the union of His own justice
with God, make void the death of those sinners whom He
justified by choosing to undergo death as they do. He was
shown forth to holy men of old that they might be saved by
faith in His Passion to come, as we by faith in His Passion
now that He has suffered it. As man, He is Mediator; but as
Word, He is not something in between, for He is equal to
God, God with God, and together one God.

How much Thou hast loved us, O good Father, *Who
hast spared not even Thine own Son, but delivered Him up
for us wicked men!* How Thou hast loved us, for whom He
who *thought it not robbery to be equal with Thee became
obedient even unto the death of the Cross,* He who alone
*was free among the dead, having power to lay down His life
and power to take it up again:* for us He was to Thee both
Victor and Victim, and Victor because Victim: for us He
was to Thee both Priest and Sacrifice, and Priest because
Sacrifice: turning us from slaves into Thy sons, by being
Thy Son and becoming a slave. Rightly is my hope strong
in Him, who sits at Thy right hand and intercedes for us;
otherwise I should despair. For many and great are my infirmities, many and great; but Thy medicine is of more
power. We might well have thought Thy Word remote from
union with man and so have despaired of ourselves, if It had
not been *made flesh and dwelt among us.*

Terrified by my sins and the mass of my misery, I had
pondered in my heart and thought of flight to the desert;

but Thou didst forbid me and strengthen me, saying: *And Christ died for all: that they also who live, may now not live to themselves but with Him who died for them.* See, Lord, I cast my care upon Thee, that I may live: *and I will consider the wondrous things of Thy law.* Thou knowest my unskilfulness and my infirmity: teach me and heal me. He Thy only One, in whom are hidden all the treasures of wisdom and knowledge, has redeemed me with His blood. *Let not the proud speak evil of me,* for I think upon the price of my redemption, I eat it and drink it and give it to others to eat and drink; and being poor I desire to be filled with it among those that eat and are filled: *and they shall praise the Lord that seek Him.*

# BOOK ELEVEN

## IN THE BEGINNING GOD CREATED . . .
### (Genesis I, 1)

B<small>UT</small>, Lord, since You are in eternity, are You unaware of what I am saying to You? Or do you see in time what takes place in time? But if You *do* see, why am I giving You an account of all these things? Not, obviously, that You should learn them from me; but I excite my own love for You and the love of those who read what I write, that we all may say: *The Lord is great, and exceedingly to be praised.* I have said before and I will say again: "It is for love of Your love that I do it." We pray [for what we want], yet Truth Himself has said: *Your Father knows what is needful for you before you ask Him.* Thus we are laying bare our love for You in confessing to You our wretchedness and Your mercies towards us: that You may free us wholly as You have already freed us in part, so that we may cease to be miserable in ourselves and come to happiness in You. For You have called us to be poor in spirit, to be meek, to mourn, to hunger and thirst after justice, to be merciful and clean of heart and peacemakers.

Thus I have told You many things, with such power and will as I had, because You, O Lord my God, had first willed that I should confess to You: for *Thou art good and Thy mercy endureth forever.*

II

But when will the voice of my pen have power to tell all Your exhortations and all Your terrors, Your consolations and the guidance by which You have brought me to be to Your people a preacher of Your word and a dispenser of Your Sacrament? Even had I the power to set down all these things duly, the drops of my time are too precious.

For a long time now I burn with the desire to meditate upon Your law, and to confess to You both my knowledge of it and my ignorance of it—the first beginnings of Your light and what re mains of my own darkness—until my weakness shall be swallowed up in Your strength. And I do not want to see scattered and wasted upon other things such time as I find free from necessary care of the body, intellectual labour, and the service which either I owe men or do not owe but render all the same.

O Lord my God, be attentive to my prayer. Let Thy mercy grant my desire, since it does not burn for myself alone, but longs to serve the charity I have for my brethren: and in my heart Thou seest that it is so. Let me offer in sacrifice to Thee the service of my mind and my tongue, and do Thou give me what I may offer Thee. For I am needy and poor, *Thou art rich unto all who call upon Thee*. Thou art free from care for Thyself and full of care for us. Circumcise the lips of my mouth and the lips of my mind of all rash speech and lying. May Thy Scriptures be for my chaste delight; let me not deceive others about them nor be myself deceived. O Lord, hearken and have mercy, O Lord my God, Light of the blind and Strength of the weak, but Light too of the clear of sight and Strength of the strong; hearken to my soul, hear it crying from the depths. Unless Thine ears are attentive to us in the abyss, whither shall we go? To whom shall we cry?

*Thine is the day, and Thine is the night:* at Thy will the moments flow and pass. Grant me, then, space for my meditations upon the hidden things of Thy law, nor close Thy law against me as I knock. Not for nothing hast Thou willed that the deep secrets of all those pages should be written, not for nothing have those woods their *stags,** which retire to them and are restored, walk in them and are fed, lie down in them and ruminate. Complete Thy work in me, O Lord, and open those pages to me. Thy voice is my joy, abounding above all joys. Grant me what I love, for I do love it. And this too is of Thy gift. Do not abandon what Thou hast given, nor scorn Thy grass that is athirst for Thee. Let me confess to Thee whatsoever I shall find in Thy books, and *let me hear the voice of Thy praise,* and drink of Thee and *consider the wondrous things of Thy law* from the first beginning, when Thou didst make heaven and earth, until our everlasting reign with Thee in Thy holy city.

* A reference to Psalm XXVIII, 9.

O Lord have mercy on me and grant what I desire. For, as I think, my desire is not of earth, not of gold and silver and gems or fine raiment or power and glory or the lusts of the flesh or the necessities of my body and of this our earthly pilgrimage: *all these things shall be added unto us who seek the Kingdom of God and Thy justice.*

See, O my God, whence comes my desire. *The wicked have told me fables but not as Thy law.* That is the source of my desire. See, Father: gaze and see and approve: and may it be pleasing in the sight of Thy mercy that I should find grace before Thee, that the inner secret of Thy words may be laid open at my knock. I beseech it by our Lord Jesus Christ Thy Son, *the Man of Thy right hand, the Son of Man, whom Thou hast confirmed for Thyself* as Mediator between Thyself and us: by whom Thou didst seek us when we sought not Thee, didst seek us indeed that we might seek Thee: Thy Word, by which Thou hast made all things and me among them: Thy Only One, by whom Thou hast called the people of the faithful, and me among them, unto adoption. I beseech it by Him who sits at Thy right hand and makes intercession for us, *in whom are hidden all the treasures of wisdom and knowledge.* These treasures are what I seek in Thy books. Moses wrote of Him: this He says, who is Truth.

### III

Grant me to hear and understand what is meant by *In the beginning You made heaven and earth.* For so Moses wrote, wrote and went his way: passed from this world to You and is no longer here before me. Were he here, I should lay hold of him, and ask him, and in Your name beg him, to explain the sense of those words to me; I should lend my bodily ear to the sounds that should issue from his mouth. If he spoke in Hebrew, his voice would beat upon my ear to no purpose, nothing of what it said would reach my mind: if he spoke in Latin, I should know what he said. But how should I know that what he said was true? And if I did know it, would it be from him that I knew it? No: but within me, in the inner retreat of my mind, the Truth, which is neither Hebrew nor Greek, nor Latin, nor Barbarian, would tell me, without lips or tongue or sounded syllables: "He speaks truth:" and I (at once assured) would say to Your servant in all confidence: "You speak truth." Since, then, I cannot question him, I ask Thee, the Truth, filled with whom Moses spoke truth: I ask Thee, my God: pardon my sins, and as Thou didst grant to Thy servant to speak those words, grant me to understand them.

### IV

We look upon the heavens and the earth, and they cry aloud that they were made. For they change and vary. (If anything was not made and yet exists, there is nothing in it that was not there before: and it is the essence of change and variation that something should be that was not there before.) They cry aloud, too, that they did not make themselves. "We exist, because we were made; but we did not exist before we existed to be able to give ourselves existence!" And their visible presence is itself the voice with which they speak.

It was You, Lord, who made them: for You are beautiful, and they are beautiful: You are good, and they are good: You are, and they are. But they neither are beautiful nor are good nor simply are as You their Creator: compared with You they are not beautiful and are not good and are not. These truths, thanks to You, we know; and our knowledge compared with Your knowledge is ignorance.

### V

But *how* did You make heaven and earth? What instrument did You use for a work so mighty? You are not like an artist; for he forms one body from another as his mind chooses; his mind has the power to give external existence to the form it perceives within itself by its inner eye—and whence should it have that power unless You made it? It impresses that form upon a material already existent and having the capacity to be thus formed, such as clay or stone or wood or gold or such like. And how should these things have come to be unless You had made them to be? It was You who made the workman his body, and the mind that directs his limbs, the matter of which he makes what he makes, the intelligence by which he masters his art and sees inwardly what he is to produce exteriorly, the bodily sense by which he translates what he does from his mind to his material, and then informs the mind of the result of his workmanship, so that the mind may judge by that truth which presides within it whether the work is well done.

All these things praise You, the Creator of them all. But how do You create them? How, O God, did You create heaven and earth? Obviously it was not *in* heaven or on earth that You made heaven and earth; nor in the air nor in the waters, since these belong to heaven and earth; nor did You make the universe in the universe, because there was no place for it to be made in until it was made. Nor had You any material in Your hand when You were making heaven and earth: for where should You have got what You had not yet made to use as material? What exists, save because You exist? You spoke and heaven and earth were created; in Your word You created them.

## VI

But *how* did You speak? Was it perhaps as when that voice sounded from the cloud saying: *This is my beloved Son?* That voice sounded and ceased to sound, had a beginning and an end. The syllables sounded and died away, the second after the first, the third after the second, and so in order, until the last after the rest, and silence after the last. From this it is clear beyond question that that voice was sounded by the movement of something created by You, a movement in time but serving Your eternal will.

These words were uttered in time and the bodily ear conveyed them to the understanding mind, whose spiritual ear is attuned to Your eternal Word. And the mind compared these words sounding in time with Your eternal Word and its silence: and it said: "It is other, far other. These words are far less than I, indeed they are not at all, for they pass away and are no more: but the Word of God is above me and endures for ever."

Thus, had it been by words sounding and passing away that You said "Let heaven and earth be made," and so created heaven and earth, there would have had to be some bodily creature before heaven and earth, by the movement of which in time that voice came and went in time.

But there was no bodily thing before heaven and earth: or if there were then certainly You did not use some still earlier utterance in time to produce it, that by it You might utter in time the decree that heaven and earth should be made. Whatever it may have been that produced such a voice, it must have been made by You, otherwise it would not have existed at all. But to produce the bodily thing capable of uttering those words, what word did You utter?

VII

Clearly You are calling us to the realization of that Word— God with You, God as You are God—which is uttered eternally and by which all things are uttered eternally.

For this is not an utterance in which what has been said passes away that the next thing may be said and so finally the whole utterance be complete: but all in one act, yet abiding eternally: otherwise it would be but time and change and no true eternity, no true immortality.

I know it, O my God, and I give You thanks. I know it, Lord, I confess it to You: and every man knows it as I do and praises You as I do who is not ungrateful for Your sure truth. We know, Lord, we know, that in the degree that anything is no longer what it was, and is now what it once was not, it is in the process of dying and beginning anew. But of Your Word nothing passes or comes into being, for it is truly immortal and eternal. Thus it is by a Word co-eternal with Yourself that in one eternal act You say all that You say, and all things are made that You say are to be made. You create solely by thus saying. Yet all the things You create by saying are not brought into being in one act and from eternity.

## VIII

Tell me, O Lord my God, how this can be? In a kind of way I see, but how to express it I do not know: save that whatever comes into being and ceases to be, begins at the moment and ends at the moment when the eternal reason—which has in itself no beginning or ending—knows that it should begin or end. That eternal reason is Your Word, *the Beginning who also speaks unto us*. This He tells us in the Gospel to our bodily ear, this He uttered exteriorly in the ears of men: that we might believe in Him, and seek Him within us and find Him in the eternal Truth, where the one good Master teaches all His disciples.

There it is that I hear Your voice, Lord, telling me that only one who teaches us is speaking to us, and that whoever does not teach us may be speaking, but not to us. Yet who teaches us save Truth unchanging? When from changing creatures we learn anything, we are led to Truth that does not change: and there we truly learn, as we stand and hear Him and rejoice with joy for the voice of the bridegroom, returning to the Source of our being. Thus it is that He is the Beginning: unless He remained when we wandered away, there should be no abiding place for our return. But when we return from error, we return by realizing the Truth; that we may realize it, He instructs us for He is the *Beginning who also speaks unto us*.

## IX

This then, O God, was the Beginning in which You created Heaven and Earth: marvellously speaking and marvellously creating in Your Word, Who is Your Son and Your Strength and Your Wisdom and Your Truth. Who shall understand this? Who shall relate it? What is that light which shines upon me but not continuously, and strikes upon my heart with no wounding? I draw back in terror: I am on fire with longing: terror in so far as I am different from it, longing in the degree of my likeness to it. It is Wisdom, Wisdom Itself, which in those moments shines upon me, cleaving through my cloud. And the cloud returns to wrap me round once more as my strength is beaten down under its darkness and the weight of my sins: for *my strength is weakened through poverty,* so that I can no longer support my good, until Thou, Lord who art merciful to my iniquities, shalt likewise heal my weakness: redeeming my life from corruption and crowning me with pity and compassion, and filling my desire with good things: *my youth shall be renewed like the eagle's. For we are saved by hope and we wait with patience for Thy promises.*

Let him who can hear Thy voice speaking within him; I, relying upon Thy inspired word, shall cry aloud: *How great are Thy works, O Lord! Thou hast made all things in wisdom.* Wisdom is "the Beginning": and it is in that Beginning that You made heaven and earth.

x

Surely those are still in their ancient error who say to us: "What was God doing before He made heaven and earth?" If, they say, He was at rest and doing nothing, why did He not continue to do nothing for ever after as for ever before? If it was a new movement and a new will in God to create something He had never created before, how could that be a true eternity in which a will should arise which did not exist before? For the will of God is not a creature: it is prior to every creature, since nothing would be created unless the will of the Creator first so willed. The will of God belongs to the very substance of God. Now if something arose in the substance of God which was not there before, that substance could not rightly be called eternal; but if God's will that creatures should be is from eternity, why are creatures not from eternity?

XI

Those who speak thus do not yet understand You, O Wisdom of God, Light of minds: they do not yet understand how the things are made that are made by You and in You. They strive for the savour of eternity, but their mind is still tossing about in the past and future movements of things, and is still vain.

Who shall lay hold upon their mind and hold it still, that it may stand a little while, and a little while glimpse the splendour of eternity which stands for ever: and compare it with time whose moments never stand, and see that it is not comparable. Then indeed it would see that a long time is long only from the multitude of movements that pass away in succession, because they cannot co-exist: that in eternity nothing passes but all is present, whereas time cannot be present all at once. It would see that all the past is thrust out by the future, and all the future follows upon the past, and past and future alike are wholly created and upheld in their passage by that which is always present? Who shall lay hold upon the mind of man, that it may stand and see that time with its past and future must be determined by eternity, which stands and does not pass, which has in itself no past or future. Could my hand have the strength [so to lay hold upon the mind of man] or could my mouth by its speaking accomplish so great a thing?

### XII

I come now to answer the man who says: "What was God doing before He made Heaven and earth?" I do not give the jesting answer—said to have been given by one who sought to evade the force of the question—"He was getting Hell ready for people who pry too deep." To poke fun at a questioner is not to see the answer. My reply will be different. I would much rather say "I don't know," when I don't, than hold one up to ridicule who had asked a profound question and win applause for a worthless answer.

But, O my God, I say that You are the Creator of all creation, and if by the phrase heaven and earth we mean all creation, then I make bold to reply: Before God made heaven and earth, He did not make anything. For if He had made something, what would it have been but a creature? And I wish I knew all that it would be profitable for me to know, as well as I know that no creature was made before any creature was made.

### XIII

But a lighter mind, adrift among images of time and its passing, might wonder that You, O God almighty and all-creating and all-conserving, Maker of heaven and earth, should have abstained from so vast a work for the countless ages that passed before You actually wrought it. Such a mind should awaken and realize how ill-grounded is his wonder.

How could countless ages pass when You, the Author and Creator of all ages, had not yet made them? What time could there be that You had not created? or how could ages pass, if they never were?

Thus, since You are the Maker of all times, if there actually was any time before You made heaven and earth, how can it be said that You were not at work? If there was time, You made it, for time could not pass before You made time. On the other hand, if before heaven and earth were made there was no time, then what is meant by the question "What were You doing *then?*" If there was not any time, there was not any "then".

It is not in time that You are before all time: otherwise You would not be before all time. You are before all the past by the eminence of Your ever-present eternity: and You dominate all the future in as much as it is still to be: and once it has come it will be past: but *Thou art always the self-same, and Thy years shall not fail.* Your years neither go nor come: but our years come and go, that all may come. Your years abide all in one act of abiding: for they abide and the years that go are not thrust out by those that come, for none pass: whereas our years shall not all be, till all are no more. Your years are as a single day; and Your day comes not daily but is today, a today which does not yield place to any tomorrow or follow upon any yesterday. In You today is eternity: thus it is that You begot one co-eternal with Yourself to whom you said: *Today have I begotten Thee.* You are the Maker of all time, and before all time You are, nor was there ever a time when there was no time!

## XIV

At no time then had You not made anything, for time itself You made. And no time is co-eternal with You, for You stand changeless; whereas if time stood changeless, it would not be time. What then is time? Is there any short and easy answer to that? Who can put the answer into words or even see it in his mind? Yet what commoner or more familiar word do we use in speech than time? Obviously when we use it, we know what we mean, just as when we hear another use it, we know what he means.

What then *is* time? If no one asks me, I know; if I want to explain it to a questioner, I do not know. But at any rate this much I dare affirm I know: that if nothing passed there would be no past time; if nothing were approaching, there would be no future time; if nothing were, there would be no present time.

But the two times, past and future, how can they *be*, since the past is no more and the future is not yet? On the other hand, if the present were always present and never flowed away into the past, it would not be time at all, but eternity. But if the present is only time, because it flows away into the past, how can we say that it *is*? For it is, only because it will cease to be. Thus we can affirm that time *is* only in that it tends towards not-being.

## XV

Yet we speak of a long time or a short time, applying these phrases only to past or future. Thus for example we call a hundred years ago a long time past, and a hundred years hence a long time ahead, and ten days ago a short time past, ten days hence a short time ahead. But in what sense can that which does not exist be long or short? The past no longer is, the future is not yet. Does this mean that we must not say: "It is long," but of the past "It was long," of the future "It will be long?"

O, my Lord, my Light, here too man is surely mocked by Your truth! If we say the past was long, was it long when it was already past or while it was still present? It could be long only while it was in existence to *be* long. But the past no longer exists; it cannot be long, because it is not at all.

Thus we must not say that the past was long: for we shall find nothing in it capable of being long, since, precisely because it is past, it is not at all. Let us say then that a particular time was long while it was present, because in so far as it was present, it was long. For it had not yet passed away and so become non-existent; therefore it still was something, and therefore capable of being long: though once it passed away, it ceased to be long by ceasing to be.

Let us consider, then, O human soul, whether present time can be long: for it has been given you to feel and measure time's spaces. What will you answer me?

Are the present hundred years a long time? But first see whether a hundred years *can* be present. If it is the first year of the hundred, then that year is present, but the other ninety-nine are still in the future, and so as yet are not: if we are in the second year, then one year is past, one year is present, the rest future. Thus whichever year of our hundred-year period we choose as present, those before it have passed away, those after it are still to come. Thus a hundred years cannot be present.

But now let us see if the chosen year is itself present. If we are in the first month, the others are still to come, if in the second, the first has passed away and the rest are not yet. Thus a year is not wholly present while it runs, and if the whole of it is not present, then the year is not present. For a year is twelve months, and the month that happens to be running its course is the only one present, the others either are no longer or as yet are not. Even the current month is not present, but only one day of it: if that day is the first, the rest are still to come; if the last, the rest are passed away; if somewhere between, it has days past on one side and days still to come on the other.

Thus the present, which we have found to be the only time capable of being long, is cut down to the space of scarcely one day. But if we examine this one day, even it is not wholly present. A day is composed of twenty-four hours—day-hours, night-hours: the first hour finds the rest still to come, the last hour finds the rest passed away, any hour between has hours passed before it, hours to come after it. And that one hour is made of fleeing moments: so much of the hour as has fled away is past, what still remains is future. If we conceive of some point of time which cannot be divided into even the minutest parts of moments, that is the only point that can be called present: and that point flees at such lightning speed from being future to being past, that it has no extent of duration at all. For if it were so extended, it would be divisible into past and future: the present has no length.

Where, then, is there a time that can be called long? Is it the future? But we cannot say of the future "It is long" because as yet it is not at all and therefore is not long. We say "It will be long." But when will it be long? While it is still in the future, it will not be long, because it does not yet exist and so cannot be long. Suppose we say, then, that it is to be long only when, coming out of the future [which is not yet], it begins to be and is now present—and thus something, and thus capable of being long. But the present cries aloud, as we have just heard, that it cannot have length.

### XVI

Yet, Lord, we are aware of periods of time; we compare one period with another and say that some are longer, some shorter. We measure how much one is longer than another and say that it is double, or triple, or single, or simply that one is as long as the other. But it is time actually passing that we measure by our awareness; who can measure times past which are now no more or times to come which are not yet, unless you are prepared to say that that which does not exist can be measured? Thus while time is passing, it can be perceived and measured; but when it has passed it cannot, for it *is* not.

### XVII

I am seeking, Father, not saying: O, my God, aid me and direct me.

Perhaps it might be said that there are not three times, past, present and future, as we learnt in boyhood and have taught boys: but only present, because the other two do not exist. Or perhaps that these two do exist, but that time comes forth from some secret place when from future it becomes present, and departs into some secret place when from present it becomes past. For where have those who prophesied the future seen the future, if it does not yet exist? What does not exist cannot be seen. And those who describe the past could not describe it truly if they did not mentally see it: and if the past were totally without existence it would be totally impossible to see it. Hence both past and future must exist.

## XVIII

Suffer me, Lord, to push my inquiry further; O my Hope, let not my purpose go awry.

If the future and the past exist, I want to know where they are. And if I cannot yet know this, at least I do know that wherever they are, they are there not as future or past, but present. If wherever they are they are future, then in that place they are not yet; if past, then they are there no more. Thus wherever they are and whatever they are, they *are* only as present. When we relate the past truly, it is not the things themselves that are brought forth from our memory—for these have passed away: but words conceived from the images of the things: for the things stamped their prints upon the mind as they passed through it by way of the senses. Thus for example my boyhood, which no longer exists, is in time past, which no longer exists; but the likeness of my boyhood, when I recall it and talk of it, I look upon in time present, because it is still present in my memory.

Whether the case is similar with prophecies of things to come—namely that images of things which are not yet are seen in advance as now existent—I confess, O my God, that I do not know. But this I do know, that we ordinarily consider our future actions in advance, and that this consideration is present, but the action we are thinking of does not yet exist, because it is future; when we have actually set about it and have begun to do what we planned, then that action will exist, because then it will not be future but present.

Whatever may be the mode of this mysterious foreseeing of things to come, unless the thing is it cannot be seen. But what now is, is not future but present. Therefore when we speak of seeing the future, obviously what is seen is not the things which are not yet because they are still to come, but their causes or perhaps the signs that foretell them, for these causes and signs do exist here and now. Thus to those who see them now, they are not future but present, and from them things to come are conceived by the mind and foretold. These concepts already exist, and those who foretell are gazing upon them, present within themselves.

Let me take one example from a vast number of such things.

I am looking at the horizon at dawn: I foretell that the sun is about to rise. What I am looking at is present, what I foretell is future—not the sun, of course, for it now is, but its rising which is not yet. But unless I could imagine the actual rising in my mind, as now when I speak of it, I could not possibly foretell it. But the dawn which I see in the sky is not the sunrise, although it precedes the sunrise; nor is the dawn the image of the sunrise that is in my mind. But both—the dawn and the image of the sunrise—are present and seen by me, so that the sunrise which is future can be told in advance. Thus the future is not yet; and if it is not yet, it is not; and if it is not, then it is totally impossible to see it. But it can be foretold from things present which now exist and are seen.

### XIX

But You, O Ruler of Your creation, how is it that you can show souls things that are to come? For such things You have told Your prophets. In what manner do You show the future to man, for whom nothing future yet is? Or do You show only present signs of things to come? For what does not exist obviously cannot be shown. The means You use is altogether beyond my gaze; my eyes have not the strength; of myself I shall never be able to see so deep, but in You I shall be able, when you grant it, O lovely Light of the eyes of my spirit.

## XX

At any rate it is now quite clear that neither future nor past actually exists. Nor is it right to say there are three times, past, present and future. Perhaps it would be more correct to say: there are three times, a present of things past, a present of things present, a present of things future. For these three exist in the mind, and I find them nowhere else: the present of things past is memory, the present of things present is sight, the present of things future is expectation. If we are allowed to speak thus, I see and admit that there are three times, that three times truly are.

By all means continue to say that there are three times, past, present and future; for, though it is incorrect, custom allows it. By all means say it. I do not mind, I neither argue nor object: provided that you understand what you are saying and do not think future or past now exists. There are few things that we phrase properly; most things we phrase badly: but what we are trying to say is understood.

## XXI

I said a little while ago that we measure time in its passing, so that we are able to say that this period of time is to that as two to one, or that this is of the same duration as that, and can measure and describe any other proportions of time's parts.

Thus, as I said, we measure time *in its passing*. If you ask me how I know this, my answer is that I know it because we measure time, and we cannot measure what does not exist, and past and future do not exist. But how do we measure time present, since it has no extent? It is measured while it is passing; once it has passed, it cannot be measured, for then nothing exists to measure.

But where does time come from, and by what way does it pass, and where does it go, while we are measuring it? Where is it from?—obviously from the future. By what way does it pass?—by the present. Where does it go?—into the past. In other words it passes from that which does not yet exist, by way of that which lacks extension, into that which is no longer.

But how are we measuring time unless in terms of some kind of duration? We cannot say single or double or triple or equal or proportioned in any other way, save of the duration of periods of time. But in what duration do we measure time while it is actually passing? In the future, from which it comes? But what does not yet exist cannot be measured. In the present, then, by which it passes? But that which has no space cannot be measured. In the past, to which it passes? But what no longer exists cannot be measured.

XXII

My mind burns to solve this complicated enigma. O Lord my God, O good Father, for Christ's sake I beseech Thee, do not shut off these obscure familiar problems from my longing, do not shut them off and leave them impenetrable but let them shine clear for me in the light of Thy mercy, O Lord. Yet whom shall I question about them? And to whom more fruitfully than to Thee shall I confess my ignorance: for Thou art not displeased at the zeal with which I am on fire for Thy Scriptures. Grant me what I love: for it is by Your gift that I love. Grant me this gift, Father, *who dost know how to give good gifts to Thy children.* Grant it because I have *studied that I might know and it is a labour in my sight* until Thou shalt open it to me. For Christ's sake I beseech Thee, in the name of Him who is the Holy of Holies, that no one prevent me. *I have believed, therefore have I spoken.* This is my hope; for this do I live, *that I may see the delight of the Lord. Behold Thou hast made my days old,* and they pass away: but how I know not.

We are forever talking of time and of times. "How long did he speak," "How long did it take him to do that," "For how long a time did I fail to see this," "This syllable is double the length of that." So we speak and so we hear others speak, and others understand us, and we them. They are the plainest and commonest of words, yet again they are profoundly obscure and their meaning still to be discovered.

### XXIII

I once heard a learned man say that time is simply the movement of the sun and moon and stars. I did not agree. For why
should not time rather be the movement of all bodies? Supposing
the lights of heaven were to cease and the potter's wheel moved
on, would there not be time by which we could measure its
rotations and say that these were at equal intervals, or some
slower, some quicker, some taking longer, some shorter? And if
we spoke thus, should we not ourselves be speaking in time:
would there not be in our words some syllables long, some short—
because some would sound for a longer time, some for a shorter?

O God, grant unto men to see by some small example the elements in common between small things and great. There are stars
and the lights of heaven *to be for signs and for seasons and for
days and years.* This is evident; but just as I would not affirm that
one turn of that little wooden wheel is a day, neither should my
philosopher say that it is no time at all.

What I am trying to come at is the force and nature of time,
by which we measure the movement of bodies and say for example that this movement is twice as long as that. A day means
not only the length of time that the sun is above the earth—so
that we distinguish day from night—but the time of the sun's
whole circuit from east to east—as we say that so many days
have passed, so many days being used to include their nights, for
the nights are not reckoned separately. Thus, since a day is con-
stituted by the movement of the sun and its completed circle from
east to east, I wish to know whether a day is that movement itself,
or simply the time the movement takes, or both.

If the movement of the sun through one complete circuit were
the day, then it would be a day even if the sun sped through its
course in a space of time equal to an hour. If the time the sun
now takes to complete its circuit is the day, then it would not be
a day if between one sunrise and the next there were only the
space of an hour: the sun would have to go round twenty-four
times to make one day. But if to constitute a day there is needed
both the movement of the sun through one circuit and the time

the sun now takes, then you would not have a day if the sun completed its whole circuit in an hour, nor again if the sun stood still
and as much time passed as the sun normally takes to complete
its journey from one morning to the next.

But I shall not at the moment pursue the question of what it
is that we call a day. I shall continue to seek what time is, by
which we measure the sun's journey: so that we should say that
it had gone round in half its accustomed time, if it went round in
a space of time equivalent to twelve hours. And comparing its
normal time with this twelve-hour time, we should say that the
latter was single, the former double; yet the sun would in the one
case have made its journey from east to east in the shorter time, in
the other in the longer [so that time is something independent of
the sun's movement].

Let no one tell me that the movement of the heavenly bodies is
time: when at the prayer of a man the sun stood still that he might
complete his victory in battle, the sun stood still but time moved
on. The battle was continued for the necessary length of time and
was finished.

Therefore I see time as in some way extended. But do I see
it? Or do I only seem to see it? Thou wilt show me, O Light,
O Truth.

XXIV

Would You have me agree with one who said that time is the
movement of a body? You would not: for I learn that no body
moves save in time: You have said it. But I do not learn that the
movement of the body is time: You have not said it. For when a
body is in motion, it is by time that I measure how long it is in
motion from the beginning of its movement till it ceases to move.
And if I did not see when the movement began, and if it moved
on without my seeing when it ceased, I should be able to measure
only from the moment I began to look until the moment I stopped
looking. If I look for a long time, all I can say is that the time is
long, but not how long it is, because when we say how long a time,
we say it by comparison: as for example: this is as long as that,
or this is twice that, and such like. But if we could note the point

of space from which a body in motion comes or the point to which it goes, or could distinguish its parts if it is moving on its axis, we should be able to say how much time has elapsed for the movement of the body, or its part, from one place to another.

Thus since the movement of a body is not the same as our measurement of how long the movement takes, who can fail to see which of these is more deserving of the name of time? A body moves at different speeds, and sometimes stands still; but time enables us to measure not only its motion but its rest as well; and we say "It was at rest for the same length of time as it was in motion," or "It was at rest twice or thrice as long as it was in motion" or any other proportion, whether precisely measured or roughly estimated.

Therefore time is not the movement of a body.

## XXV

I confess to You, Lord, that I still do not know what time is. And again I confess to You, Lord, that I know that I am uttering these things in time: I have been talking of time for a long time, and this long time would not be a long time unless time had passed. But how do I know this, since I do not know what time is? Or perhaps I do know, but simply do not know how to express what I know. Alas for me, I do not even know what I do not know! See me, O my God, I stand before You and I do not lie: as my speech is, so is my heart. *For Thou lightest my lamp, O Lord; O my God, enlighten my darkness.*

## XXVI

Does not my soul speak truly to You when I say that I can measure time? For so it is, O Lord my God, I measure it and I do not know what it is that I am measuring. I measure the movement of a body, using time to measure it by. Do I not then measure time itself? Could I measure the movement of a body— its duration and how long it takes to move from place to place— if I could not measure the time in which it moves?

But if so, what do I use to measure time with? Do we measure a longer time by a shorter one, as we measure a beam in terms of cubits? Thus we say that the duration of a long syllable is measured by the space of a short syllable and is said to be double. Thus we measure the length of poems by the lengths of the lines, and the lengths of the lines by the lengths of the feet, and the lengths of the feet by the lengths of the syllables, and the lengths of long syllables by the lengths of short. We do not measure poems by pages, for that would be to measure space not time; we measure by the way the voice moves in uttering the poem, and we say: "It is a long poem, for it consists of so many lines; the lines are long for they are composed of so many feet; the feet are long for they include so many syllables; this syllable is long for it is the double of a short syllable."

But not by all this do we arrive at an exact measure of time. It may well happen that a shorter line may take longer if it is recited slowly than a longer line hurried through. And the same is true of a poem or a foot or a syllable.

Thus it seems to me that time is certainly extendedness—but I do not know what it is extendedness of: probably of the mind itself. Tell me, O my God, what am I measuring, when I say either, with no aim at precision, that one period is longer than the other, or, precisely, that one is double the other? That I measure time, I know. But I do not measure the future, for it is not yet; nor the present, for it is not extended in space; nor the past, which no longer exists. So what do I measure? Is it time in passage but not past? So I have already said.

### XXVII

Persevere, O my soul, fix all the power of your gaze. *God is our helper. He made us, and not we ourselves.* Fix your gaze where truth is whitening toward the dawn.

Consider the example of a bodily voice. It begins to sound, it sounds and goes on sounding, then it ceases: and now there is silence, the sound has passed, the sound no longer is. It was future before it began to sound, and so could not be measured, for as yet it did not exist; and now it cannot be measured because now it exists no longer. Only while sounding could it be measured for then it was, and so was measurable. But even then it was not standing still; it was moving, and moving out of existence. Did this make it more measurable? Only in the sense that by its passing it was spread over a certain space of time which made it measurable: for the present occupies no space.

At any rate, let us grant that it could be measured. And now again imagine a voice. It begins to sound and goes on sounding continuously without anything to break its even flow. Let us measure it, while it is sounding. For when it has ceased to sound, it will be past and will no longer be measurable. Let us measure it then and say how long it is. But it is still sounding and can be measured only from its beginning when it began to sound to its end, when it ceased. For what we measure is the interval between some starting point and some conclusion. This means that a sound which is not yet over cannot be measured so that we may say how long or short it is, nor can it be said either to be equal to some other sound or single or double or any other proportion in relation to it. But when it *is* over, it will no longer be. Then how will it be possible to measure it? Yet we do measure time—not that which is not yet, nor that which is no longer, nor that which has no duration, nor that which lacks beginning and end. Thus it seems that we measure neither time future nor time past nor time present nor time passing: and yet we measure time.

*Deus creator omnium:* This line is composed of eight syllables, short and long alternately: the four short syllables, the first, third, fifth, seventh are single in relation to the four long syllables, the second, fourth, sixth, eighth. Each long syllable has double the time of each short syllable. I pronounce them and I say that it is so, and so it is, as is quite obvious to the ear. As my ear distinguishes I measure a long syllable by a short and I perceive that it contains it twice. But since I hear a syllable only when the one before it has ceased—the one before being short and the one following long—how am I to keep hold of the short syllable, and how shall I set it against the long one to measure it and find that the long one is twice its length—given that the long syllable does not begin to sound until the short one has ceased? And again can I measure the long one while it is present, since I cannot measure it until it is completed? And its completion is its passing out of existence.

What then is it that I measure? Where is the short syllable by which I measure? Where is the long syllable which I measure? Both have sounded, have fled away, have gone into the past, are now no more: yet I do measure, and I affirm with confidence, in so far as a practised sense can be trusted, that one is single, the other double, in the length of time it occupies. And I could not do this unless they had both passed away and ended. Thus it is not the syllables themselves that I measure, for they are now no more, but something which remains engraved in my memory.

It is in you, O my mind, that I measure time. Do not bring against me, do not bring against yourself the disorderly throng of your impressions. In you, I say, I measure time. What I measure is the impress produced in you by things as they pass and abiding in you when they have passed: and it is present. I do not measure the things themselves whose passage produced the impress; it is the impress that I measure when I measure time. Thus either that is what time is, or I am not measuring time at all.

But when we measure silences, and say that some particular silence lasted as long as some particular phrase, do we not stretch our mind to measure the phrase as though it were actually sounded, so as to be able to form a judgment of the relation between the space of the silence and that space of time? For without voice or lips we can go through poems and verses and speeches in our minds, and we can allow for the time it takes for their movement, one part in relation to another, exactly as if we were reciting them aloud. If a man decides to utter a longish sound and settles in his mind how long the sound is to be, he goes through that space of time in silence, entrusts it to his memory, then begins to utter the sound, and it sounds until it reaches the length he had fixed for it. Or rather I should say [not that it sounds but] that it has sounded and will sound: for as much of it as has been uttered at a given moment has obviously sounded, and what remains will sound: and so he completes the sound: at every moment his attention, which is present, causes the future to make its way into the past, the future diminishing and the past growing, until the future is exhausted and everything is past.

### XXVIII

But how is the future diminished or exhausted, since the future does not yet exist: or how does the past grow, since it no longer is? Only because, in the mind which does all this, there are three acts. For the mind expects, attends and remembers: what it expects passes, by way of what it attends to, into what it remembers. Would anyone deny that the future is as yet not existent? But in the mind there is already an expectation of the future. Would anyone deny that the past no longer exists? Yet still there is in the mind a memory of the past. Would anyone deny that the present time lacks extension, since it is but a point that passes on? Yet the attention endures, and by it that which is to be passes on its way to being no more. Thus it is not the future that is long, for the future does not exist: a long future is merely a long expectation of the future; nor is the past long since the past does not exist: a long past is merely a long memory of the past.

Suppose that I am about to recite a psalm that I know. Before I begin, my expectation is directed to the whole of it; but when I have begun, so much of it as I pluck off and drop away into the past becomes matter for my memory; and the whole energy of the action is divided between my memory, in regard to what I have said, and my expectation, in regard to what I am still to say. But there is a present act of attention, by which what was future passes on its way to becoming past. The further I go in my recitation, the more my expectation is diminished and my memory lengthened, until the whole of my expectation is used up when the action is completed and has passed wholly into my memory. And what is true of the whole psalm, is true for each part of the whole, and for each syllable: and likewise for any longer action, of which the canticle may be only a part: indeed it is the same for the whole life of man, of which all a man's actions are parts: and likewise for the whole history of the human race, of which all the lives of all men are parts.

## xxix

But *Thy mercy is better than lives,* and behold my life is but a
scattering. *Thy right hand has held me up* in my Lord, the Son of
Man who is the Mediator in many things and in divers manners—
that *I may apprehend by Him in whom I am apprehended* and
may be set free from what I once was, following your Oneness:
*forgetting the things that are behind* and not poured out upon
things to come and things transient, but *stretching forth to those
that are before* (not by dispersal but by concentration of energy)
*I press towards the prize of the supernal vocation,* where *I may
hear the voice of Thy praise* and contemplate Thy delight which
neither comes nor passes away.

But now my years are wasted in sighs, and Thou, O Lord, my
eternal Father, art my only solace; but I am divided up in time,
whose order I do not know, and my thoughts and the deepest
places of my soul are torn with every kind of tumult until the
day when I shall be purified and melted in the fire of Thy love
and wholly joined to Thee.

## xxx

And I shall stand and be established in You, in my own true
form, in Your truth. I shall no longer suffer the questions of men
who, by a disease they have merited for their punishment, ever
thirst for more than they can drink. Thus they ask: "What was
God making before He made Heaven and earth?" "Or how did
the idea of creating something come into His mind whereas He
had never created anything before?"

Grant them, Lord, to think well what they are saying, and to
realize that one cannot use the word "never" when there is no
time. If you say that he "never" made anything, obviously this
means that He did not make anything "at any time." Let them
see then that there can be no time apart from creation, and let
them cease to talk such nonsense. *Let them stretch forth to the
things that are before,* and let them realize that before all times
You are the Eternal Creator of all times, and that no times are

co-eternal with You, nor is any creature, even if there were a creature above time.

### XXXI

O Lord, My God, how deep is the abyss of Thy secret, and how far from it have the consequences of my sins held me? Cleanse my eyes and let me rejoice in Thy Light. Assuredly if there were a mind of such vast knowledge and fore-knowledge that all the past and all the future were as clearly known to it as some familiar canticle is known to me, such a mind would be marvellous beyond measure, would strike us silent with awe. For to such a mind nothing would be hidden of ages past or ages still to come, any more than when I am singing my canticle anything is unknown to me of what I have sung from the beginning, of what remains to me to sing to the end. Yet far from me be it to think that You, O Creator of the Universe, Creator of souls and bodies, had only such knowledge as that of the future and the past. Far more marvellously, far more mysteriously, do You hold Your knowledge. For when a man is singing a song he knows, or hearing a song he knows, his impressions vary and his senses are divided between the expectation of sounds to come and the memory of sounds already uttered. No such thing happens to You, the immutable and eternal, the eternal Creator of minds. In the beginning You knew heaven and earth without any element of change in your knowledge; and similarly in the beginning You created heaven and earth without any element of change in Your action. Let him who understands praise You, and let him who does not understand praise You likewise. You are the highest, and the humble of heart are Your dwelling place. For You *lift up them that are cast down,* and those do not fall who have You for their high place.

# BOOK TWELVE

## . . . HEAVEN AND EARTH
### (Genesis I, 1–2)

## I

MY HEART is deeply wrought upon, Lord, when in the neediness of this my life the words of Your Holy Scripture strike upon it. Thus it is that so often the poverty of the human intellect uses an abundance of words: for seeking uses more words than finding, petitions take longer to utter than to obtain, and knocking means more work for the hand than receiving. But we have the promise: who shall destroy it? *If God be for us, who is against us? Ask and you shall receive, seek and you shall find, knock and it shall be opened to you. For everyone that asks, receives: and he that seeks, finds: and to him that knocks, it shall be opened.*

These are Your promises, and who need fear to be deceived when Truth gives the promise?

## II

The lowliness of my tongue confesses Your loftiness, in that *You created heaven and earth*—the heaven I see, the earth I tread, the earth of which is made the body I bear. You created them.

But where, O Lord, is the heaven of heaven of which we have heard in the voice of the psalm: *the Heaven of Heaven is the Lord's: but the earth He has given to the children of men.* Where is that heaven which we do not see, by comparison with which all that we do see is but earth? For the whole corporeal creation, which is not wholly everywhere, bears loveliness to its utmost parts, even to our earth which is lowest of all; but compared to that heaven of heaven, the heaven above our earth is but earth. Thus it is not absurd to call each of these two great bodies "earth," in comparison with that mysterious heaven which is the Lord's, and not for the children of men.

## III

Assuredly this earth was *invisible and without form,* a profound abyss, upon which there was no light, for it was altogether formless. That is why You commanded to be written that *darkness was upon the face of the deep*: for darkness is only absence of light. If light had been, where should it have been save above, dominating and illumining? But since light was not yet, what could the presence of darkness be, save the absence of light? Darkness was over the deep because there was no light over it, just as where there is no sound there is silence. For what is the presence of silence save the absence of sound?

Was it not You, Lord, who instructed this soul which now makes confession to You? Was it not You, Lord, who taught me that before You gave form and outline to that formless matter, there was not anything, neither color nor shape nor body nor spirit? Yet was there not utterly nothing; there was a certain formlessness without anything to specify it.

## IV

What can we call that formlessness, how convey it to men's sluggish minds, save by finding some word already familiar? In the whole of the world what can be found closer to total formlessness than "earth" and "deep"? They are least in beauty because of the lowly grade they hold, below all higher things that shine so brilliantly. Why then should I not take it that this formless matter, which You created without beauty and yet made of it a world so beautiful, is meant to be conveyed to me with sufficient accuracy under the name of *earth, invisible and without form.*

## V

When our mind seeks something for thought to take hold of [in this concept of formless matter], it says: "It is neither an intelli-

gible form like life or justice, for it is the matter of which bodies
have been made; nor is it a sensible form, for there is nothing
that can be seen or otherwise perceived in a thing invisible and
formless." Thus speaking, the human mind can but aim at a sort
of lightless knowledge—or, if you prefer, enlightened ignorance.

VI

But I, Lord—if I am to say and write in confession to You all
that You have taught me about this formless matter—[I admit
that] when I used to hear its name without understanding, as
others without understanding spoke of it to me, I tried to conceive
it under a great number and variety of forms, so that in fact I
was not conceiving it at all. My mind was in a whirl of hideous
and horrible forms which utterly denied the order of nature; yet
they were forms all the same; and I conceived the formless not
as totally lacking form but as possessing such a form that, if it
were seen, my senses would recoil from its strangeness and gro-
tesqueness and my human weakness be utterly confounded.

But in fact the concept I had was formless not by the absence
of all forms, but only by comparison with forms more beautiful.
Right reason urged that if I wished to conceive the formless, I
should strip away every smallest vestige of every sort of form. But
I could not do it. I should have found it easier to think that whatever is totally without form cannot exist at all, than to conceive
something between form and non-being, lacking form yet not
nothing, formless and almost nothing.

So my mind ceased to question my spirit, which was full of
images of bodily forms which it changed and re-arranged as it
willed. I fixed my mind upon the bodies themselves, and looked
deeper into the mutability by which they cease to be what they
were and begin to be what they were not. And it occurred to
me that this transition from one form to another might be by
way of something formless, and not by way of absolute non-
being.

But I wanted to know, not merely to conjecture that it might be
so; and if my voice and pen were to confess to You all that You

untangled for me upon this question, which of my readers would have the endurance to take it all? Yet my heart will not cease to give You honor, and raise its canticle of praise for things which it has not the power to express.

For the mutability of mutable things is simply their capacity for all the forms into which mutable things can be changed. But what *is* this? Is it soul? Is it body? Is it any species of soul or body? If it were allowable to say that it is a nothing which is in some way something, or that it is and yet is not, that is what I should say. Certainly in some manner it must have been, in order to receive those visible and composite forms.

## VII

Whatever it is, whence could it be save from You, from whom all things are in whatever degree they are? But the less a thing resembles You, the further it is from you (I do not mean in space!). Thus Lord, You who do not change as things and circumstances change but are the Self-same, and the Self-same and the Self-same, Holy, Holy, Holy, Lord God Almighty—You, Lord, in the Beginning, which is from You, in Your wisdom, which is born of Your substance, made something and made it of nothing.

You created *heaven and earth,* but not of Your own substance: for in that event they would have been equal to Your only-begotten Son and hence to Yourself; and it would have been altogether unjust that something not proceeding from You should be equal to You. But, apart from You there was no other thing existent to make them of, O God, Trinity that is One, Unity that is Three. Therefore it was of nothing that You made heaven and earth, the great thing and the small thing: for You are almighty and good and must make all things good, the great heaven and the small earth. You were and nothing else was, and of nothing You made *heaven* [*the heaven of heaven*] *and earth,* these two, one close to You, the other close to nothing, one than which You alone are higher, the other than which nothing is lower.

## VIII

That *heaven of heaven* is Yours, O Lord; but the earth, *which You gave to the children of men* to be seen and touched, was not such as we now see it and touch it. It was *invisible and without form,* an abyss over which was no light. *Darkness was over the face of the deep,* that is darkness greater than was in the deep. The abyss of waters that we can now see has even in its depths a certain light of its own kind perceptible to the fish and the living things that creep upon the sea-bottom. But then all was close to nothingness, for it was still utterly formless; yet it was not nothing, for it could receive form.

Thus, Lord, You created the world out of formless matter: and it was of nothing that You created this almost-nothing, out of which You have made the mighty things which we children of men marvel at. For truly wonderful is that material Heaven, which on the second day—after the creation of light on the first— You set as a firmament between the water above and the water below, with the words: *Let it be made*: and it was made. This firmament You called heaven, [not the *heaven of heaven* but] the heaven over our earth and sea, which You created on the third day by giving visible form to the formless matter which You had created before any day. You had indeed made heaven before any day—for *in the Beginning You made heaven and earth—* but it was the heaven of our heaven.

But the earth which You made [in the beginning, along with the heaven of heaven] was formless matter, because *it was invisible and formless, and darkness was over the deep.* It was of this *invisible and formless earth,* of this formlessness, of this almost nothingness, that You made all those things wherein our mutable world subsists so far indeed as it can be said to subsist at all, in which the mutability appears whereby time can be perceived and measured. For time is made by the changes of things, as their forms vary and are changed, and the matter of these is that *invisible earth* of which we are speaking.

## IX

That is why the Holy Spirit, the teacher of Your servant, when he relates that *in the beginning You made heaven and earth,* says nothing about times or days. Clearly the *heaven of heaven* which You made *in the beginning* [and not on any numbered day] is in some way an intellectual creature; although in no way co-eternal with You, the Trinity, it is yet a partaker in your eternity. It holds its mutability in check because of the joy and delight of contemplating You; and from the moment of its creation it adheres to You with never a lapse and so escapes all the fleeting vicissitudes of time.

Nor was the creation of that formlessness, *the invisible and formless earth,* included in the numbering of the days. For where there is no form and no order, nothing comes and nothing passes away, and as a consequence there are no days nor any changes to mark the duration of time.

## X

Let Truth, the Light of my heart, speak to me, not my own darkness! I fell away and my sight was darkened; but from that depth, even from that depth, I loved Thee. I wandered afar, but I remembered Thee. I heard Thy voice behind me calling me to return, but I could scarcely hear it for the tumult of my unquieted passions. And now behold I return to Thy fountain panting and with burning thirst. Let none bar my way: I shall drink of it and so I shall live. Let me not be my own life: of myself I lived evilly and to myself I was death. In Thee I live again. Do Thou speak to me, do Thou instruct me. I have trusted Thy books and their words are deep mysteries.

## XI

Already, Lord, You have said with strong voice in the ear of my spirit that You are eternal, *who only have immortality*: for You change neither in form nor by motion, nor is Your will changed as the times change, for a will which is now one thing and now another is not eternal. In Your presence this truth shines clear to me: and I beg of You that it may shine ever clearer, and that under Your sheltering wings I may continue with wisdom in that clear knowledge.

Again, O Lord, You said with strong voice in the ear of my spirit that all natures and substances, which are not what You are and which yet exist, were made by You: only what is not at all, is not from You. Such, for example, is the movement of a will away from You, who are, towards some other thing, of less being than You: such a movement is a fault and a sin, and no one's sin can either harm You or disturb the order of Your rule in the greatest things or the smallest. In Your presence this truth shines clear to me: and I beg of You that it may shine ever clearer, and that under Your sheltering wings I may continue with wisdom in that clear knowledge.

Again You said with strong voice in the ear of my spirit that that creature [*the heaven of heaven*] is not co-eternal with You: You are its sole delight and it tastes of Your delight in purity unfailing: never and in no way does it lose its quality of mutability, yet, being ever in Your presence and held to You with utter love, having no future in anticipation nor passing away into any past for memory, it suffers no variation and its being is not spread out over time.

Happy creature, if such there be, because it inheres in Your beatitude, with You ever indwelling and illumining it. I find nothing that would seem to me more worthy to be called the *heaven of heaven which is the Lord's* than such a dwelling-place of Yourself, which ever contemplates Your delight without ever falling away from Your contemplation upon lesser things, a pure mind united in perfect harmony in a binding union of peace with those holy spirits, the citizens of Your City which is in heaven far above the heavens we see.

From this let the mind that wanders far from You understand if now it thirsts for You, if now *tears have been its bread, while it is said to it daily: where is Thy God; if one thing it asks of Thee and this seeks after, that it may dwell in Thy house all the days of its life?* And what is its life but Thee? And what are Thy days but Thy eternity, *Thy years which shall not fail, because Thou art always the Self-same?* From this, I say, let the mind understand, so far as it can, how far above all times You are in Your eternity, when Your dwelling-place, which has never gone away from You, is so endlessly and unfailingly united with You that it suffers no vicissitude of time: yet it is not co-eternal with You. This truth shines clear to me: and I beg of You that it may shine ever clearer, and that under Your sheltering wings I may continue with wisdom in that clear knowledge.

In the changes of the last and lowest things I see that there must be involved some kind of formless matter. Now, unless a man is all wandering and whirled about with empty fantasies in the emptiness of his heart, would he dare assert that if every form were taken away and made utterly naught—so that only this formlessness remained, thanks to which beings [endowed with form] change and pass from one form to another—this sheer formlessness could show any changes of time? Obviously it could not, for where there is no change of movement there is no time: and there is no change where there is no form.

## XII

I consider all these things as far as You give me the power, O my God, as far as You incite me to knock and open to my knocking. And I find two things made by You upon which time has no hold, although neither is co-eternal with You. The one because You so formed it that, without any wavering in its contemplation, without any intervention of change, though it is mutable it yet suffers no mutation and delights in Your eternity and immutability; the other because it was so formless that it could not change from one form to another, whether of motion or rest, and so time has no hold upon it. But You did not leave it formless. In the beginning, before all days, You made heaven and earth, the two beings of which I speak. *The earth was invisible and formless, and darkness was over the abyss.* By these words **there is** conveyed—in such a way that minds may gradually be

won which are unable to conceive a complete and utter absence of
form which is yet not a reduction to sheer nothingness—the suggestion of that formlessness out of which the second heaven [the
firmament] was made, and the visible and ordered earth, and the
beauty of water and in short whatever in the constitution of this
world we are told was made, and made on given days. And all
these are of such sort that the changes of time affect them by
reason of the ordered succession of movements and forms.

### XIII

When, O my God, I hear your Scripture say *In the beginning
God made heaven and earth, and the earth was invisible and
formless, and darkness was over the abyss,* and I observe that
Scripture does not say on what day You made these things, I
assume that it is because by "heaven" is meant the *heaven of
heaven,* the intellectual heaven, where it is given to the intellect
to know in one act, and not part by part, *not in a dark manner,
not through a glass,* but wholly, in full sight, *face to face*: not to
know now one thing, now another but, as has been said, to know
in one act without any succession of time; and because by "earth"
is meant *the invisible and formless earth,* which knows nothing
of the succession of times with their changes from this to that
because where there is no form, there is no this and no that.

It is with reference to these two, the one formed from the
beginning, the other utterly without form, the one heaven [*the
heaven of heaven*] the other earth [the invisible formless earth]
that I take it Your Scripture says, without specifying the day,
*In the beginning God made Heaven and earth.* It goes on to add
of what earth it spoke. And since it says that on the second day
the firmament was made and called heaven, it suggests what that
"heaven" was of which it first spoke without specifying a day.

### XIV

Marvellous is the profundity of Thy Scriptures. Their surface
lies before us, flattering us as we flatter children. But marvellous

is their profundity, O my God, marvellous is their profundity. To gaze into it is a shuddering, the shudder of awe, the shudder of love. I hate its enemies mightily: O, if Thou wouldst slay them *with a two-edged sword,* that it might have no enemies. I should love them to die to themselves that they might live to Thee.

But there are those, not enemies of the book of Genesis but admirers, who say: "The Spirit of God, which wròte these words by his servant Moses, did not mean by them what you say, but some other thing which we say." Thus I answer them, O God of us all: do Thou judge between us.

## XV

Will you say that that is false which Truth told me with strong voice in the ear of my spirit concerning the true eternity of the Creator—namely that His substance suffers no change whatever in time and that His will is not something additional to His substance? The consequence of this is that He does not will now one thing now another: what He wills He wills once and in one act and eternally; He does not will by a succession of acts, nor does He will a succession of objects, or come to will what He had not willed or cease to will what He had willed before: for a will of that sort would be mutable, and nothing mutable is eternal: but our God is eternal.

Or again, would you deny what He told me in the ear of my spirit—namely that the expectation of things to come turns into attention to them when they have come, and attention turns into memory when they have passed away: obviously every mental act which thus varies is mutable, and nothing mutable is eternal: but our God is eternal. I gather these truths and put them together, and I find that my God, the eternal God, did not create by any new will and that His knowledge admits nothing that is passing.

What then will you say, you who oppose me? Are these things false? "No," they say. What then? Is it false to assert that every nature which has a form, and likewise matter capable of receiving

a form, had received their existence from Him alone who is
supremely good because He supremely is? "We do not deny this
either," they say. What then? Perhaps you deny that there exists
a sublime creature cohering to the true and truly eternal God with
love so pure that, though not co-eternal with Him, yet it does not
detach itself and flow away from Him into any variation or
vicissitude of time but reposes in the utterly sure contemplation of
Him alone: because You, O God, show Yourself to him who
loves You as much as You command, and are sufficient unto him,
so that he never swerves away from You nor toward self? This is
the *house of God*, not an earthly house nor of any material
heaven, but spiritual, a sharer of Your eternity because for
eternity it remains without sin. *You have established it for ever
and for ages and ages: you have a decree, and it shall not pass
away*. Yet it is not co-eternal with You, for it is not without
beginning: it too was made.

Certainly we do not find any time before it, for *wisdom has
been created before all things*. Of course I do not mean that Wisdom who is co-eternal and equal, O our God, with You, His
Father, and by whom all things were created, the Beginning in
whom You made heaven and earth. I refer to created wisdom,
that intellectual nature which by the contemplation of light
is itself light: for this, though created, is likewise called wisdom:
there is as much difference between the Wisdom which creates
and the wisdom which is created as between the Light which gives
light and the light that is so only by reflection, or between the
Justice which justifies and the Justice which results from being
justified. Have we not been called Your justice: as Your servant
Paul says: *that we might be made the justice of God in Him?*
There was then a certain created wisdom created before all things,
the reasonable and intellectual mind of Your pure City, *our
mother, which is above and is free and eternal in heaven*: and
what could be meant by heaven here save the *heaven of heaven*
which praises you, the *heaven of heaven which is the Lord's?* We
do not find any time before it, because it precedes the creation of
time, *being created before all things*: yet before it lies the eternity
of its Creator, made by whom it drew the beginning, not of its

time, because as yet there was no time, but of its condition of being.

Thus it is from you, our God, yet in such a way as to be utterly other than You and not the Self-same. Yet we not only find no time before it, we find no time in it, because it is fitted to gaze always upon Your face nor ever to be turned away: so that it is subjected to no change. But mutability abides in its essence, so that it could fall into darkness and coldness unless it cohered to You in a love so great that Your noonday ever shone upon it and warmed it with its heat.

O lovely and luminous house, *I have loved your beauty and the place where the glory dwells of my Lord,* who made it and possesses it. In my pilgrimage may I sigh for you; and I ask of Him who made you that He should possess me too in you, because me too He made. *I have gone astray like a sheep that is lost,* but I hope that I may be brought back to You upon the shoulders of my Shepherd, your Builder.

You whom I answer as my opponents, what have you to say to me? You believe that Moses was a pious servant of God and his books oracles of the Holy Spirit. Is not that the house of God, not indeed co-eternal with God yet in its own mode eternal in heaven, where you look in vain for the changes of time because you will not find them? It rises beyond all extension and all the fleeting space of time, for its good is to adhere to God for ever. "Agreed," they say. Then which of the things that *my heart cried to my God* when it *heard the voice of Thy praise* within, which of them do you charge as false? Is it because I have said there was a formless matter, in which there was no order, because there was no form? But where there was no order, there could be no succession of time; yet this almost-nothing, since it was not absolutely nothing, must have been from Him from whom all is that in any way is. "Nor do we deny this either," they say.

## XVI

I would have some discourse in Your presence, O my God, with those who grant that all these things are true which Your

Truth has uttered inwardly in my mind. As to those who deny them, let them bark away as they will and deafen themselves: yet I shall strive to persuade them to silence, shall strive to open a way by which Your word may come to them. But if they refuse and repulse me, I beseech You, O my God, *be not Thou silent to me.* Do Thou speak truly within my heart, for Thou alone dost so speak. Let me leave them outside, breathing into the dust and filling their eyes with earth, and let me *enter into my chamber* and sing my songs of love to Thee, groaning with inexpressible groaning in my pilgrimage, and remembering Jerusalem with my heart stretching upwards in longing for it: Jerusalem my Fatherland, Jerusalem which is my mother: and remembering Thee its Ruler, its Light, its Father and Tutor and Spouse, its pure and strong Delight, its Joy unshakable and the sum of all ineffable good because Thou alone art the one supreme and true Good. So that I shall not turn away but shall come to the peace of that Jerusalem, my dear mother, where are the first-fruits of my spirit, from which all certitude comes to me, and there Thou shalt collect from my present scatteredness and deformity all that I am, and Thou shalt re-form me and confirm me unto eternity, O my God, my Mercy.

But there are some who do not say that all these truths are false, but honour Your holy Scripture given us through Moses, Your Saint, and are one with us in regarding it as the pinnacle of authority to be followed: yet they make certain objections to my interpretation. And I say: Do you, Our God, judge between my confession and their objections.

### XVII

They say: "Though all this may be true, yet it was not of these two beings that Moses was thinking when by the revelation of the Holy Spirit he said: *In the beginning God made heaven and earth.* By the word *heaven* he did not signify that spiritual or intellectual creature which always contemplates the face of God, nor by the word *earth* formless matter."

What then did he signify? "What we say ourselves is what he

meant and expressed in those words." And what is that? "By the words *heaven and earth*," they reply, "he meant first to signify comprehensively and in brief the whole visible world, and afterwards to detail point by point—listing the days—the same totality which it pleased the Holy Spirit so to express. The unlettered and carnally-minded people to whom he spoke were the kind of men to whom he judged that only the visible works of God could be conveyed." As to the *invisible and formless earth* and *the abyss* of darkness—from which we are shown successively that during those days all the visible things that we all know were made and set in order—they grant me that this may very well be understood as the formless matter I have called it.

But another may say that the phrase *heaven and earth* signifies this same formless and confused matter, because from it this visible world with all the natures so clear to be seen in it—all of which is commonly enough styled "heaven and earth"—was established and perfected.

Or again, another may say that the phrase *heaven and earth* quite properly signifies nature visible and invisible so that the whole creation which God made in Wisdom, that is to say in the Beginning, is comprised under these two words. Yet all things were made of nothing and not of the actual substance of God— because they are not the same as God and in them all there remains a principle of mutability, whether they abide changeless, like the eternal house of God, or suffer change like the soul and body of man. Therefore the common matter of all things visible and invisible—a matter still formless but capable of receiving a form, the matter of which heaven and earth were to be made, meaning by heaven and earth the invisible and visible creation but each now endowed with form—this common matter is signified by the terms *invisible and formless earth* on the one hand and *darkness over the deep* on the other: the distinction being that *invisible and formless earth* applies to corporeal matter before it is determined by form, *darkness over the deep* to spiritual matter before a boundary was set to its boundless flow and the light of Wisdom shone upon it.

There is still one more possibility. There might be one who says

that in the text *In the beginning God made heaven and earth,*
the phrase *heaven and earth* does not signify invisible and visible
natures already perfected and endowed with form, but a still
formless inchoation of things, a matter capable of receiving form
and of being used for creation, because in it already existed—
though confusedly and as yet without any distinction of qualities
and forms—the two creatures, one spiritual, the other corporeal,
which in the order now given them are called heaven and earth.

### XVIII

I hear all these objections and weigh them, but I have no desire
to contend in words *for it is to no profit, but to the subverting of
the hearers. The law is good for edification, if a man use it lawfully,* because *its end is charity from a pure heart and a good conscience and an unfeigned faith;* and our Master knows *on which
two commandments He made the whole law and the prophets
depend.* How am I who ardently confess this law of love, O my
God, Light of my eyes in darkness, injured when in these words
different meanings are found which may very well be true?

What harm is it to me, I ask again, if I think the writer had
one meaning, someone else thinks he had another? All of us who
read are trying to see and to grasp the meaning of the man we
are reading: and given that we believe him a speaker of the truth,
we should obviously not think that he was saying something that
we know or think to be false. While therefore each one of us is
trying to understand in the sacred writings what the writer meant
by them, what harm if one accepts a meaning which You, Light
of all true minds, show him to be in itself a true meaning, even
if the author we are reading did not actually mean that by it:
since his meaning also, though different from mine, is true.

### XIX

What certainly is true, O Lord, is that *You made heaven and
earth.* It is true that the Beginning was Your Wisdom, in which
You made all things. It is likewise true that this visible world is

in two great parts, heaven and earth, which two words briefly summarize all natures created and endowed with form. And it is true that anything subject to change suggests to our mind a certain formless element, by which it receives form or by which it is changed and transformed. It is true that a being which is so closely united with the immutable that, though mutable, it does not change is not subject to time. It is true that formlessness, which is almost nothingness, cannot have any succession of time. It is true that that of which something is made can by a usage of language be given the name of the thing that is made from it: so that the formless matter of which heaven and earth are made can be called heaven and earth. It is truth that of all things endowed with form nothing is nearer to the formless than earth and the abyss. It is true that not only whatever has been created and given form but all that can be created and given form is of Your creation, *of whom are all things*. It is true that whatever is formed from formless being, was itself first formless, then endowed with form.

## XX

Of all these truths—none of which are doubted by those to whom You have granted to see them with the eye of the spirit and who believe unshakeably that Your servant Moses spoke in the spirit of truth—of all these truths he chooses one who says: *In the beginning God made heaven and earth,* that is in His Word co-eternal with Himself God made the intelligible and sensible or, to put it another way, the spiritual and corporeal creation.

He chooses another who says: *In the beginning God made heaven and earth,* that is in His Word co-eternal with Himself God made the universal mass of this corporeal world with all the natures visible and known to us that it contains.

He chooses another who says: *In the beginning God made heaven and earth,* that is in His Word co-eternal with Himself, God made the formless matter of the spiritual and corporeal world.

He chooses another who says: *In the beginning God made*

*heaven and earth,* that is in His Word co-eternal with Himself God made the formless matter of the corporeal creation, in which heaven and earth—which we now see distinct and endowed with form in the structure of our universe—then formlessly were.

He chooses another who says: *In the beginning God made heaven and earth,* that is in the actual first movement of His making and working, God made a formless matter in which heaven and earth were indistinctly contained, and out of which they were formed and now exist and are to be seen with all that is in them.

### XXI

Likewise with regard to the meaning of the words that follow, of all the truths I have already stated, he chooses one who says: *The earth was invisible and formless, and darkness was upon the face of the deep,* meaning that this corporeal thing which God made, was as yet only the formless matter of corporeal things, without order, without light.

He chooses another who says: *The earth was invisible and formless, and darkness was upon the face of the deep,* meaning that the totality which is called heaven and earth was still only formless and lightless matter, of which the material heaven and material earth were to be made with all the things in them that can be known by the bodily senses.

He chooses another who says: *The earth was invisible and formless, and darkness was upon the face of the deep,* meaning that the totality which is called *heaven and earth* was the matter still formless and lightless, of which were to be made the intelligible heaven—elsewhere called the *heaven of heaven*—and the earth, that is to say the whole of corporeal nature, under which name is to be included the material heaven—in other words the matter of which the whole of creation visible and invisible was to be made.

He chooses another who says. *The earth was invisible and formless, and darkness was upon the face of the deep,* meaning that Scripture did not call that original formlessness by the name of *heaven and earth,* for that formlessness already was in existence, and is referred to as *the invisible and formless earth and the abyss of darkness*: of which, as Scripture had already said, God made heaven and earth, that is the spiritual and corporeal creation.

He chooses another who says: *The earth was invisible and formless, and darkness was upon the face of the deep,* meaning that there already was a formlessness as the matter of which Scripture teaches that God made heaven and earth, made, that is, the corporeal mass of the world divided into its two great parts upper and lower, with all the creatures known to us and familiar which they contain.

XXII

To these last two opinions some one might wish to object: If you will not have it that formless matter is signified by the phrase heaven and earth, then there must have been something, not made by God, of which He made heaven and earth. For Scripture does not say that God made that formless matter, unless we take it as signified either by the phrase *heaven and earth* or by the word *earth* alone when it says: *In the beginning God made heaven and earth*. Thus in that which follows: *The earth was invisible and formless,* although it pleased Moses thus to call formless matter, yet we can only understand by it that which God made, as written in the verse before: *God made heaven and earth*.

The champions of the last two opinions set out above, or of either of them, will reply to these objections: We do not deny that this formless matter was made by God, from whom are *all things very good*: because as we hold that what is created and endowed with form is a higher good, we also hold that what is made capable of being created and endowed with form, though a lesser good, is still a good. Scripture has not mentioned that God made this formless matter: but there are many other things it does not say God made, for example Cherubim and Seraphim, and other orders of angels which the Apostle sets out as distinct— Thrones, Dominations, Principalities, Powers: yet it is clear that God made them all. If in the phrase: *God made heaven and earth,* all things are held to be included, what are we to say of the waters, over which *the spirit of God moves?* For if these are held to be included under the name earth, how can the same name be applied to formless matter, since we see that the waters are so beautiful? And again if we read it thus, why is it written that of that formless mass the firmament was made and given the name of heaven, but it is not written that the waters were created? For they are not still formless and invisible, for we see the order and the beauty of their flow. Or if you argue that they received this beauty when God said: *Let the waters that are under the heaven be gathered together into one place,* thus taking their gathering together as their reception of form, what is to be said of the waters which are above the firmament? They cannot be formless since they have merited to occupy so honourable a place, yet Scripture does not tell us by what word they were endowed with form. Thus if Genesis does not mention that God made some particular thing, yet no sound faith or clear intelligence doubts that He made it. Again no rational doctrine would dare to teach that those waters are co-eternal with God because we find them mentioned in the Book of Genesis but do not find any statement as to where or when they were made. Why then should we not under the teaching of truth hold that this formless matter which Scripture calls *invisible and formless earth and abyss of darkness* was made by God of nothing (and thus is not co-eternal with Him), though the scriptural account omits to mention where it was made?

## XXIII

I hear these opinions and examine them as well as my weakness, which I confess to You, my God, though You already know it, will allow. And I see that two kinds of disagreement can arise when something is told us in words by truthful messengers. One of these arises if there is any question of the truth of the things themselves, the other if there is any dispute as to the meaning of the person who gives the message. It is one thing to seek out the truth as to the mode of creation, quite another thing to seek what Moses, that splendour of the household of Your faith, wished the reader or hearer to understand by his words. As to the first sort far from me be all who think they know things that are in fact false. As to the second, be likewise far from me all who think Moses said things that are false. May I be with those in You, Lord, and rejoice with them in You who are nourished by Your truth in the breath of Your charity; and may they and I together approach the words of Your book and in them seek Your meaning through the meaning of Your servant by whose pen You gave them to us.

XXIV

Thus different meanings are extracted from these words by different enquirers. Among so many meanings—each of them true in itself—can any of us find one of which he would dare to affirm that Moses meant this, or wished that to be understood from what he wrote, as confidently as he would affirm that this or that is true, whether Moses meant it or not? As for me, O my God, Your servant, I have vowed to You the sacrifice of my confession in what I am now writing, and I pray that in Your mercy it may be given me to pay my vows to You. But though I affirm with all confidence that You created all things visible and invisible in Your immutable Word, would I say as confidently that this and not some other truth was in the mind of Moses when he wrote: *In the beginning God made heaven and earth*? No, I do not see that this was the thought in his mind when he wrote these words as clearly as I see in Your truth that it certainly is so.

It is possible that when he said *in the beginning,* he meant "in the beginning of creation"; it is possible that when he said *heaven and earth* he had not in mind any nature, whether spiritual or corporeal, already formed and perfected, but both of these inchoate and not as yet endowed with form. I see quite clearly that, whichever of these he meant, it would be true; but which of them he had in mind in writing these words I do not so clearly see. All the same whether so great a man saw either of them in his mind when he was writing these words or perhaps some other truth still which I have not suggested here—I cannot doubt that what he saw was true and that he wrote it truly.

Let no one then go on bothering me with such words as: "Moses did not mean what you say, he meant what I say." If he said to me: "How do you know that Moses meant by these words what you say?"—I should take the question with complete calmness, and should answer perhaps as I have just answered, or at rather more length if he were slow of understanding. But when he says: "He did not mean what you say, he meant what I say," yet does not deny that what each of us says is true, then, O Life of the poor, O my God, in whose bosom is no contradiction, rain down the gift of moderation upon my heart, that I may bear such talk with patience. For what they say, they say not because they are godly men and have seen it in the mind of Your servant Moses, but because they are proud men: it is not that they know the opinion of Moses but that they love their own opinion, and this not because it is true but because it is their own. Otherwise they would have as much love for the truth uttered by another: just as I love what they say when they say truth—not because it is theirs but because it is truth: from the mere fact that it is true it ceases to be theirs. But if they love it because it is true, then it is not only theirs but mine too, it is the common property of all lovers of truth.

But in that they contend that Moses did not mean what I say but what they say, I will have none of them, I do not love them, because even if what they say is so, yet their boldness is not the boldness of knowledge but of rashness, it is born not of vision but of arrogance.

Your judgments, Lord, are to be feared with trembling. For Your truth is not mine or this man's or that man's; it belongs to all of us because publicly You call us to share it, warning us most terribly not to possess it as our private property, lest we be deprived of it. For whoever claims for himself what You have given for the enjoyment of all, and would have as his own what is meant for everyone, is driven forth from the wealth of all to his own poor wealth, that is from truth to a lie. *When he speaks a lie, he speaks of his own.*

Give heed, O excellent Judge, O God, Truth Itself, give heed to the reply I shall make to such an opponent. Give heed, for I speak in Your presence and in the presence of my brethren, who *use the law lawfully unto the end of charity*. Give heed and mark what I say to him, if it is Your pleasure.

This is the fraternal and peaceable language I use to him: "If we both see that what you say is true, and we both see that what I say is true, then tell me, wherein do we see it? Not I in you certainly, nor you in me, but both of us in that immutable truth which is above our minds. Since therefore we are in no disagreement about the Light itself of the Lord our God, why do we dispute about the thought of one who is a man like ourselves: for we cannot see that as we see the immutable Truth. Even if Moses himself appeared to us and said "This is what I meant," we should not actually see that he meant it but should take his word for it. Let *one be not puffed up against the other for another, above that which is written. Let us love the Lord our God with our whole heart and our whole soul and our whole mind and our neighbor as ourself*. Whatever Moses meant in his books, he meant according to these two commandments of charity—unless we believe this, we make the Lord a liar, for we should judge of the soul of His servant otherwise than He taught. Now see how foolish it is, in such a flood of true meanings which can come from those words, rashly to assert that Moses especially intended one or other of them, and in sinful contention to offend that charity by reason of which he, whose words we are seeking to explain, said all that he said.

### XXVI

But a further thought comes to me, O my God, Loftiness of my lowliness and Repose in my labor, You who hear my confessions and forgive my sins, You command me to love my neighbor as myself. Therefore I cannot think that Moses Your most faithful servant was given by you lesser gifts than I should have wished and longed to have for myself if I had been born at the same time as he, and established in the same place—that is, if by the service of *my* heart and tongue writings were to come forth which for so long after should be to all nations and over the whole world so towering in authority over the words of all doctrines of falsehood and pride.

Now if I had been Moses—*for we all come from the same lump* and *what is man that Thou art mindful of him*—if I had been the same as he and You had given me the book of Genesis to write, I should have wished that You would grant me such a skill in writing, such an art for the construction of what I had to say, that not even those who cannot as yet grasp how God creates would reject my words as too much for their strength; and again that those who can grasp so much, would find fully contained in the few words of Your servant whatever truths they had arrived at in their own thinking; and if in the light of truth some other man saw some further meaning, that that too would be discoverable in those same words of mine.

### XXVII

A spring enclosed in a narrow space is more abundant and pours its flow by more streams over a wider countryside than any single one of those same streams however long its course. Similarly the writing of the dispenser of Your word, since it was meant to be of service to many who later should preach upon it, sets flowing in its brevity of utterance torrents of clear truth from which each may draw such truth as he can, one man this, another that, but with far lengthier windings of words.

There are those who when they read or hear the words [*In the beginning God created heaven and earth*] picture God as a kind of man, or some corporeal mass of immense power, who by some new and sudden decision created heaven and earth apart from Himself and in some sense at a distance from Himself, heaven and earth being two great bodies, one above, one below, in which all things are contained. And when they come to *God said: Be it made: and it was made,* they think of these words as words that had a beginning and an end, sounding in time and passing away, so that the moment they had passed away there existed immediately what they had commanded to exist. All this they imagine and much more of the same sort through their material way of thinking.

Such people are still like infants with minds barely existent—yet it is as though on the utterly simple language of Scripture their weakness is upborne as on a mother's breast: and their faith is built up unto salvation in that they see and hold as certain that God made all the natures which their senses look upon in such marvellous variety.

But if any man, despising as poverty the simplicity of Your words, is so foolish in his pride as to leap from the nest in which You nourish him, the poor wretch, alas, will fall: do You, O Lord God, have pity lest those who pass by the way should tread upon that poor unfeathered nestling: send Your angel to put him back in the nest that he may not perish before he has learnt to fly.

### XXVIII

There are others to whom these words are not so much a nest as a thick-leaved orchard, in which they see fruit hidden, and they flutter about it with joy, and gaze upon it chattering, and eat of the fruit.

For when they read or hear these words, they see that all the past and all the future are over-towered in Your eternal and changeless abiding, O God, yet that there is no creature of time not made by You: that Your will being one with Yourself was in no way changed or other than it had been before; yet by it You made all things: [and this] not as drawing them out of Yourself in Your own likeness, the form of all things, but producing from nothing a being utterly unlike You and utterly without form, which yet could be formed in Your likeness, by a recourse to Your unity in the measure ordained by You and given to each being according to its kind: and that all things are very good, whether they abide close to You, or else, at various degrees removed from You in time and place, they cause or undergo all the lovely changes of the world.

These things they see and they rejoice in the light of Your truth, so far as their small strength allows.

One man studying the words: *In the beginning God made,*
understands "the beginning" as meaning Wisdom, *who also
speaks unto us.* Another studying the same words understands
"the beginning" as simply the commencement of creation, and
thus takes *In the beginning God made* as meaning *first God made.*

Of those who take the word "beginning" as meaning that *in
Wisdom You made heaven and earth,* one thinks that *heaven and
earth* signifies the matter of which heaven and earth were to be
created, another thinks the words refer to natures already formed
and distinct, another thinks that *heaven* means a formed and
spiritual nature, and *earth* the formless nature of corporeal matter. Those who take the words *heaven and earth* as meaning the
matter still without form of which heaven and earth were to be
formed, do not all attach the same meaning even to this: for
one sees it as that from which the intelligible and sensible creation
are alike produced, another only as that from which the sensible
corporeal world is produced containing in its mighty bosom all
natures visible and shown to us.

Nor do those agree who think that *heaven and earth* signifies
created things already formed and given their places: one thinks
they refer to the invisible and the visible world, another only to
the visible, in which we see both heaven shining with light and
earth wrapped in darkness, with all that they contain.

XXIX

Now if a man takes *In the beginning God made* as meaning
*first God made,* it is not possible properly to understand *heaven
and earth* save as the matter of heaven and earth, that is of the
whole of creation, spiritual and corporeal. For if he holds that the
universe was created already formed, we might well ask him: If
God made this first, what did He make afterwards? And since he
will not find anything after everything, he will have to face the
question: How could it be first, if nothing came after?

If he says that God first created matter formless and then gave
it form, this would not be absurd provided he is able to distinguish between priority in eternity, priority in time, priority in

choice, priority in origin: priority in eternity, as God is before all
created things: in time, as the flower is before the fruit: in choice,
as the fruit is before the flower: in origin, as sound is before song.

Of these four, those I have mentioned the first and last are very
difficult to understand, the middle two quite easy. It is a rare and
very arduous act of sight, O Lord, to see Your eternity immutable
yet creating things mutable, and thus prior to them. And again
who is so piercing of mental vision as to be able to grasp without
very great effort how sound is prior to song: for song is ordered
sound, and though obviously a thing can exist unordered, that
which does not exist cannot be ordered. Thus matter is prior to
that which is made of it, not prior in the sense that it makes it—
since it would be truer to say that it is itself made [into the new
thing]—nor prior by any interval of time. For we do not begin by
uttering formless tuneless sounds and then later fit and shape these
into a song as we shape wood into a box or silver into a vase. Such
materials as these do precede in time the forms of the things which
are made of them. But with song it is not so. For when we sing,
the sound of the song is heard: it does not first sound in a dis-
ordered way and then get shaped into a song. For whatever the
sound is, as soon as it has sounded it ceases to be, and you will
not find anything left of it that you could take up and shape:
thus a song is embodied in its sound, yet that sound is the matter
of the song. The sound comes forth ordered, that it may be a
song. Thus, as I said, the material, which is sound, is prior to the
form, which is song: not prior as having the power to make it,
for sound is not the maker of songs, but is put by the body at the
disposal of the singer's mind for him to make a song of it; nor
prior in time, for sound and song are uttered together; nor prior
in choice, for sound is not worth more than song, since song is
nothing but sound, sound made beautiful. It is simply prior in
origin, because the song is not formed in order that there should
be a sound, but the sound in order that there should be a song.

By this example let him who is able understand that the matter
of things was made first and called heaven and earth, because of
this matter heaven and earth were made: but first does not mean
first in time, because the forms of things give rise to time, and this

matter was formless and only manifested itself in time at the same time as time. Yet one cannot speak of this formless matter save as first in time, though it is last in value—since formed things clearly are better than unformed—and it is preceded by the eternity of the Creator, so that that of which things were to be made should itself be made of nothing.

xxx

In this diversity of true opinions, let Truth itself bring harmony; and may our God have pity upon us that we may *use the law lawfully, for the end of the commandment which is pure charity.*

Thus if anyone asks me which of these was the meaning in the mind of Moses, Your servant, these would not be my confessions if I did not confess to you that I do not know. But I know that all these are true meanings, except those carnal meanings of which I have said just what I think. Yet those who hold these carnal meanings are little children of good hope, and the words of Your Book, so deep in their humility, saying so much in their brevity, have no terrors for them.

But let all of us who, as I confess, see and say truth in these words, love one another and likewise love You, O Fount of truth to those who thirst for truth and not for vanity; and so let us honor Moses Your servant, the dispenser of Your Scripture, as to believe that when under Your inspiration he wrote these words, he had in his mind whatever is most excellent in them by the illumination of truth and their fruitfulness for our profit.

xxxi

Thus when one man says to me: "Moses meant what I think," and another "Not at all, he meant what I think," it seems to me the truly religious thing to say: Why should he not have meant both, if both are true; and if in the same words some should see a third and a fourth and any other number of true meanings, why should we not believe that Moses saw them all, since by him the one God tempered Sacred Scripture to the minds of many who should see truths in it yet not all the same truths.

Certainly—and I say this fearlessly and from my heart—if I had to write with such vast authority I should prefer so to write that my words should mean whatever truth anyone could find upon these matters, rather than express one true meaning so clearly as to exclude all others, though these contain no falsehood to offend me. This being so, I would not be so rash, O my God, as to believe that so great a man did not merit this gift at Your hands. When he was writing these words he wholly saw and realized whatever truth we have been able to find in them—and much beside that we have not been able to find, or have not yet been able to find, though it is there in them to be found.

### XXXII

Lastly, O Lord, You who are God and not flesh and blood, even if a man [like Moses] did see less than is there, could Your *good Spirit, which shall lead me into the right land,* have failed to see whatever You Yourself were to reveal in those words to later readers, even if Moses, through whom the words were uttered, may possibly have seen only one out of many true meanings? If this is so, granted that the meaning Moses saw was nobler than the others, then, Lord, either show it to us or at Your pleasure show us some other true meaning: so that whether You discover to us the same meaning as to Moses Your servant or some other meaning arising out of the same words, it may be You feeding us and not error mocking us.

Behold, O Lord my God, how much I have written on those few words, how much! What strength of mind, what time would be required to discuss the whole of Your Scripture at the same rate!

But let me summarize my confession to You upon these words, and choose one meaning which You have breathed into my soul as true and certain and good, even though many others may come into my mind, where so many are possible: and let my confession be made in the assurance that if I have said what Your servant meant, that is truest and best, and for that I must strive: yet if I have not succeeded, that I shall at least say what Your Truth willed to say to me by His words, just as He said what He willed to Moses.

# BOOK THIRTEEN

## THE DAYS OF CREATION
### (Genesis I, 2–31)

I CALL upon Thee, O my God, my Mercy, who didst create me and didst not forget me when I forgot Thee. I call Thee into my soul, which Thou dost make ready to receive Thee by the desire that Thou dost inspire in it: do Thou not abandon me now when I call upon Thee, for it was by Thy aid going before me that I called upon Thee; and Thou hadst urged me over and over, in a great variety of ways, to hear Thee from afar off and be converted and call upon Thee who wert calling me.

It was You, Lord, who destroyed all my acts that deserved ill, that You might not have to punish me for what my hands have done, the hands by which I had fallen away from You; and You went before all my deeds that deserved well, that You might give recompense for what Your hands have done, the hands by which You had made me: for, before I was, You were, nor was I anything at all that You should grant me existence: yet behold I am, and the reason is Your goodness which made provision for all that You have made me to be, and all that You made me of. You had no need of me, nor am I a being so good as to be of any aid to You, my Lord and my God: I do not exist to serve You as though to save You from weariness in action, or that Your power would be less for lack of my service: nor is the cult I pay You like the cultivation of a field, so that You would be the poorer for lack of it:* but I serve You and worship You that I may be happy in You, to whom I owe that I am a being capable of happiness.

II

It is from the plenitude of Your goodness that Your creature subsists, that a good should not remain out of existence, which, although it benefits You in no way and is not of You and equal to You, yet can be given existence by You.

* I do not see how to reproduce the pun in English. The Latin is: "neque ut sic te colam quasi terram, ut sis uncultus si non te colam."

What had *heaven and earth,* which You *created in the beginning,* merited of You? Let spiritual and corporeal nature say what they had deserved of You, which You made *in your Wisdom,* that by it all things inchoate and formless whether in the spiritual or corporeal order should be held in being in spite of their tendency away from You into disorder and utter unlikeness to You: the spiritual, even though formless, being more excellent than if it were a body endowed with form, and the corporeal though formless more excellent than if it were utterly nothing: and all the things *that are very good* would have remained upheld by Your Word but formless still, unless by the same Word they had been recalled to Your unity and given form and being by You the one supreme Good. But what had they deserved of You that they should exist even formless, for they would not have existed even thus but for You?

What had corporeal matter deserved of You that it should exist even invisible and void, for it would not have existed even thus save because You made it? It was not: therefore it could not deserve of You that it should be.

And what had that first inchoation of the spiritual creation deserved of You, that it should have even its wavering lightless existence [doomed to remain] like the abyss and unlike You, if by the same Word it had not been turned toward the Word by which it was made: and, illumined by It, become light—not in equality with You, but conformed to the Image which is Your equal.

For a body, to be is not the same thing as to be beautiful, otherwise a body could not be ugly; similarly, for a created spirit, to live is not the same thing as to live wisely: otherwise such a spirit would remain immutable in wisdom. *But it is good for it to adhere to You* always, lest the light it had gained by turning towards You, it might lose by turning away from You, and so fall back into a life similar to the abyss of darkness.

But we, who by our souls are a spiritual creation, have turned away from You our light. In this life *we were heretofore darkness,* and we labor in what is still left of our darkness until *we are made*

*Thy justice* in Thy only-begotten Son, until we are made *as the mountains of God: for thy judgments are as a great deep.*

### III

On the first day of creation You said: *Be light made. And light was made*: it seems to me that this properly applies to the spiritual creation, which was already in some sense life, capable of receiving light from You. But just as it had not deserved of You that it should be the kind of life that could receive light, so, now that it existed, it did not deserve of You that light should actually be given it. Its formlessness would not have been pleasing in Your sight unless it had become light: and it became light not from the mere fact of existing, but by turning its face to the light that enlightened it and cohering to it: so that it owed solely to Your grace both that it lived and lived happily, being turned, by a change for the better, toward that which can suffer no change for worse or for better. For You alone are, because You alone simply are: for to You, to live and to live happily are one thing, because You are Your own beatitude.

### IV

What then would have been wanting to that goodness which You are unto Yourself, if those things either had not come into existence at all, or had remained formless? For You created them not out of any need of them but out of the plenitude of Your goodness, shaping and turning them to form though Your joy was not increased by them. You are perfect and their imperfection displeases You: they are perfected by You and they please You, but not as though You were imperfect and needed to be perfected by their perfection. For Your good Spirit *moved over the waters*, but was not upborne by them, as though resting upon them. When the Holy Spirit is said to rest in any, He makes them to rest in Him. But Your incorruptible and immutable will, sufficient in itself to itself, moved over that life that You had made, to which living and beatitude are not one, because it lives still even when tossing about in its own darkness: yet it is possible to it to be turned to Him by whom it was made, and more and more to live by the Fountain of life, and in His light to see the light and to be made perfect and glorified and brought to beatitude.

v

And now [in these opening verses of Genesis] *in a dark manner* I see the Trinity, which You are, O my God: for You, the Father *created heaven and earth in the Beginning* of our Wisdom, which is Your Wisdom, born of you, equal to You and co-eternal, Your Son. I have said a good deal about *the heaven of heaven* and *the earth invisible and formless* and *the abyss* which would have remained dark according to the aimless drift of its spiritual formlessness if it had not been turned to Him from whom comes whatever is life, and by His illumination it became living and beautiful, and the heaven came to be of that [lower] heaven, which was created afterwards between the waters and the waters.

Already in the word "God," who did these things, I recognized the Father, and in the word "Beginning," in which He did these things, I recognized the Son; and believing that my God is Trinity, following my belief I sought in His sacred words, and behold I found Your Spirit *moving over the waters*. Thus I found the Trinity, My God, Father, and Son, and Holy Spirit, the Creator of every creature.

vi

O true Light, to You I lift up my heart lest it should teach me vanities, do You cleave its darkness and tell me, I beseech You by Charity our Mother, tell me, I beseech You, why it was that Your Scripture named Your Spirit, only after having named *heaven and earth invisible and formless* and *the darkness over the abyss?* Was it because He had to be first shown to us as *moving over,* and this could not be said unless something had already been mentioned over which Your Spirit could be understood as moving? He did not move over the Father and the Son and He could not properly be said to be *moving over* if He were not moving over anything. Thus that over which He was moving had to be mentioned before Him, since He had to be first shown to us as *moving over*. But why was it necessary that He should be first shown to us thus?

VII

Now let whoever can, follow in his intelligence Your Apostle when he says that Your *charity is poured forth in our hearts by the Holy Spirit who is given to us,* and again when, teaching us concerning spiritual things, he *shows us the yet more excellent way* of charity, and bends his knees for us to You that we may know the *knowledge surpassing all other of the charity of Christ.* Thus from the beginning He, the surpassing one, was shown moving *over* the waters.

To whom shall I tell, how shall I tell, of the weight of concupiscence dragging us down that steep abyss, and of charity which lifts us up by Your Spirit, who *moved over the waters?* To whom shall I tell it? How shall I tell it? Shall I say that we sink, and we rise again? But it is not in any space-occupying abyss that we sink and we rise again. The reality is at once like this and quite unlike. It is our passions, our loves, the uncleanness of our spirit that bear us downward under the weight of the cares we are so much attached to; and it is Your sanctity that bears us upward by our attachment to peace of spirit: so that we lift up our hearts to You, where *Your spirit moves over the waters,* and we come to supreme peace when *our soul has passed through a water insupportable.*

VIII

The angel fell, the soul of man fell, showing us in what utter darkness the abyss which contained the whole spiritual creation would have been if You had not said on the first day: *Be light made: and light was made,* and if the whole intelligence of the Celestial City had not remained obedient, cleaving to You, and at rest in Your Spirit which moves immutably over all things mutable. Otherwise the very *heaven of heaven* would have been an abyss of darkness; *but now it is light in the Lord.*

For in the restless misery of fallen spirits, which expose their darkness stripped of the vesture of Your light, You clearly show how great You made the rational creature, since for its repose and beatitude nothing less than You suffices. Thus it does not suffice for itself. Thou, O God *wilt enlighten my darkness*: from Thee shall arise our vesture of light, and *our darkness shall be as the mid-day.*

Give Thyself to me, O my God, give Thyself once more to me. I love Thee: and if my love is too small a thing, grant me to love more intensely. I cannot measure, to know how much my love falls short of sufficiency, that my life should run to Thy embrace and never be turned away until it is *hidden in the secret of Thy face.* This only do I know, that it is ill with me when Thou art not with me—I do not mean *by* me, but *in* me; and that all abundance which is not my God to me is neediness.

## IX

But did not Father and Son also *move over the waters*? If we take this movement as of a body moving in space, then it is not true even of the Holy Spirit; but if we take it as referring to the changeless super-eminence of divinity over all things mutable, then Father and Son and Holy Spirit moved over the waters.

But why then is only the Holy Spirit mentioned here? Why in regard to Him alone is there mention of a place where He was—though in fact it was no place—He of whom alone it was said that He is your gift? It is in Your gift that we rest, it is there that we enjoy You. Our rest is our place.

So high does love raise us up, and Your Holy Spirit lifts up our lowness *from the gates of death.* In goodness of will is our peace. A body tends by its weight towards the place proper to it— weight does not necessarily tend towards the lowest place but towards its proper place. Fire tends upwards, stone downwards. By their weight they are moved and seek their proper place. Oil

poured over water is borne on the surface of the water, water
poured over oil sinks below the oil: it is by their weight that
they are moved and seek their proper place. Things out of their
place are in motion: they come to their place and are at rest.
My love is my weight: wherever I go my love is what brings me
there.* By Your gift we are on fire and borne upwards: we flame
and we ascend. *In our heart we ascend and sing the song of
degrees.* It is by Your fire, Your beneficent fire, that we burn and
we rise, rise towards the peace of Jerusalem, since I have rejoiced
in those who said to me: *We shall go to the house of the Lord.*
There our good will shall place us, so that we shall desire nothing
but to remain there forever.

X

Happy the creature which has no other condition [but this
beatitude]: though it would have been other, unless by Your Gift,
moving over all things changeable, it had been lifted up in the
moment of its creation, with no lapse of time between, in that
summoning by which You said: *Be light made,* and had become
light. For in us there is a distinction between the time when we
were darkness and the time when we became light: but in it we
are not told what it would have been if it had not been made
light. It is spoken of as though it had before been flux and darkness, that the cause might appear by which it was made to be
otherwise, the cause, that is, by which it was turned towards light
unfailing and became itself light. He who can understand let him
beg of You to understand this. Why bother me about it, as
though it were I that *enlighten every man that comes into this
world*?

XI

Who can understand the omnipotent Trinity? And who does
not speak of the Trinity, if indeed it truly is the Trinity that he
speaks of? Rare is the soul, whatever it says of the Trinity, that

* The translation is so clumsy that the Latin must be given: Eo
feror, quocumque feror.

knows what it is saying. Men quarrel, and men fight, but without peace no one sees that vision.

It would be good if men would meditate upon three things to be found in themselves. These three are very far different from the Trinity, but I mention them that men may exercise their minds and test and realize how far different they are. The three things of which I speak are existence, knowledge, will. For I am, and I know, and I will. I am a being that knows and wills: I know that I am and that I will: I will to be and to know. In these three there is inseparable life, one life, one mind, one essence: so that it is impossible to effect separation: yet the three are distinct. Let him see this who can. At any rate the fact is within himself; let him look attentively at himself, and see and tell me.

But when a man has found and stated what truth he can in all this, he must not think that he has found that which is above such things and immutable, which exists immutably, and knows immutably, and wills immutably. For whether there is Trinity there because these three are in the one God, or whether all three are in each Person so that they are each triple; or whether both things are true and in some marvellous manner, at once simple and multiple, the Infinite is in Itself its own object: so that by Itself It is and knows Itself and suffices to Itself immutably the Self-same in the superabundant magnitude of Its unity, who can easily conceive? Who can attain to express it? Who would have the rashness to claim to know the manner of it?

## XII

Proceed in Your confession, O my faith; say to your Lord God: Holy, Holy, Holy, O Lord my God: in Your name were we baptized, O Father, Son, and Holy Ghost, in Your name do we baptize, O Father, Son, and Holy Ghost. For among us also God has in his Christ created a *heaven and earth,* the spiritual and carnal members of His Church. And our "earth," before it received the form of doctrine, was *invisible and formless,* and wrapped in the darkness of ignorance, for *Thou hast corrected man for iniquity* and *Thy judgments are a great deep.*

But because your Spirit moved over the waters, Your mercy did not abandon our wretchedness; and You said: *Be light made; Do penance, for the Kingdom of God is at hand. Do penance; be light made.* And because our soul was troubled within us, we remembered you, O Lord, from the land of Jordan and from that mountain high as Yourself but made low for us, and our darkness grew displeasing to us and we turned our face to You and light was made. *And we were heretofore darkness, but now light in the Lord.*

## XIII

Yet [though we are light in the Lord] we are still so by faith and not by sight. *For we are saved by hope. But hope that is seen is not hope.* Still *deep calls on deep,* but now *at the noise of Thy floodgates.* Still even he who said: *I could not speak to you as unto spiritual, but as unto carnal,* does not yet *count himself to have apprehended*; but *forgetting the things that are behind, he stretches himself forth to those that are before and groans being burned,* and *his soul thirsts after the living God as the hart after the fountains of water,* and says: *when shall I come?* He desires *to be clothed with his habitation that is from heaven,* and he calls upon the lower abyss, saying: *Be not conformed to this world but be reformed in the newness of your mind,* and *do not become children in sense, but in malice be children* that you *may in sense be perfect,* and: *O senseless Galatians, who has bewitched you?* But it is no longer the voice of the apostle that speaks thus, it is Thine, who *sent Thy Holy Spirit from above* upon him, who ascended on high and opened the floodgates of his gifts, that *the stream of the river may make your city joyful.*

For that City the friend of the bridegroom sighs, *who has the first fruits of the spirit,* but still *groaning within himself, waiting for adoption, the redemption of his body.* He sighs for it, for he is a member of the Spouse of Christ; and he is jealous for it, for he is the friend of the bridegroom; he is jealous for it and not for himself, because it is *in the noise of Thy floodgates* and not in his own voice that he calls upon that other abyss, of which he is jealous and in fear. For he fears *lest, as the serpent seduced Eve by his subtlety, so their minds should be corrupted* from the purity which is in our Spouse, Thy only-begotten Son. What will be the light of that beauty, when *we shall see Him as He is,* and there shall be no more of the tears which *have been my bread day and night, while it is said to me: Where is Thy God?*

## XIV

And I too say: O my God, where art Thou? Tell me where Thou art? *I take breath a little* in Thee, when *I pour out my soul in Thee with the voice of praise and confession, the noise of one feasting.* And my soul is still sad, because it falls back and becomes an abyss, or rather it feels that it is still an abyss. My faith, which Thou hast *lighted in the night before my feet* says to it: *why are you sad, O my soul, and why do you trouble me?* and *Hope in God, Thy word is a lamp to my feet.* Hope and persevere until the night passes, which is the mother of sinners: until the wrath of the Lord passes, for we were *the children of wrath* and *were sometime darkness;* of this darkness we trail the remains in our body which is dead in sin *till the day break and the shadows retire. Hope in the Lord: in the morning I shall stand and contemplate Him; I shall not cease to confess Him. In the morning I shall stand and I shall see the salvation of my countenance, my God,* who *shall quicken also our mortal bodies because of His Spirit that dwells in us,* because over the dark and storm-tossed waters within us He moves in mercy. Thus in our pilgrimage we have received a sign that we are now light, for we are still *saved by hope* and children of the light and children of the day, not children of night and darkness which once we were.

Between them and us in the continuing uncertainty of human knowledge You alone distinguish, who prove our hearts and *call the light day and the darkness night.* For who distinguishes us but You? *What have we that we have not received from Thee, who hast of the same lump made one vessel unto honor, of which others are made unto dishonor?*

## XV

Or who but You, our God, made a firmament of authority over us in Your divine Scripture? For *the heavens shall be folded together as a book* which now are *stretched out like a pavilion over us*. The authority of Your divine Scripture is all the more sublime because the mortals by whom You gave Scripture to us have died the death. And You know, Lord, You know how You clothed men with skins when by sin they had become mortal. Thus it was as a skin that you stretched out the firmament of Your Book, the firmament of Your words ever in harmony which, by the ministry of mortal men, You placed over us. By their death the firmament of the authority that was in the words You uttered through them was stretched more sublimely over all that lies below; while they were living that force and authority were not spread so high. You had not yet *stretched out the heaven like a pavilion,* You had not yet spread all through the world the fame of their death.

Let us, O Lord, *behold Thy heavens, the works of Thy fingers*: clear away from before our eyes the cloud with which You have covered them. In them is *Thy testimony giving wisdom to little ones*. O, my God, *out of the mouth of infants and of sucklings perfect Thy praise*. I know no books so destructive of pride, so destructive of the enemy who stands up in the justification of his sins, resisting reconciliation with You. I know, Lord, no writings so pure, none that have so powerfully persuaded me to confession, and bent my neck to Your yoke, and invited me to worship You for worship's sake alone. Grant me in my subjection to understand these words, O good Father, because it is for those in subjection that You have established them.

There are, as I believe, other waters above this firmament [of Scripture] waters immortal and kept clear of earthly corruption. Let the super-celestial hosts of Your angels praise Your name, let them praise You for they have no need to look upon this firmament nor to read it in order to know Your word. For they ever see Your face, and in Your face they read without syllables spoken in time what is willed by Your eternal will. They read it and they choose it and they love it; they read it without ceasing, and what they read never passes away. For by choice and love they read the very immutability of Your counsels. Their scroll is not closed, their book is not folded together, for their book is Yourself and You eternally are: because You have established them above that firmament which You have established above the infirmity of the peoples below : and there they may look up and know Your mercy, that mercy which ever announces You in time, who made time. *O Lord, Thy mercy is in heaven and Thy truth reaches even to the clouds.* The clouds pass, but heaven remains. The preachers of Your word pass from this life to the next, but Your Scripture is stretched over the peoples until the end of time. *Heaven and earth shall pass, but Thy words shall not pass;* the scroll shall be folded, and the grass over which it was spread shall pass with its glory, *but Thy word endures forever*; now we see in the darkness of clouds and in the mirror of heaven, and not *as it is*: because though we are now beloved by Your Son, *it has not yet appeared what we shall be.* He has seen us through the lattice of flesh and has caressed us and inflamed us, and *we run after the odor of his ointments.* But *when He shall appear, we shall be like to Him, because we shall see Him as He is.* It will be ours, O Lord, to see Him as He is: but it is not for us yet.

## XVI

Just as You alone absolutely are, You alone have knowledge: for You *are* immutably, and You know immutably, and You will immutably: and Your Essence knows and wills immutably, Your Knowledge is and wills immutably, Your Will is and knows immutably. It does not seem proper in Your eyes that immutable Light should be known by the mutable being which it illumines, as that Light knows itself. Therefore *my soul is as earth without water unto Thee,* for just as it cannot of itself illumine itself, so it cannot of itself quench the thirst that it has. *For with Thee is the fountain of life, and in Thy light we shall see light.*

## XVII

Who gathered the bitter ones into one society? They have the same end, the happiness of earth and of time; and for this single end they do all that they do, though the anxieties in which they are tossed are innumerably various. It was You, Lord, and none other who said: *Let the waters be gathered together into one place, and let the dry land appear; the sea is Thine and Thou hast made it and Thy hands formed the dry land.* The word *sea* here means the gathering together of the waters, not the bitterness of men's wills. For even upon the ill desires of souls You impose Your order, setting limits how far the waters shall be allowed to go, so that their waves break upon themselves: thus You create the sea by the order of Your power which is over all things.

But the souls which thirst for You and which You behold as separated by different bounds from the gathering-together of the sea, these souls You water from Your secret fount of loving kindness, *that the earth may bring forth fruit.* And it does bring forth its fruit: by the command of You its Lord God, our soul brings forth works of mercy according to their kind. Thus we love our neighbor in bringing help to his bodily needs, for our soul bears in itself seed, by reason of the likeness [between our neighbour and ourself], so that from our infirmity pity moves us to bring aid to the poverty of those in need, helping them as we would wish help given us if we were in the same great need: and the help we are moved to give is not only in easy matters, comparable to *the herb bearing seed,* but in the protection of our aid powerfully given, like *the tree bearing fruit*—of avail, for example, to rescue one who suffers injury from the hand of the mighty, and lending the shadow of our protection, with the strong aid of judgment that is just.

## XVIII

O Lord, I beseech You, just as it is You who make joy and strength and give them to men, so let *truth spring out of the earth, and justice look down from heaven,* and let *lights be made in the firmament. Let us break our bread with the hungry* and *bring into our own house the needy and the harbourless: let us clothe the naked and despise not those of our own flesh.*

By the fruits that are born in our earth, see how good it is. *Let our light break forth as the morning,* and from that lower harvest of action, poor as it is, may we wing upward to the Word of Life in the delights of contemplation, and, established in the firmament of Your Scripture, shine like lights in the world.

For there You discuss with us, so that we can distinguish between things spiritual and things of sense, between souls given to spiritual things and souls given to earthly things, as between day and night. Thus now not You alone distinguish in the mystery of Your judgment between light and darkness, as before the firmament was made; but now that Your grace has been manifested over the earth, Your spiritual ones also, established and ranged in the same firmament, shine upon the earth and divide day and night, and are *for signs and for seasons*: for *the old things are passed away and behold all things are made new, and our salvation is nearer than when we believed: the night is passed, the day is at hand*: and *Thou dost bless the crown of Thy year, sending labourers into Thy harvest,* in which *others have laboured at the sowing,* and sending labourers also to new sowing, whose harvest shall not be till the end of time.

Thus do You grant the prayers of him who beseeches, and bless the years of the just; but You are always *the self-same,* and in Your *years which do not fail* You prepare a granary for the years that pass.

In your eternal design You spread over the earth the good things of heaven in their proper season, since *to one indeed by the Spirit is given the word of wisdom* as a greater light for those who rejoice in the light of clear truth as in the dawn of day; *to another, the word of knowledge according to the same Spirit,* as a lesser light; *to another faith, to another the grace of healing, to another the working of miracles, to another prophecy, to another the discerning of spirits, to another divers kinds of tongues,* and all these are as stars. But *all these things one and the same Spirit works, dividing to everyone according as He wills,* making these stars shine before men for the profit of souls.

But the word of knowledge, in which are contained all the mysteries which change with the seasons like the moon, and the other gifts listed, which I have described as like stars, differ from the glory of that Wisdom with which the coming of day rejoices, as if they were but the beginning of night. Yet they are necessary for those to whom Your most prudent servant Paul *could not speak as unto spiritual, but as unto carnal,* he who *speaks wisdom among the perfect.*

But the sensual man like a little one in Christ must be given milk to drink, until he is able to take solid meat; and until his eye is strengthened upon the sun, he must not have his night utterly lightless, but must be content with the light of moon and stars.

These are the things You discuss with us most wisely, O our God, in Your Book, Your firmament, that in the wonders of contemplation we may distinguish all things, though we are still under *signs and seasons and days and years.*

### XIX

But first *wash yourselves, be clean, take away the evil from your eyes* and from the sight of my eyes, that the dry land may appear. *Learn to do well, judge for the fatherless and defend the widow,* that the earth may bring forth the grass of pasture and the fruit-tree. Come, says the Lord, let us consider together, *that there may be lights made in the firmament of heaven to give light upon the earth.*

The rich man asks the good Master what he should do to gain life everlasting. And the good Master—in whom the rich man saw only a man and nothing more, whereas He is good because he is God—answers him that *if he will enter into life he must keep the commandments,* cut away the bitterness of malice and wickedness, *not kill, not commit adultery, not steal, not bear false witness,* that the dry land may appear and bring forth honour of mother and father and love of neighbour. And the young man said to him: all these things have I done. But where do so many thorns come from, if the earth is fruitful? Go, root out the thick bushes of avarice, *sell what you have*, win harvest by giving to the poor, and *you shall have treasure in heaven*; and *follow the Lord, if you will be perfect,* be in the company of those among whom He speaks wisdom, who know what He gives to day and what to night, that you too may know and that for you too there may be lights in the firmament of heaven: but this will not be unless your heart is there too: and your heart will not be there unless your treasure is there, as you have heard from the good Master. But the barren earth *became sorrowful,* and the thorns choked the word.

But you, O chosen race, *weak things of the world,* who have given up all things to follow the Lord, go after Him and confound the strong, go after Him, O beautiful feet [of them that preach the gospel of peace], and shine in the firmament that the *heavens may show forth His glory,* for you shall divide the light of the perfect who are not yet as the angels, from the darkness of the little ones who yet are not without hope: shine over the whole earth, and *day* all glorious with the sun *will utter* the *speech* of wisdom *to day, and night* lit by the moon *will show* the word of *knowledge to night.* The moon and stars shine by night, but night does not darken them: rather they give it light so far as it can be lightened. It is as though when God said *let there be lights made in the firmament of heaven, suddenly there came a sound from heaven, as of a mighty wind coming, and there appeared parted tongues as it were of fire, which sat upon every one of them,* and they became lights in the firmament of heaven having the word of life. Run over the world, holy fires, glorious fires. For *you are the light of the world* and you are not *under a bushel.* He is raised on high, to whom you have adhered, and He has raised you on high. Go forth and be known to all nations.

## XX

Let the sea too conceive and bring forth Your works, *let the waters bring forth the creeping creatures having life. Separating the precious from the vile, you shall be as the mouth of God,* by which He said: *let the waters bring forth* not the *living creatures,* which the earth brings forth, but *creeping creatures having life, and the fowl that fly over the earth.* For by the work of Your saints, O God, Your sacraments have made their way through the midst of the waves of this world's temptations to endue the peoples with Your name in Your baptism.

Meanwhile mighty miracles were worked, figured by *the great whales,* and the words of your messengers went *flying* over the earth high in the firmament of Your Book, which is placed over them as the authority beneath which they must fly wherever they go. *There are no speeches nor languages, where their voices are not heard,* since *their sound has gone forth into all the earth, and their words unto the ends of the world,* for You, Lord, blessing them have multiplied them.

Can it be that I am speaking falsehood or mixing together and failing to distinguish the luminous knowledge of these things *in the firmament of heaven,* and the corporeal works accomplished in the tossing sea and *under the firmament of heaven?*

Now there are things of which the notions are established and completed with no increase of generations, like the lights of wisdom and knowledge; but there are many and various material operations of these same things; and, each giving the other increase, they are multiplied in Your blessing, O my God. You have made up to us for the too rapid weariness of our bodily senses, by so making us that in the knowledge of the mind one single thing may be figured and uttered in a great variety of ways by bodily motions.

Such things the waters have brought forth, but in Your Word. They have been brought forth by the needs of peoples alienated from Your eternal truth, but in Your gospel: for it was those waters that cast them out, whose unpleasing bitterness was the reason why Your Word brought them forth.

All things are beautiful because You made them but You are inexpressibly more beautiful, who made all things. If Adam had not fallen away from You, there would not have flowed forth from him the bitter sea of the human race, with the depths of its curiosity, the storms of its pride, and the restless tossing of its instability; and there would have been no need for the dispensers of Your word to show forth corporeally and sensibly and in the midst of many waters the mysteries of Your words and deeds. For thus I understand the *creeping creatures* and the *fowl that fly*: but men taught and initiated by these signs and made dependent upon material sacraments, would not make progress beyond them, if their soul did not begin to live spiritually on another level and after the *word of the beginning* tend towards perfection.

XXI

Thus in Your word it was not the depth of the sea but the earth separated from the sea's bitterness that brought forth *the living soul*, and not merely *creeping creatures having life* and *the fowl that fly*. And this soul no longer has need of baptism, as the heathen need it, as itself needed when the waters covered it. For not otherwise can the Kingdom of heaven be entered since You ordained that so we should enter. Nor does such a soul demand great miracles, that it may have faith: of such it is not true that *unless it sees signs and wonders it believes not*: for the faithful earth is now distinct from the waters of the sea which are bitter with infidelity, and *tongues are for a sign not to believers but for unbelievers*. Nor has the earth, which You have established above the waters, any need of the race of winged creatures which by Your Word the waters produced. Send Your Word upon the earth by Your messengers. We recount their works, but it is You who work in them that they may bring forth a living soul.

The earth is said to produce a living soul, because the earth is the cause that Your messengers do such things in it, just as the sea was the cause of the production of creeping creatures having life and the fowl that fly under the firmament of heaven. But these things the earth does not need, although, at that table which You have prepared before those that believe, it eats the Fish [Christ our Lord] drawn from the deep: that Fish, indeed, was drawn from the deep to nourish the barrenness of earth. And although birds are sprung from the sea, yet they *are multiplied upon the earth*. The first preaching of those who brought the gospel was caused by man's infidelity; yet the faithful too are exhorted and blessed by them in a thousand ways daily. But the living soul has its origin from earth, because only to the faithful is there any profit in refraining from the love of this world, that their soul may live to You, which was dead while it was living in pleasures—pleasures, O Lord, that bring death: for You are the living delight of a pure heart.

Let Your servants then operate upon "the earth," not as in the waters of infidelity by preaching and speaking with miracles and mysterious signs and tongues, for at that level ignorance, the mother of wonder, is held attentive in fear of mysterious signs. This is the way of approach to faith for the sons of Adam when they have forgotten You, while they *hide themselves from Your face* and are become an abyss. But let Your servants work as upon dry land lifted above the whirlpools of the deep, let them be a pattern to the faithful, by living among them and stirring them to imitation.

Thus men hear the words *Seek Ye God, and your soul shall live,* not merely as something to listen to but as something to do, that the earth may bring forth a living soul. *Be not conformed to this world, but refrain yourselves from it.* The soul lives by avoiding those things which if they are sought bring death. Refrain from the ugly savagery of pride, from the slothly pleasure of lust, from all that lyingly bears the name of science, that the wild beasts may be tamed, the cattle brought to subjection, and the serpents made harmless. For these animals are an allegory for the movements of the mind. The pomp of pride and the delight that is in lust and the poison of curiosity are the movements of a soul that is dead—not dead so that it has lost all movement, but dead by departing from the fountain of life so that it is taken up by the world that passes away and conformed to it.

But Your word, O God, is a fountain of life everlasting and does not pass away: therefore in Your word we are forbidden to separate ourselves from it: *Be not conformed to this world,* that in the fountain of life the earth may bring forth a living soul, in Your word uttered by the evangelists a soul made continent by imitation of those who imitate Your Christ. For this is what is meant *according to their kinds,* for a man's imitation is of his friend: as St. Paul says *Be ye as I because I also am as you.*

Thus in the living soul the beasts will be good, acting with gentleness. For You have given the command: *do thy works in meekness and thou shalt be loved by all men.* And the cattle will be good, for *neither if they eat shall they have the more; nor if they eat not shall they have less.* And the serpents will be good, not poisonous to do harm, but cunning only in watchfulness, and gliding through temporal nature only in so far as may be necessary that by means of the things that are made, eternity may be seen and understood. These animals obey reason when, turned from their death-bringing ways, they live and are good.

XXII

Thus, O Lord our God and our Creator, when the passions, in which we were dying by evil living, have been turned from the love of this world, and our soul by living well begins to be a living soul, and the word You spoke by Your apostle has been accomplished: *Be not conformed to this world,* then indeed will that have come to pass which You added immediately to those words: *but be reformed in the newness of your mind.* You did not add *according to your kind,* as though we should imitate another who has gone the same road before us or live by the authority of some better man. For You did not say "Let man be made according to his kind," but: *Let us make man to our image and likeness,* that we may prove what is Your will.

Thus it is that [Paul] the dispenser of Your word generated children by the gospel, but, not wishing them to remain always children to be fed with milk and suckled at the breast, said: *Be reformed in the newness of your mind, that you may prove what is the good and the acceptable and the perfect will of God.*

Thus you do not say: *Let man be made,* but: *Let us make man;* nor do you say: *according to his kind,* but *to our image and likeness.* For when in newness of mind he sees and understands Your truth, man does not need any other man to teach him to imitate his kind: but with You to teach him he sees for himself *what is*

*Your will, what is good and acceptable and perfect.* And now that he has the capacity You teach him to see the Trinity of Unity or equally the Unity of Trinity. Thus to the phrase in the plural: *Let us make man,* there is added in the singular: *and God made man*; and to the phrase in the plural: *to our image,* there is added in the singular: *to the image of God.* Thus *man is renewed unto knowledge according to the image of Him that created him,* and having become spiritual, he judges all things— all things that is which are to be judged—*and he himself is judged of no man.*

**XXIII**

The statement that he judges all things means that he has *dominion over the fishes of the sea and the fowls of the air and the beasts* and wild animals *and of the whole earth and of every creeping creature that moves upon the earth.* This he does by the understanding of his mind, by which he *perceives the things that are of the Spirit of God.* But *man when he was in honour did not understand: he has been compared to senseless beasts and made like to them.*

Thus it is that in Your Church, O my God, according to Your grace which You have given it, *for we are Your workmanship created in good works,* not only do those judge spiritually who are in spiritual authority but also those who according to the spirit are subject to these—for *You created man male and female,* but all one in Your spiritual grace, where there is neither male nor female according to sex, just as *there is neither Jew nor Greek nor bond nor free.* Thus spiritual men, whether those who have authority or those who obey, judge spiritually: they judge not of the spiritual truths which shine in the firmament, for it would not be fitting for men to judge of an authority so sublime; nor do they judge of Your Book, even such matters as are not clear in it, since we submit our intellects to it and hold it certain that even what is closed to our gaze is rightly and truly said. A man, although he is now spiritual and *renewed unto knowledge of God according to the image of Him who created him, must be a doer of the law, not a judge.* Nor does he judge which men are spiritual and which are carnal: for these, O my God, are known to Your eyes, whereas they have not appeared to us by any works so that *we may know them by their fruit*: but You, Lord, already knew them, and separated them and called them in secret, before the firmament was made. Nor does any man though spiritual judge of the troubled citizens of the world [outside God's grace]. *For what* has he in his ignorance *to do to judge them that are without,* as to which of them will come into the fragrance of Your grace and which will remain in the everlasting bitterness of enmity to You?

Likewise man, whom You made to Your image, has not received dominion over the lights of heaven, nor over that mysterious heaven itself, nor over day and night, which you called into being before the creation of heaven, nor over the gathering-together of the waters which is the sea; but over *the fishes of the sea and the fowls of the air and all beasts, and the whole earth, and every creeping creature that moves upon the earth.*

He judges, and approves what he finds good, and blames what he finds evil, whether in the ministration of the sacraments by which those are initiated whom Your mercy has sought out from the midst of many waters: or in that ceremony figured by the Fish raised from the depths which the pious "earth" eats: or in the significations of words, and the voices subjected to the authority of your Book which fly like the fowls of the air under the firmament—interpreting, expounding, discussing, disputing, praising You and calling upon You, words coming from the mouth and sounding forth that the congregation may answer Amen. That all these words have to be corporeally uttered is by reason of the abyss of this world and the blindness of our flesh, whereby thoughts cannot be seen but need to be sounded in our ears. Thus, although birds *are multiplied upon the earth,* their origin is from the waters.

The spiritual man judges also by approving what he finds good and blaming what he finds evil in the works and morals of the faithful, in their almsgiving which is symbolized by the fruitful earth: and he judges of the living soul whose passions are brought under control by chastity, by fasting, by pious thoughts concerning the things which are perceived by the bodily senses. In a word he is said to judge of those things in which he has the power to correct.

### XXIV

But now we come to something profoundly mysterious. You bless men, Lord, *that they may increase and multiply and fill the earth.* Surely You intend us to see some special meaning in the fact that You did not thus bless the light, which You called day, nor the firmament of heaven, nor the heavenly lights, nor stars nor earth nor sea? I would say, O my God, who created us to Your image, that You had chosen to give the gift of this blessing to man especially, if You had not in the same way blessed the fish and the great whales, that they should *increase and multiply and fill the waters of the sea,* and the birds that they should *be multiplied upon the earth.* Again I would say that this blessing pertained especially to those kinds of beings which are propagated by generation from themselves, if I found it given likewise as a blessing to trees and plants and the beasts of the earth. But *increase and multiply* was not said to plants or trees nor to beasts and serpents, although all these, as well as fishes and birds and men increase by generation and so preserve their kind.

What then am I to say, O Truth, my Light? That the fact means nothing, that it was said for no particular reason? Far be it from the servant of Your word, O Father of piety, to say such a thing. Even if I do not understand what You mean by the phrase, let those make better use of it who are better than I, that is more intelligent than I, in the degree that You have given each one to be wise, O my God. At least let my confession be pleasing in your sight: I confess, O Lord, that I believe You did not speak thus to no purpose, and I shall say what was suggested to me by reading it. What I think is true in itself, and I do not see what hinders me from thinking that it is what the words of your Scripture signify. I know that corporeal signs can signify in multiple ways what is understood in the mind in one way, and that the mind can understand in multiple ways what is signified by the body in one way.

For example, the single idea of love of God and our neighbor is expressed in countless symbols and countless tongues, and in each tongue by innumerable modes of speech. Similarly, the creatures of the sea increase and multiply. On the other hand, let readers consider something which Scripture expresses in one manner, and the voice utters in one manner: *In the beginning God made heaven and earth*: can this not be understood in various ways—I do not mean erroneously, but by different interpretations each of which is true? Similarly, the offspring of men increase and multiply.

If we consider the natures of things not allegorically but properly, the phrase *Increase and multiply* is proper to all creatures born of seed. But suppose we regard it as used figuratively, as I think that Scripture meant us to regard it, since it cannot be for nothing that it attributes this blessing only to the offspring of creatures of the sea and men: if we do so, we find multitudinousness both among spiritual and corporeal creatures, represented by *heaven and earth*; and in just and unjust souls, represented by *light and darkness*; and in the sacred writers by whom the law is uttered, represented by *the firmament established between the waters and the waters*; and in the society of peoples spoiled with bitterness, represented by *the sea*; and in the zeal of pious souls represented by *dry land*; and in the works of mercy carried out in our present life, represented by *herbs yielding seed* and *fruit-bearing trees*; and in spiritual gifts shown forth for our profit, represented by the *lights of heaven*; and in men's passions brought under control as represented by *the living soul*.

In all these things we find multitude, and fertility, and increase. But the special kind of increase and multiplication whereby one meaning is expressed in many ways, and one mode of expression is understood in many meanings, we find only in signs made corporeally, and in the concepts of the intellect.

I take it that corporeal signs, since they are made necessary by the depth of our immersion in the flesh, are represented by the generation of creatures of the waters; and things thought out in our mind, since they are due to the fertility of reason, are represented by human generation.

That is why, O Lord, as I think, You said to these two kinds: *Increase and multiply*. In this blessing I take it that you granted us the faculty and the power both to express in many ways what we understand by one single idea, and to understand in many ways what we find expressed obscurely in a single way. Thus the waters of the sea are filled, and their waves stand for the various meanings of signs; and the land is filled with new generations of men: its dryness is shown in its thirst for truth, and reason dominates it.

xxv

Now, O Lord my God, I would say what the next phrase of Your Scripture tells me. I shall say it and I shall not fear. With Your inspiration I shall utter the truth You have willed me to say of these words. For I do not think that I could utter truth save by your inspiration, seeing that You *are true, and every man a liar. And when he speaks a lie, he speaks of his own*. Thus that I may speak truth, I shall speak [not of my own but] of Yours.

*Every herb bearing seed upon the earth, and all trees that have in themselves fruit of their own kind* You gave to us for our food. And not only to us, but *to all beasts of the earth and to every fowl of the air* and to serpents; but You did not [say that You] give these things to the fish and the monsters of the sea. [What does this omission signify?]

I have said that by *the fruits of the earth* were signified and allegorically figured the works of mercy, which are brought forth by the *fruitful earth* for the necessities of this life. An "earth" in this sense was the pious Onesiphorus, *to whose house* You *gave mercy* because *it had often refreshed* Paul and *had not been ashamed of his chain*. The same was true also of the brethren who *from Macedonia supplied what was wanting to him* and thus produced so great a harvest. But see how the Apostle grieves for certain "trees" which had not given him the fruit that was due. He writes: *At my first answer no man stood with me, but all forsook me: may it not be laid to their charge*. For we do owe fruits to those who minister spiritual doctrine to us through their understanding of the divine mysteries. We owe these to them as *men*. We owe these fruits also to them as to the *living creatures* in that they offer themselves for our imitation in all continence. And again we owe these to them as to *flying creatures*, because of their blessings *which are multiplied upon the earth*: for *their sound has gone forth into all the earth*.

### XXVI

Those are fed by this food who find their joy in it; but those find no joy in it *whose God is their belly*. And in those who bring us these fruits, the fruit is not what they give, but the spirit in which they give it.

Thus in that Paul served God and not his belly, I see clearly the source of his joy, I see it and I rejoice with him greatly: he had received from the Philippians what they had sent by Epaphroditus. And I see the reason for his joy. He is fed by what he finds his joy in, as he says in truth: *I rejoice in the Lord exceedingly, that now at length your thought for me has flourished again, as you did also think: but you had grown weary.* These men had grown too faint and dried up from a weariness that had lasted over long to go on producing the *fruit* of a good work; and his rejoicing was for them because they *flourished again*, and not for himself because they had come to the aid of his need. Thus he continues: *I speak not as it were for want. For I have learned, in whatsoever state I am, to be content therewith. I know both how to be brought low, and I know how to abound; everywhere and in all things I am instructed both to be full and to be hungry; both to abound, and to suffer need. I can do all things in Him who strengthens me.*

What then is the cause of your joy, great Paul? What is the cause of your joy, upon what do you feed, *O man renewed to the knowledge of God according to the image of Him who created you, O living soul* of such self-mastery, *winged* tongue that spoke mysteries? To such souls that food is due. What is it that you feed upon? Joy. Observe what follows: *Nevertheless you have done well in communicating to my tribulation.* This is the cause of his joy, this is his food: that they have done well, not that his need has been relieved. For he says: *In tribulation you opened my heart,* for he *knew how to abound and how to suffer need* in You who strengthened him. He says further: *And you also know, O Philippians, that in the beginning of the gospel when I departed from Macedonia, no church communicated with me as concerning giving and receiving, but you only, for unto Thessalonica also you sent once and again for my use.* He now rejoices that they have returned to these good works, he is glad because they flourish again, as at a field returning to fertility.

Was it on account of the advantage to himself—for he says: *you sent for my use*—that he was glad? Assuredly not. How do we know this? Because he goes on to say: *Not that I seek the gift, but I seek the fruit.*

I have learned from you, O my God, to distinguish between *gift* and *fruit.* The gift is the thing itself given by one who supplies another with necessaries—money, food, drink, clothing, shelter, help. But the fruit is the good and right will of the giver. For our good Master did not say only: *He that receives a prophet,* but added *in the name of a prophet, he that receives a just man,* but added: *in the name of a just man*; the one *shall receive the reward of a prophet,* the other *shall receive the reward of a just man.*

Nor did He say only: *Whosoever shall give to drink to one of these little ones a cup of cold water,* but added: *in the name of a disciple,* and proceeded to say: *Amen I say to you he shall not lose his reward.*

The gift consists in receiving the prophet, receiving the just man, giving a cup of cold water to the disciple; but the fruit is in doing these things specifically for a prophet, and a just man, and a disciple. It was upon the fruit that Elias was fed by the widow, who knew that she was feeding a man of God and fed him for that reason; it was only upon the gift that he was fed by the raven: and it was not the spirit of Elias that was fed by the raven, but the body which might have died for the need of that food.

## XXVII

So, Lord, I will say what is true in Your sight. By the words *fish* and *sea-monsters* are signified, as I think, unlearned persons and infidels, who need sacraments of initiation and notable miracles to win them to the church. Such men may provide bodily refreshment for your children, or give them aid in some other matter of this earthly life; but they do not know why they are bound to do it nor the true meaning of what they do. Therefore they do not really give, nor do Your children receive from them, true good: because the givers do not act from a right and holy will, and the recipients take no joy in the gifts since they see that there is as yet no fruit. Thus it is that a soul is fed by what it finds joy in. That is why the *fish* and the *sea-monsters* are not [said to be] fed with food, because the earth germinates food only when it is divided and set apart from the bitterness of the sea's waters.

## XXVIII

*And You saw, O God, all the things that You had made, and they were very good.* We see them too, and they are very good. With regard to each order of things, when You had said that they were to be made and they were made, You saw one by one that they were good. Seven times, I have counted, is it written that You saw that what You made was good; and this is the eighth, that You saw all that You had made, and You saw that all things as a totality were not only good but very good. For taken one by one they were simply good; but taken altogether they were not only good but very good. Beautiful bodies utter the same truth: because the body, all of whose members are beautiful, is much more beautiful than the individual members by whose harmonious arrangement the whole is completed, although taken one by one these members are beautiful.

## XXIX

I scrutinized the Book closely to see whether it was seven or eight times that You saw that Your works were good, when they pleased You; and I realized that there could be no time in Your seeing to help me understand in what sense You had looked so many times at what You had made. And I said: "O Lord, surely Your Scripture is true, for You are true and Your Truth has uttered it? Why then do You tell me that there is no time in Your seeing, yet Your Scripture tells me that You saw each day that what You had made was good, and I counted and found how often You had done it?"

And upon this You told me, for You are my God: You told me with strong voice in the ear of Your servant's spirit, breaking through my deafness and crying: "O man, what My Scripture says, I say. But it says things in terms of time, whereas time does not affect My Word, because it abides with Me equal in eternity. Thus the things you see by My Spirit, I see, just as what you say by My Spirit, I say. But while you see those things in time, I do not see them in time, just as you say those things in time, but I do not say them in time."

### xxx

I heard, O Lord my God, and from Your truth I sucked in a drop of its loveliness, and I understood. There are those who find displeasing the things You have made, and they assert that You made many of them—the structure of the heavens, for example, and the courses of the stars—under the constraint of necessity: and that You did not make them of material of Your own making, but that they had already been created elsewhere and by some other means: and all You did was to bring them together and build them in and set them in order—all this when You had conquered Your enemies and built the ramparts of the world, so that held down in defeat by these ramparts they could not again rebel against You. Further they assert that there are other beings —all flesh, for example, and very small living creatures and all things rooted in the earth—which were not made by You nor even arranged by You: a hostile mind and an alien nature, not created by You but opposed to You, produced and formed these things in the lowest levels of the world.

They are mad who talk thus, for they do not see Your Works by Your Spirit, nor do they recognize You in them.

XXXI

But as to those who do by Your Spirit see these things, it is You who see in them. Thus when *they* see that these works are good, it is You who see that they are good; when anything pleases us because of You, You are what pleases us in that thing, and when by Your Spirit something pleases us, it pleases You in us. *For what man knows the things of a man, but the spirit of a man, which is in him? So the things also that are of God, no man knows, but the spirit of God. Now we have received not the spirit of this world, but the spirit that is of God, that we may know the things that are given us from God.*

And I am moved to add: Assuredly no one knows the things of God, but the Spirit of God. How then do we know the *things that are given us from God?* The answer has been given me: Even those things which we know by His Spirit, no one knows but the Spirit of God. For just as it had been rightly said to those who speak in the Spirit of God: *It is not you that speak,* so it may be rightly said to those who know in the Spirit of God: It is not you that know. And just as rightly may it be said to those who see in the Spirit of God: It is not you that see. Thus whatever a man sees in the Spirit of God as good, it is not he but God who sees that it is good.

It is one thing then to think like the men spoken of above that what is good is evil; it is quite another to see that what is good is good—like many whom Your creation pleases because it is good, yet what pleases them in it is not You, so that they prefer to take their joy in it rather than in You. And it is another thing again when a man sees that something is good, but it is God in him seeing that it is good, and it is God that is loved in the thing that He made. He would not be loved save through the Spirit which He has given, *because the charity of God is poured forth in our hearts by the Holy Ghost who is given to us*: by whom we see that whatever exists in any mode is good: for it is from Him who does not in this or that mode exist but *is* absolutely.

XXXII

Thanks be to You, O Lord! We see *heaven and earth,* that is the upper and lower parts of the material world, or perhaps the spiritual and material creations; and for the adornment of these two—whether they constitute the whole mass of the material world or the whole of creation altogether—we see *light made* and *divided from darkness.* We see the *firmament of heaven,* whether this means the first body of the world, between the spiritual waters above and the material waters below, or that space of air, likewise called heaven, through which the birds of the air take their wandering flight between the waters which rise as vapor and are distilled as dew in the quiet of the night, and the heavier waters that flow upon the earth. We see the beauty of the *waters gathered together* in the plains of the sea; and the dry land, first bare, then formed so that it is *visible and organized,* the mother of plants and trees. We see the great *lights* shining above, the sun sufficing to the day, moon and stars comforting the night, time's movements marked and signified by them all. We see water spread all about us and swarming with fish and great monsters and birds, for the density of the air which supports birds in their flight results from the evaporation of water. We see the face of the earth diversified with land-animals. And we see man, made to Your image and likeness, dominating all the irrational animals by reason of that same image and likeness, that is by the power of reason and understanding; and just as in the human soul there is one element which takes thought and dominates, another which is subjected to obedience, so woman has been created corporeally for man: for though she has indeed a nature like that of man in her mind and rational intelligence, yet by her bodily sex she is subjected to the sex of her husband, much as appetite, which is the source of action, must be subjected to reason if it is to learn the rules of *right* action. We see these things, and each thing is good and the whole is very good.

## XXXIII

Let Your works praise You that we may love You, and let us love You that Your works may praise You. For they have a beginning and end in time, a rising and setting, growth and decay, beauty and defect. Thus they have their succession of morning and evening, in part secretly, in part plainly to be seen. They were made by You of nothing—not of Yourself, not of some matter not made by You or of some matter previously existent: but of a *concreated* matter, that is a matter created by You in the same act [as the things You made of it], because You gave form to its formlessness without any interval of time.

For the matter of heaven and earth is not the same as the form of heaven and earth: You made formless matter of absolutely nothing, and the form of the world from this formless matter: yet You created both simultaneously, so that form came upon matter with no space of time intervening.

## XXXIV

I have considered also the figurative signification of Your choosing that things should be made in that particular order and related in that particular order. And I have seen that Your works individually are good and all together are very good. In Your Word, Your only-begotten Son, were *heaven and earth,* signifying the Head and the body of the church, predestined before all time, when as yet morning and evening were not. Then You began to work out in time what You had predestined outside time, that you might show forth things hidden and bring order to our disorder: for our sins were *over* us and we had gone away from You into *the abyss* of darkness, and *Your good Spirit moved* over us to raise us up in due time. And You *justified the wicked,* and *divided* them from the rest of sinners, and You established the authority of Your Book between those higher ones who were obedient to You, and the lower ones who were subjected to them; and You *gathered together* the whole body of the faithless into a society of one mind, that the zeal of the faithful might appear, that they might *bring forth* works of mercy unto You, distributing their earthly goods to the poor to acquire heavenly.

Next you set certain lights *in the firmament,* Your saints, having the word of life and shining with the sublime authority given them by their spiritual gifts; then for the conversion of pagan peoples—and for the blessing also of the faithful—You brought forth out of corporeal matter sacraments and visible wonders and voices in harmony with the firmament of Your Book; then You formed the *living soul* of the faithful by bringing their passions into control under the strength of continence: and then the mind, subject to You alone and needing no human authority for its imitation, You renewed *to Your image and likeness;* You subjected rational action to the higher excellence of the intellect as woman to man; and you ordained that all Your ministers, necessary for the perfection of the faithful in this life, should from those same faithful receive what is necessary for their temporal use, as a work that will later *bring forth fruit.*

All these things we see, and all together *they are very good,* for You see them in us; it is You that have given us the Spirit whereby we see them and love You in them.

### XXXV

O Lord God, grant us peace, for Thou hast granted us all things, the peace of repose, the peace of Thy Sabbath, the peace that has no evening. For this gloriously beautiful order of things that are very good will pass away when it has achieved its end: it will have its morning and its evening.

### XXXVI

But the seventh day is without evening. It has no sunset, for You sanctified it that it may abide forever. After all Your works which were very good, You rested on the seventh day—although You made them with no interruption of Your repose. And likewise the voice of Your Book tells us that we also, after our works —which are only very good because You have granted us to

accomplish them—will rest in You in the Sabbath of life everlasting.

## XXXVII

For then also You will rest in us, as now You operate in us, so
that it will then be Your rest in us as it is now Your work in us.
But You, Lord, are ever in action and ever at rest. You do not
see in time nor move in time nor rest in time. Yet You make the
things we see in time, and You make both time while time is and
rest when time is no more.

## XXXVIII

We see the things You have made, because they are; and they
are, because You see them. Looking outside ourselves we see that
they are, and looking into our own mind we see that they are
good: but You saw them as made when You saw that they were
to be made.

At the present time we move towards doing good, since our
heart has so conceived by Your Spirit; but at an earlier time we
moved towards doing ill, for we had gone away from You. But
You, God, who alone are good, have never ceased to do good.
Some indeed of our works are good through Your grace, but they
are not eternal: after them we hope that we shall find rest in the
greatness of Your sanctification. But You, the Good, who need no
good beside, are ever in repose, because You are Your own
repose.

What man will give another man the understanding of this, or
what angel will give another angel, or what angel will give a
man? Of You we must ask, in You we must seek, at You we must
knock. Thus only shall we receive, thus shall we find, thus will it
be opened to us.